Based on the Ballet by Igor Stravins

APOLLO

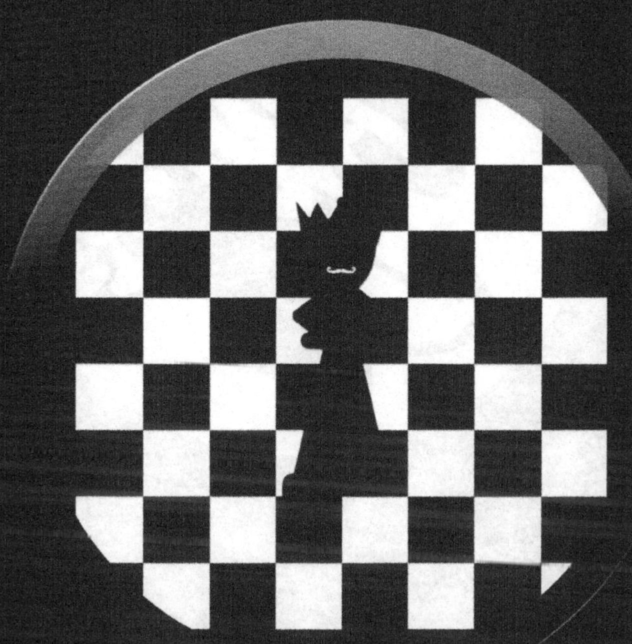

One Night Only

A CONCEPTUAL POEM

Principal Dancers: Marcel Duchamp / Rrose Sélavy, Leonora Carrington, Dorothea Tanning & Gertrude Abercrombie; Orchestra conducted by Max Ernst; featuring Solo Trumpeter: Dizzy Gillespie

BY GEOFFREY GATZA

Presented by BlazeVOX Ballet

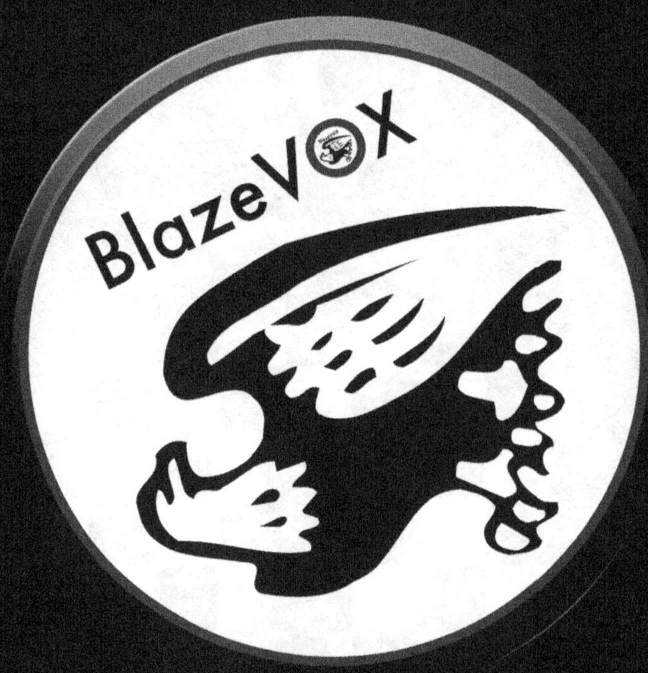

Apollo by Geoffrey Gatza
Copyright © 2014

Published by BlazeVOX [books]

All rights reserved. No part of this book may be reproduced without
publisher's written permission, except for brief quotations in reviews.

Printed in the United States of America
Cover art, interior design and typesetting by Geoffrey Gatza
First Edition
ISBN: 978-1-60964-154-2
Library of Congress Control Number: 2013911032

BlazeVOX [books]
131 Euclid Ave
Kenmore, NY 14217
Editor@blazevox.org

publisher of weird little books

BlazeVOX [books]

blazevox.org

21 20 19 18 17 16 15 14 13 12 01 02 03 04 05 06 07 08 09 10

Image Credits:

Page: 7

Marcel Duchamp 1950. © Jacqueline Matisse Monnier

Rrose Sélavy (Marcel Duchamp). 1921. Photograph by Man
Ray. Art direction by Marcel Duchamp. Silver print. 5-7/8"
x 3-7/8"

Max Ernst and Dorothea Tanning Photograph by Robert
Bruce Inverarity, 1948

Max Ernst and Leonora Carrington, St Martin d'Ardèche
(France), 1939 -by Lee Mille

Page: 8

Leonora Carrington Photograph by Alejandro Jodorowsky,
1955.

Gertrude Abercrombie with her painting Slaughterhouse,
ca. 1945 / unidentified photographer. Miscellaneous
photographs collection, Archives of American Art,
Smithsonian Institution.

Dizzy Gillespie with Gertrude Abercrombie on his
birthday, 1964.Photographer unknown. Gertrude
Abercrombie papers, Archives of American Art,
Smithsonian Institution.

BlazeVOX ballet presents

Apollo
a ballet by Igor Stravinsky

Orchestra conducted by Max Ernst
Feature trumpet soloist Dizzy Gillespie

Featured Principal Dancers:
Marcel Duchamp / Rrose Selavy,
Leonora Carrington,
Gertrude Abercrombie
Dorothea Tanning.
Choreography: Geoffrey Gatza

One Night Only

Seating starts at 5:30PM
Sponsored by the BlazeVOX [ballet]
For tickets call 716-873-5454

WEDNESDAY, JUNE 19 2013
At the Studio Center, Buffalo NY
www..blazeVOXballet.org

APOLLO

A VARIATION ON STRAVINSKY'S
APOLLON MUSAGÈTE

BlazeVOX ballet presents
Apollo, a ballet by Igor Stravinsky

WEDNESDAY, JUNE 19 2013
At the Studio Center, Buffalo, NY

Orchestra conducted by Max Ernst
Feature trumpet soloist Dizzy Gillespie

Principal Dancers: Marcel Duchamp / Rrose Sélavy,
Leonora Carrington, Gertrude Abercrombie,
and Dorothea Tanning.

Choreography: Geoffrey Gatza

Seating starts at 5:30PM
For tickets call 716-873-5454

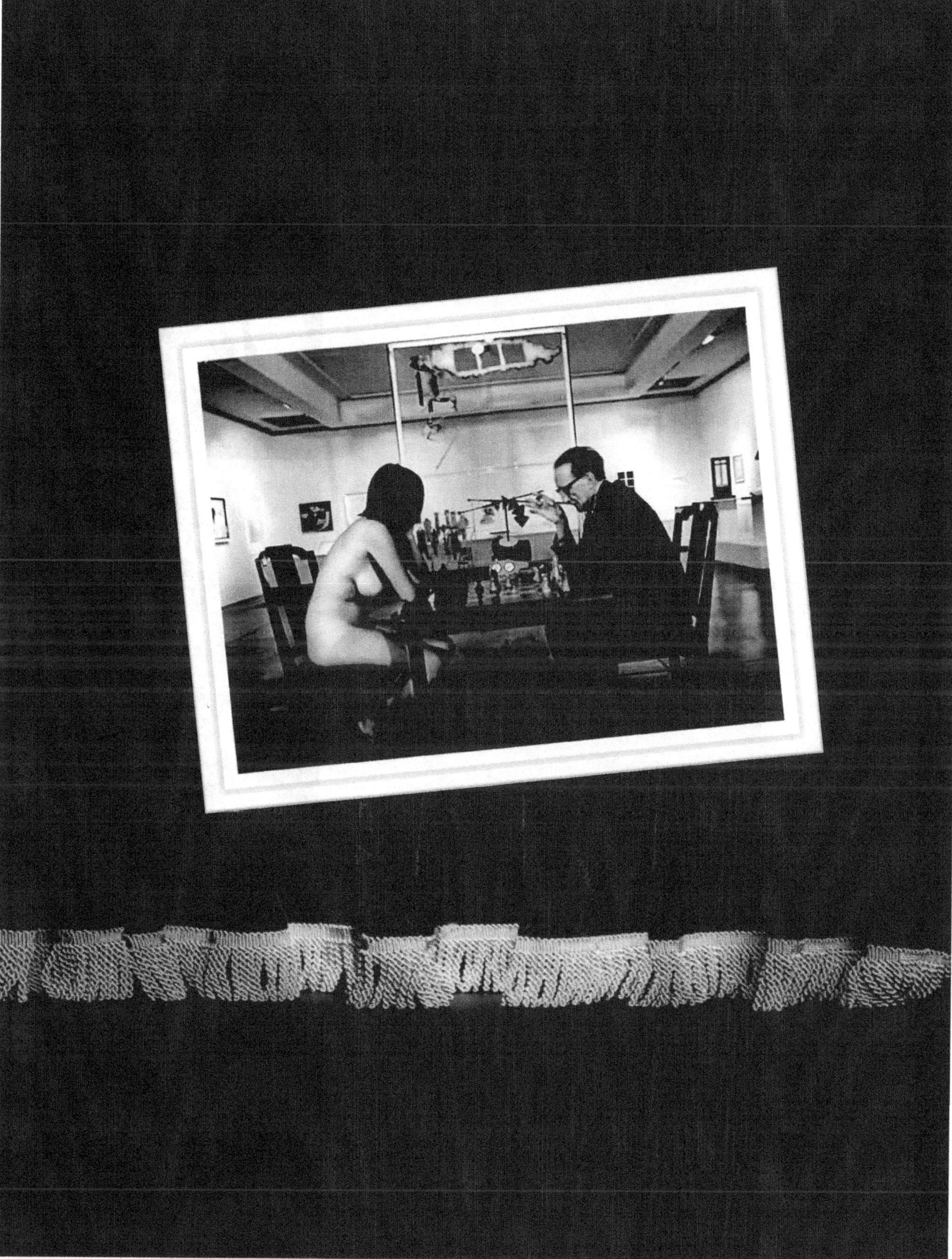

Marcel Duchamp
Apollo, the god of the sun || King

Rrose Sélavy
Tiresias, the blind prophet of Thebes || Queen

July 28, 1887 – October 2, 1968

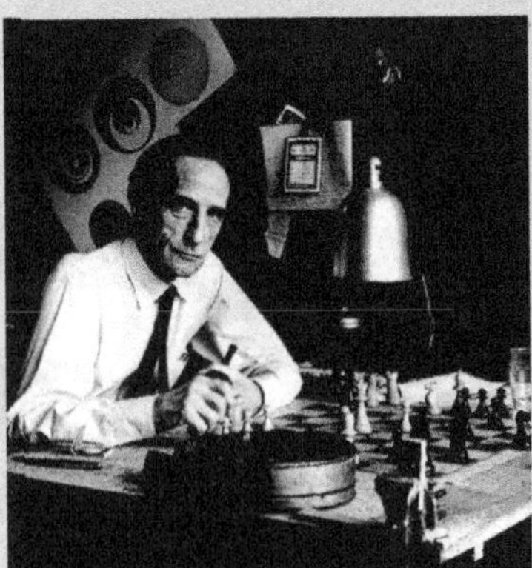

Marcel Duchamp was a French-American painter, sculptor and writer whose work is associated with Dadaism and conceptual art. Duchamp is considered one of the most significant artists of the 20th century. His grave bears the epitaph, "D'ailleurs, c'est toujours les autres qui meurent," or "Besides, it's always the others who die".

"Rrose Sélavy", also spelled Rose Sélavy, was one of Duchamp's pseudonyms. The name, a pun, sounds like the French phrase "Eros, c'est la vie", which may be translated as "Eros, such is life". It has also been read as "arroser la vie" ("to make a toast to life"). Sélavy emerged in 1921 in a series of photographs by Man Ray showing Duchamp dressed as a woman. Through the 1920s Man Ray and Duchamp collaborated on more photos of Sélavy. Duchamp later used the name as the byline on written material and signed several creations with it.

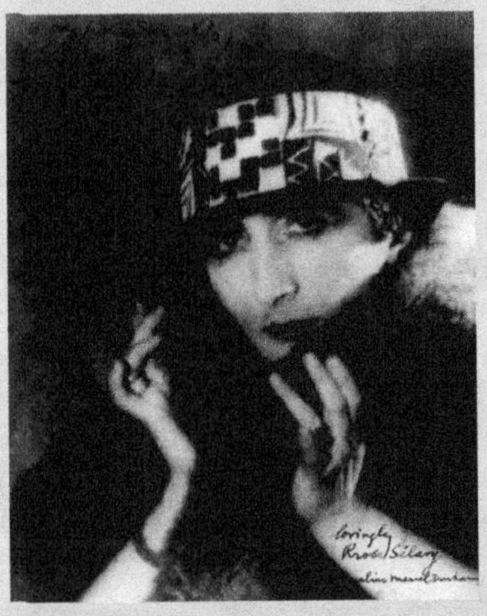

Dorothea Tanning
Calliope, the muse of poetry \\ Rook
Logopoeia, the play of Meaning in poetry

August 25, 1910 – January 31, 2012

Dorothea Margaret Tanning was an American painter, printmaker, sculptor and writer. She created ballet sets and costumes for George Balanchine's "Night Shadow," at the Metropolitan Opera House and others. She also appeared in Hans Richter's avant-garde films. As she recounts in her memoirs, Birthday and Between Lives, when Max Ernst visited her studio in 1942, they played chess, fell in love, and embarked on a life together that soon took them to Sedona, Arizona, and later to France.

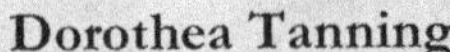

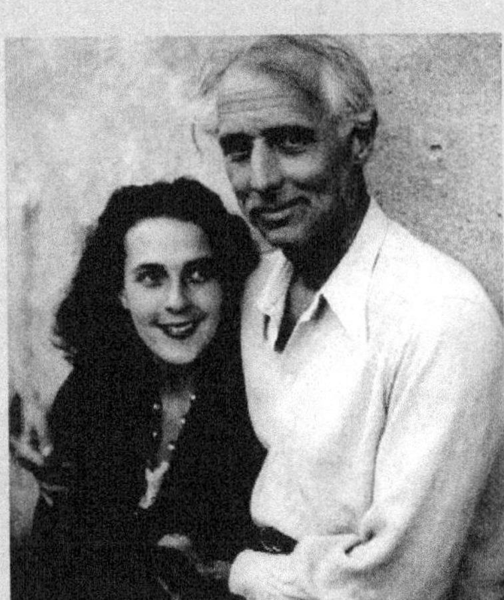

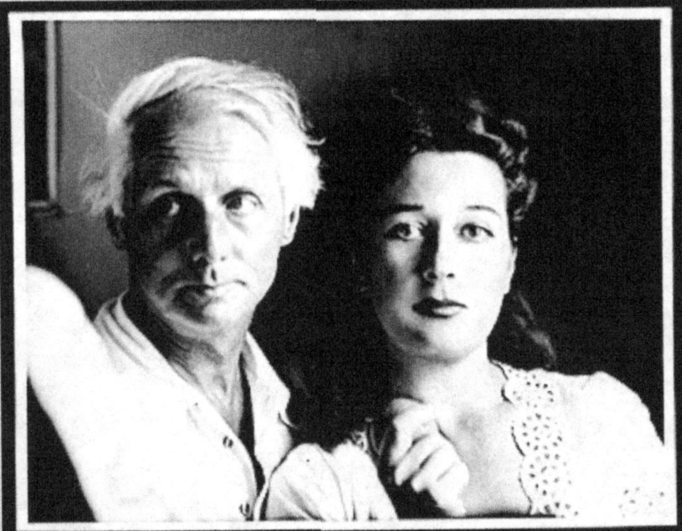

Leonora Carrington
Polyhymnia, the muse of rhetoric \\ Bishop
Phanopoeia, the play of Image in poetry

April 6, 1917 – May 25, 2011

Leonora Carrington was a British-born Mexican artist, a surrealist
painter and a novelist. She lived most of her life in Mexico City,
and was one of the last surviving participants in the Surrealist
movement of the 1930s.

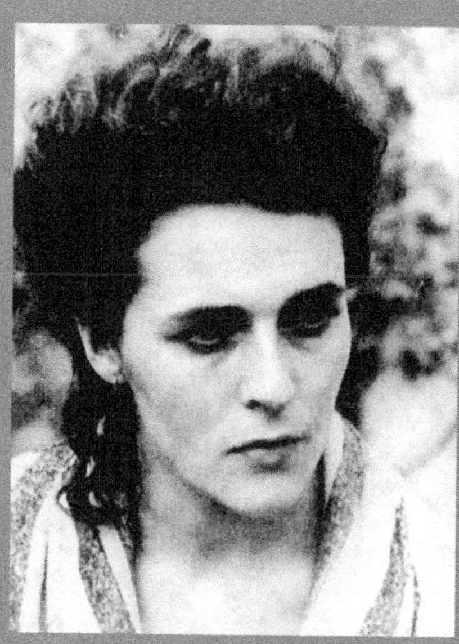

Gertrude Abercrombie
Terpsichore, the muse of dance \\ Knight
Melopoeia, the play of Music in poetry
February 17, 1909 – July 3, 1977

Gertrude Abercrombie was an American illustrator, painter and
musician. She was born in Austin, Texas, on February 17th, 1909,
but spent most of her life in Chicago. Her work combines both
fantasy and reality. Called "the queen of the bohemian artists,"
Abercrombie was involved in the Chicago jazz scene and friends
with musicians such as Dizzy Gillespie, Charlie Parker, and Sarah
Vaughan, whose music inspired her own creative work.
Abercrombie was influenced by European Surrealists but
identified herself as a Midwestern artist.

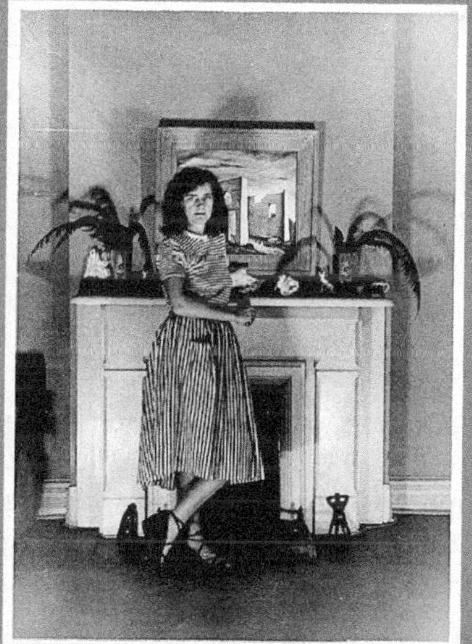

Max Ernst
Conductor
April 2, 1891 – April 1, 1976

Max Ernst was a German painter, sculptor, graphic
artist, and poet. A prolific artist, Ernst was a primary
pioneer of the Dada movement and Surrealism.

Dizzy Gillespie
Solo Trumpeter

October 21, 1917 – January 6, 1993

John Birks "Dizzy" Gillespie was an American jazz trumpeter,
bandleader, composer and occasional singer. Dizzy's solo is
featured in Variation of Terpsichore: Donna di Scalotta.

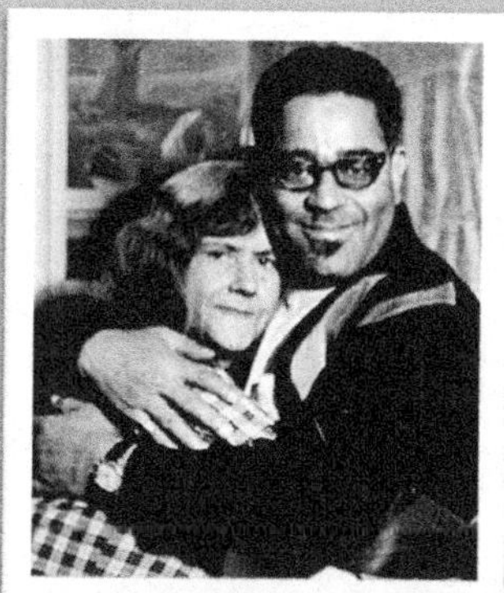

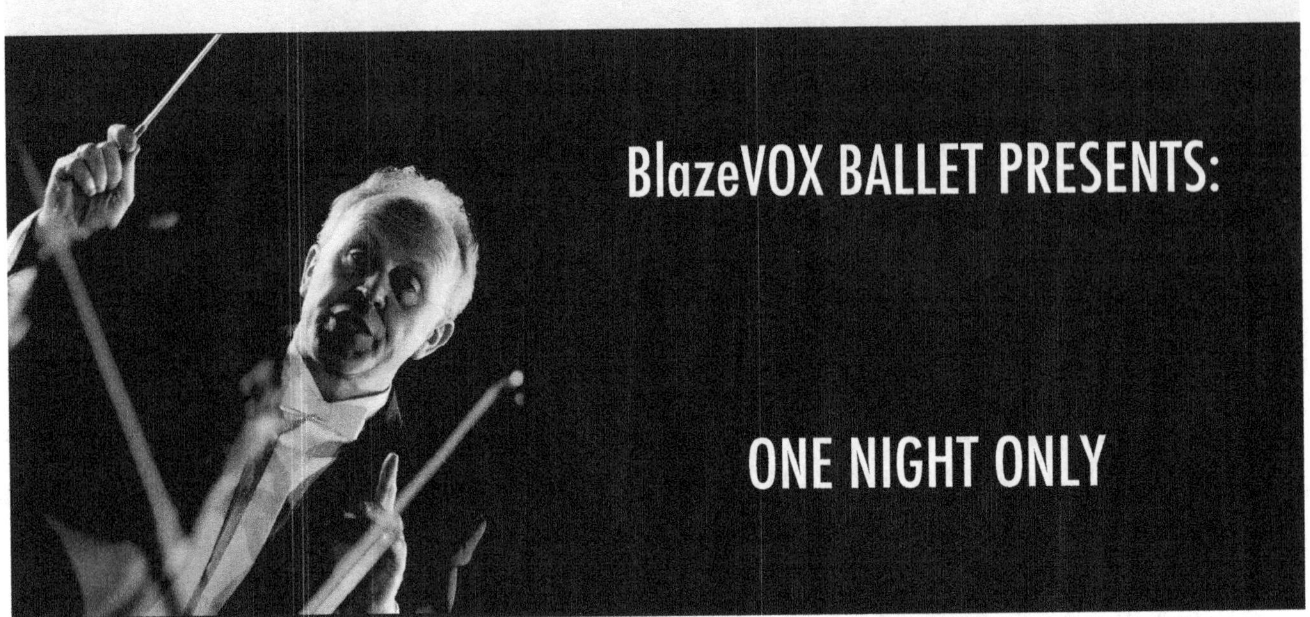

Apollo, once titled Apollon Musagete, is a ballet by Igor Stravinsky and is based on the story of Apollo, as the conductor of the muses. The god instructs the muses in their arts and leads them to Parnassus. Stravinsky was commissioned to write Apollo in 1927 for a festival of contemporary music to be held at the Library of Congress, in Washington, D.C. Originally choreographed by George Balanchine, it is his oldest surviving ballet, and his first public success.

Choreographed for five dancers in definitively modern 'black and white' leotard ballet; this work has been revived by Geoffrey Gatza, his second work for BXB, as part of the Umbrella Project. In angular, contemporary choreography this striking and inventive performance is paired to a modernist score arranged and conducted by Max Ernst. Gatza states. 'The ballet itself means nothing. It's a conceptual piece about art and chess that will be a lot of fun.'

Although the score is based on ideas of Ezra Pound's notions of poetry: Logopoeia, Melopoeia and Phanopoeia, neither the music nor the ballet itself makes specific or literal interpretation of these ideas. An understanding of these ideas was merely a point of departure for the choreography.

WEDNESDAY, JUNE 19 2013
At the Studio Center, Buffalo, NY

Seating starts at 5:30PM
For tickets call 716-873-5454

Contents

APOLLO

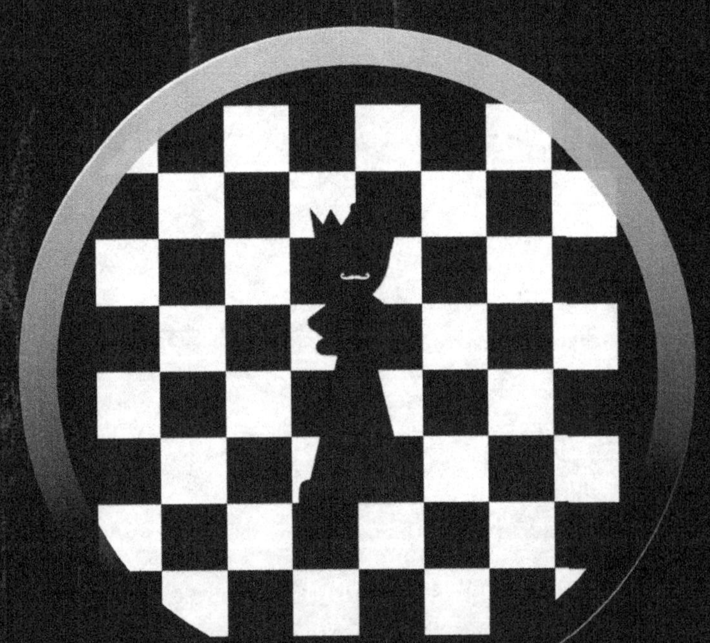

AN INTRODUCTION:

from Rrose Sélavy

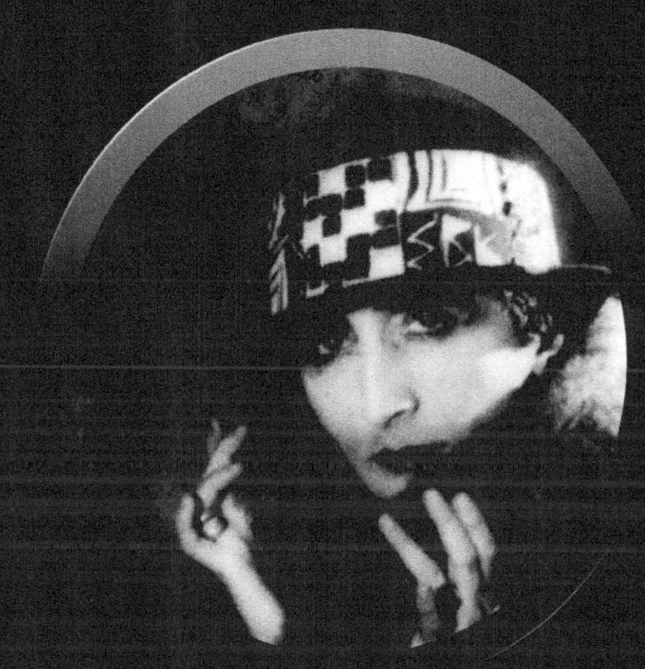

WELCOME TO OUR BALLET

Principal Dancers: Marcel Duchamp / Rrose Sélavy, Leonora Carrington, Dorothea Tanning & Gertrude Abercrombie; Orchestra conducted by Max Ernst; featuring Solo Trumpeter: Dizzy Gillespie

An Introduction:

Welcome to our Ballet, from Rrose Sélavy

A deep voice from above states, please welcome, Rrose Sélavy.
The audience rises up in applause. Following a spotlight, she walks
To center stage, waving her hands in gratitude and appreciation.
She is waiting for the audience to wind down but there is no relenting.
The preeminent artist of the 20th century is taking stage with three
Surrealist painters. It will be an evening not soon forgotten.

'Welcome, welcome, thank you for coming to our performance.
My name is Rrose Sélavy and I will be your host for this evening.
Of course you can plainly see that it is I, voilà, Marcel Duchamp
Dressed in women's clothing as my alter ego and loving colleague.
Yes, thank you, a voice from the audience said, coconspirator.
That unfortunate phrase may be true. Well done. Now that said,
We are going to go into our performance, a ballet of Stravinsky's
Entitled Apollo. Originally titled Apollon Musagete and eventually
Shortened in the nineteen-fifties to be somewhat less pretentious.

We shall use the game of chess as a working metaphor for this ballet.
Our dancers and I shall take on the characteristics of chess pieces;
Their movements and rules will emulate image, music and meaning.
This ballet tells the story of Apollo, the conductor of the muses.
Polyhymnia, the muse of rhetoric, Terpsichore, the muse of dance
And Calliope, the muse of poetry are ingénues, new to being muses.
You can imagine this as their first day at being muses. A frightening
Prospect by any standard. Apollo instructs them in their virtuosities
And leads them to Parnassus. There they guide the world's artists.

This piece of music is written for thirty-four instruments.
We chose the metaphoric representation that each musician
Shall parallel a chess piece. The thirty-two pieces of regular
Game play and the two extra queens used in tournament play.
Now, I would like to properly introduce tonight's conductor
Whose baton will lead the orchestra, the famed surrealist painter
And poet, Max Ernst. His wife, Dorothea Tanning will be dancing
As Calliope. So please, ladies and gentlemen, a round of applause!

Tonight's feature trumpet soloist is the great Dizzy Gillespie,
Whose new composition will accompany Gertrude Abercrombie,
Who is dancing as Terpsichore, during in her variation. Leonora
Carrington is cast in the role of Polyhymnia. The players are painters,
Sculptors, and musicians and I want to thank them for coming together
To make this ballet a reality. I would also like to thank those who funded
Our endeavor, without them this project would remain blank paper.

Now to begin. I will enact two roles in this performance. As Marcel, Apollo.
As myself, Rrose; will guide, narrating the proceedings as Tiresias, the blind
Prophet of Thebes. If you recall your Greek mythology, Tiresias was renown
For his extraordinary prophetic powers, his ability to interpret the language
Of the birds and his longevity. According to one legend, Tiresias lived for nine
Generations interchanging genders as man and woman. A descendant of the
Spartoi, a people who they say were crafted from dragon's teeth. Born a man,
The son of Everes and the Nymph Chariclo. His mother was a close friend
of Athena, goddess of wisdom. So our young man had many fine prospects.

Tiresias has many attributes, a transgendered mythological figure, a blind seer,
With great wisdom cultivated through the agony of an exceptionally long life.
How did this happen you may wonder, very simple. The goddess Hera cursed
Him several times for not being as calculating as maybe he might have been.
When Tiresias was a young man, while walking home to his mother, he caught
Sight of two snakes intertwined, mating near Mount Cyllene in Peloponnese.
Heartlessly, as young men can be, their morality taking shape, still forming,
He took up his walking stick and furiously beat at the snakes forcing them
To break part. In an instant he transformed into a woman...

Seven years later, Tiresias again saw another a couple of snakes entangled, mating.
This time, being a bit more cautious she lay down her staff, knelt to the ground
And bowed. In that moment she was changed back into a man. One can imagine
The sorrow she must have felt by the loss. It is said he was a husband and father,
A mother, a daughter and a wife. The range of experiences this person was exposed to
Is truly something to ponder. We were not the only ones to think of this. High on
Mount Olympus, Zeus, the king of the gods, and his wife Hera were arguing
Whether men or women take more pleasure from love. "Let's ask the wise Tiresias
From Thebes. He knows best. After all, in his life he has been both man and woman."

With a clap, they evaporated from Mount Olympus and appeared in a garden.
The summertime flowers were in bloom and the scent of rose hung in the air.
In a snap of their fingers Tiresias was brought before them. "Now tell us,
With an honest open heart, do men or women take more pleasure in love?"
Tiresias was naturally afraid to answer; this was a question with no answer.
"My dear Hera, My wonderful Zeus, I cannot say how any one sex can love.
I have loved with pleasure as both man with woman and woman with man.
Both were lovely and fulfilling; exotic and warm sensations please both sexes.
It is up to each person to love as they can love and seek the love within the self.

But that would not do. Zeus called him a prevaricator. Hera called him an evader.
"You must do better than that my dear Tiresias," Hera proclaimed; punishment
Laced in her tone. "It was I that turned you into a woman all those years ago.
In that time you were a priestess of mine, then you were forced into prostitution
From there you were purchased and married to a man, kind though he be, you
Were bought. Sex was never your own once you were transformed into woman.
I have insinuated over and over again, that men are the ones who are pleasured
Most." "Do not listen to this," Zeus interrupted. "My boy, we have seen their faces.
The plastic faces of orgasm, that grimace of ecstasy is all the evidence we require."

Tiresias was about to answer in favor of men, but stopped. Hera scowled, "how dare
You both!" She clicked her fingers changing Tiresias again into a woman. From there
Hera sent her from the garden to the bathhouse, sold once again as rightful property.
She wept and wept and wept. It was her sorrow that woke the bathing goddess
Athena. Seeing the woman crying on the stoop below she decided to offer her
Assistance. Athena, completely naked came down the stairs to hug the woman,
But as soon as Tiresias lifted her head, she saw him as a man, disguised. Shamed,
She tried to cover his eyes with her hands but her rage routed intention leaving
Tiresias struck blind. Tiresias fell to the floor with yet another misery to contend.

What else is there do but cry? Blind, cursed, misunderstood by even the gods;
She was outmaneuvered. Resigned to perish, she lay prostrate on the floor.
Once Athena's anger subsided, she recognized this woman as Chariclo's son.
Taking strength from her tears, the drops of wisdom that comes from suffering
Tiresias became bold, and recounted to Athena all the strange events in the garden.
Athena restored her to a man, but regrettably, could not reverse his blindness.
She gave him a cornel-wood staff, enabling him to walk as if he had sight. She
Took hold of a snake and purified his ears enabling him to receive divinations
Spoken by the birds. Thus granting him the gifts of prophesy as well as long life.

A long life is a curse as evil as a fine memory. Forgetting the past is as reassuring
As knowing that there is a finality to the madness that is our lives. To pass on
Into the dark recesses of whatever is after this frozen moment. There is an end.
And we all shall inherit that gift; to make small what was once great, reduce to ash
The golden temples we cloister. It is why we are performing, to know we are alive.
Initially commissioned for a festival of contemporary music at the Library of Congress,
In Washington, D.C. Stravinsky's ballet Apollo is one of the finest achievements in
Modernism. A triumph for its choreographer, ballet master George Balanchine.
The set was designed by André Bauchant, with costumes by Coco Chanel.

Choreographed in Balanchine's neoclassical style, Apollo was a direct response
To the excesses of romanticism and modernity. Stripped of its detailed narrative
And heavy theatrical setting, we are left with the only the dance itself, refined, chic,
Modern, retaining fine pointe work, while avoiding the traps of over the top drama,
The gambits of caricature typical of the technique often found in 19th century dance.
The theme of this story is outmoded by today's standards, a male figure leading female
Muses towards a dreamtime mountain for them to become objects for artists to swoon.
But not this night. Tonight, in my part as narrator, Tiresias will direct, guide the dancers.
As Apollo, I shall dance with our muses, three bold women, as equals on a chessboard.

The very idea of gods and goddesses are antique relics, as are the Freudian ideas
So often associated with chess, that unconscious need for father-murder. Royalty
Carved into box wood armies. Wooden family romances enacting out forgotten
Desires for omnipotence recaptured in elements of creative arts, sport and *unio mystica,*
That special union of the believer with the sacred. As Apollo was for Stravinsky,
The chessboard will be our medium to meet the divine halfway, that gray line resting
Between black squares and white squares. The tiles will be the floor upon which our
Dance will master, will ignore restrictions of classical rules and burst forth, break out
And announce that which exists within our reality as more kinetic than stationary.

We have worked long and hard and it is a real honor to say, 'Now on with the show!'

FIRST TABLEAU

THE BIRTH OF APOLLO

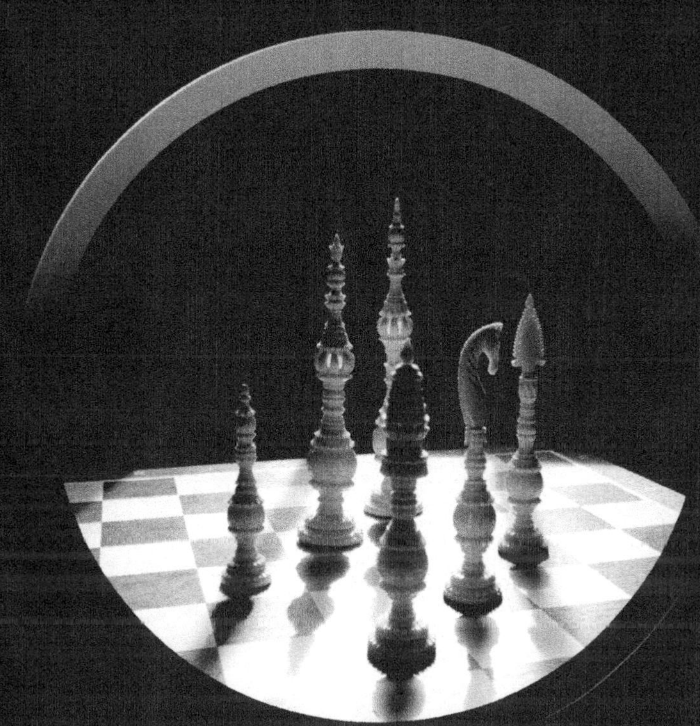

PROLOGUE

Dancers: Marcel Duchamp, Leonora Carrington, Dorothea Tanning & Gertrude Abercrombie

Narrator: Rrose Sélavy

The Birth of Apollo

After *Schaccia, Ludus* By Marcus Hieronymus Vida, 1527 and Caïssa by William Jones, 1763

Now I am ready to tell you of birth of Apollo,

How he fell in love with the charming dryad,
Caïssa and how the game of chess was invented for her.

The only arbiter in chess is salient victory.
Life's victory is surviving; avoiding death.

This is how Leto found victory, living her life.
In constant movement, ever hiding from Hera

The queen of the gods. Leto, a goddess in her own right
Is the lithe daughter of the Titans Coeus and Phoebe.

Her beauty was her prominence as jealousy was Hera's.
She was kept, hidden away on the island of Kos for fear

That Hera would kill her if ever she had the chance.
This threat was real. Leto was repulsed from all lands

Upon earth. And as these things happen, Leto conceived
After her splendor inadvertently caught the eye of Zeus.

Leto was devastated. How could this happen? She shrieked
Into the emptiness where she hid. Hera certainly will find her,

Kill her and her unborn children. She is going to have twins,
A son, the god, Apollo and a daughter, the goddess, Artemis.

Now as never before did Leto take action. She called out to
Her sister, Asteria, the goddess of falling stars for sanctuary.

The year before Leto went into hiding, Asteria had transformed
Into an elegant quail, a tiny speckled bird, to avoid Zeus' advances.

In her rage, sorrow and fear, Asteria gave Leto a final tender hug
And flew high up into the sky, transformed once again, changing

Her form into a falling star, and fell to earth in a blaze of water.
Her body fell into the Aegean Sea and smoothed into a small island.

She became the quail island of Ortygia. Since this island was not
Attached to the ocean floor, Leto could refuge in her sister's arms

And give birth in the goodwill that she deserved. The vengeful Hera
Was in check. She could not do anything other than watch her fear

Come to life. Apollo, the god of music, playing a golden lyre is born.
Artemis, the goddess of the wildlands, mistress of animals is born.

And poor Leto, having played her part withdraws,
To remain in the dim, shadowy corners of Olympus.

*   *   *   *

Some children grow up and do
The most extraordinary things,
Other simply just grow. Apollo
The sun god, the silver archer
Of light did the extraordinary.

Being bound to truth and prophecy,
He cannot speak a lie. And as the leader
Of the choir of muses, Apollon Musegetes
He guides them while plucking his golden
Lyre as the patron of art, music and poetry.

Each morning, at each sunrise,
It is Apollo we see driving
The sun across the blue-black sky,
Yoked to his four-horsed chariot.

His tree is the laurel.
The crow his bird.
The dolphin his animal.

He brought the world
The arts of medicine.
He also brought into
The world black plagues.

And it is to him
We offer heartfelt
Homage in tonight's
Performance.

*　　*　　*　　*

When Sylvia Plath wants to bring the idea of nature
Into her poetry, she calls upon the Dryad for help.

Consider her poem, 'On the Difficulty of Conjuring
Up a Dryad.' The title tells us everything; they are difficult.

The dryads are tree nymphs, specific to the oak tree.
Their spirit protects the tree over their long oaky lives.

They scatter their acorns in the best places for squirrels
To bury for winter meals or perhaps take root and grow.

They dance in their whirling branches to calm the trees
When the winds become too fearsome and untamed.

And it was this dance that Apollo happened to see
Conveying the sun over a storm shattered morning.

Apollo lost his heart to the beautiful dryad Caïssa.
In her swirling ballet she was a gyre of fascination.

*   *   *   *

Dryads are very shy creatures,
With one exception, Artemis,
Apollo's sister, they adore.
She was a friend to all nymphs.
She was wild, free, and unclean.
In uncivilized splendor she hid.

Caïssa could not hide from Apollo
Although she tried innocently, incessantly.
Each day he would make his advances
And each day she would run away
In fear. Caïssa found him repulsive.
He embodied everything she hated.

Stood solidly against. He was a dandy
With that golden lute, foppish with no
Beard on his chin, and smelled of laurel.
He also had the worst habit of telling
The truth outright when sometimes she
Sought a pleasant lie to delicate questions.

She wanted go to a field and play when he wanted to read.
He took her to the sun; she wanted to go to the garden.
She wanted silence when he wanted to preform a paean.
So after a string of rejections, he conferred with Artemis.
She sent him to seek advice from Euphron, god of sport.
Euphron knew what to do, create a game to win her heart.

In one moment, or a minor eternity, Euphron
Called Apollo to his workshop. His job done,
The game of kings, Chess, had been invented.
Euphron brought out a black and white checkered
Board containing eight rows up, eight files down
Each row containing eight squares totaling sixty-four.
From a leather case, Euphron placed thirty-two
Pieces on the board, describing each character's role.

There is a malignant, latent energy boxed up
In these armies, he told Apollo, but delights
That rival even the creative arts are here
To behold for any player of any ability.
All that is required is a courageous mind.
On these squares these pieces will move or
Be captured in due course by your opponent.
Controlling the game is the king, not unlike

Your father, it is a very powerful piece. But
When cornered and attacked, the game is lost.
The other pieces work to prevent this attack
While trying to capture the other side's king.
The queen has the greatest ability to move
Around the board. Able to use any course
She is a piece with which to take notice of
And fear. These are the bishops, they move

On the oblique. These are the knights who
Move up two squares and over one. They
Form a circle of sorts in their attack.
On the ends are the rooks that move
Up, down or across and over the board.
Standing in front are the pawns, they are
The soul of the game. They move only
One step forward and attack on the flanks.
Though small, their fate lies at the center

Of the game. For they represent the societies
for whom this game of squares is performed.
This game personifies the arts of war while
Stimulating the basic need to fight or hide.
Capturing the subtle arts found in the wild.
Apollo looked down at the board, and considering
All the possibilities was sad, there is nothing
But sorrow and grief to be found in this game.

*   *   *   *

Apollo thanks Euphron.
He decorates his head
With the laurel he wore
To honor his achievement.

He went to find Caïssa
She was dancing in an oak tree.
Apollo sits under the tree
Without acknowledging her.

There he sets up the chessboard.
He explains the chess rules into the air.
She is shy, secreted behind a branch,
And watches the horrible god play.

All night Apollo played chess by himself
And Caissa watched from above,
Head tilted in wonder, lip quivering
In anxious, nervous passion. Desire

Brought sweat to her palms as she
Watched and contemplated positions.
Slowly the game transmutes her image
Of Apollo, who seems now, less repulsive.

She crawls down from her tree
As might an orange cat confident
In her fear of everything and nothing.
Slowly, with care, she sits next to Apollo.

He touches her fingers
Uses his hand to guide
Her fingers over the board
To move, direct her pleasures.

Together they play the game
Over days and weeks, sitting
Under the oak tree neither one
Eating or sleeping, consumed

With their play. Or rather
To be more accurate Caïssa
Held the passion for Chess.
Apollo wanted another game.

She blocked his advances once
Again, but this time not due
To lack of love, no she loved
Apollo, he brought this game

Into her life. She felt so full
Brave, decisive in ways she
Never felt before. Control
Beyond the irrational world
In which she constantly tread.

Here was a world safe in its logic.
Here she could fight as well as hide.
With shrugged shoulders Apollo
Left the shade of the oak tree.

He left Caïssa with her game,
Becoming the muse of chess.
And Apollo became the very
First chess widow in history.

SECOND TABLEAU

VARIATION OF APOLLO

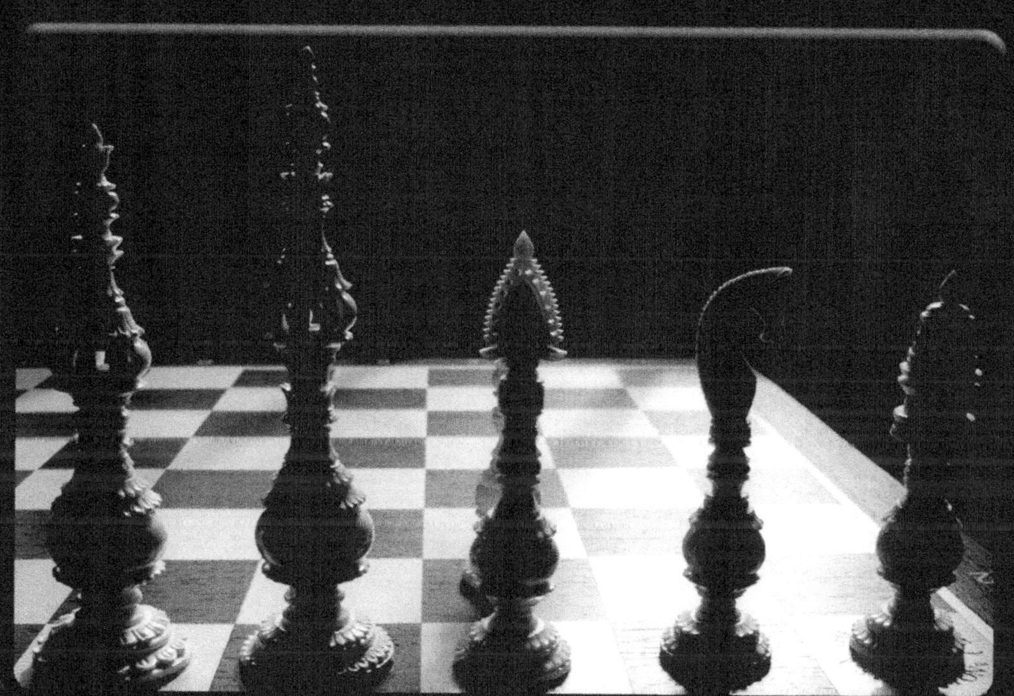

The Moment Duchamp Broke with Painting

Dancers: Marcel Duchamp, Leonora Carrington, Dorothea Tanning & Gertrude Abercrombie

Narrator: Rrose Sélavy

The Moment Duchamp Broke with Painting

In the 1920s Duchamp stopped painting, instead
he set out to explore 'the retinal boundaries
which had been established with Impressionism
into a field where language, thought, vision
act upon one another. There it changes form
through a complex interplay of new mental
and physical materials, heralding many of the
technical, mental and visual details found in recent art.'[1]

1. A new thought for that object.

The empty need of fame
Set in an imagined scene,

Set at night, with the Queen
In the state of undress; over

A chair lay the crimson velvet
Robe worn at her coronation.

It is the human face staring outwards
The mind behind that face is changing.

On canvas she is so lovely,
So unlike herself.

The great mystery of being
Is trying to capture real life.

Sound allows for silence, stillness.
Life's movements predict passing.

In one moment
One still second

Caught in oil
Representing

The time its subject stood
For hours, days at attention.

---

[1] from Dialogues with Marcel Duchamp, by Pierre Cabanne, 1987, pp.109-10

2. Propel

In 1912 Marcel Duchamp, Fernand Léger and Constantine Brancusi
Visiting the Salone de la Locomotion Aerienne saw a propeller in motion.

According to Marcel Duchamp, Brancusi
Exclaimed 'Now that is what I call sculpture!
From now on, sculpture must be nothing less than that.

Fernand Léger's version of that day differed.
'Before the Great War, I went to see the Air Show
With Marcel Duchamp and Brancusi.
Marcel was a dry fellow who had something elusive
About him. He was strolling amid the motors and propellers,
Not saying a word. Then, all of a sudden, he turned to Brancusi,

'It's all over for painting.
Who could better that propeller?
Tell me, can you do that?'

3. Flames

In 1913 at his Paris studio Duchamp mounted
A front bicycle fork with its wheel onto a stool.

It had no purpose
He simply enjoyed
Watching gyration.

'Just as I enjoy looking
At the flames dancing
In the fireplace.'

The flame spoke
No words
But illuminated
All the same.

It was years later
In New York
Bicycle Wheel
Was realized as
A readymade.

4. Astronautica

One does not
Simply choose
To stop painting.

Analogous to
Breaking one's leg.
It just happens.

The mind
Moves
Beyond
Being there.

Disobeying
Its confines
To portray
New ideas
Upon new
Substances.

To produce
A believable
Kinetic reality,
Merging
Two styles
Under one
Umbrella

From the
Mundane,
Ad Astra.

SECOND TABLEAU

PAS D'ACTION

(APOLLO AND THE THREE MUSES)

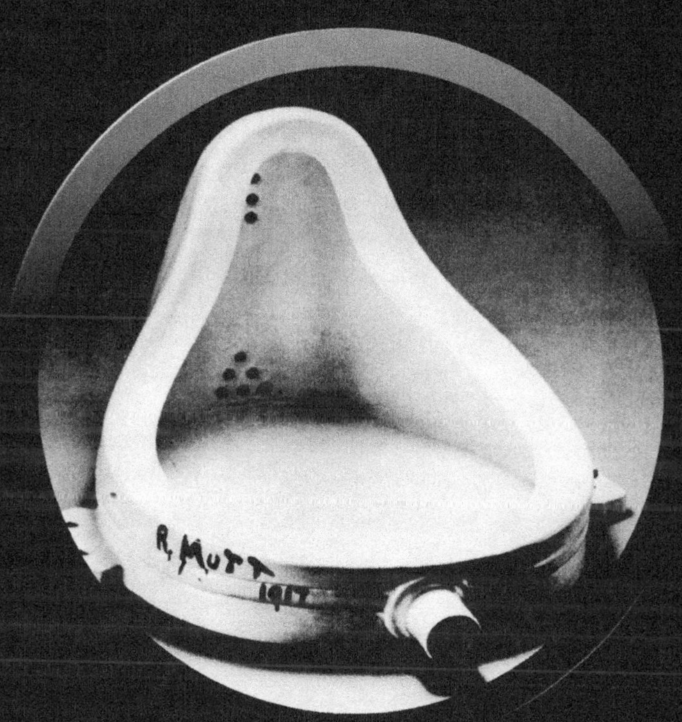

Playing Chess with Marcel Ducham (sic)

Dancers: Marcel Duchamp, Leonora Carrington, Dorothea Tanning & Gertrude Abercrombie

Narrator: Rrose Sélavy

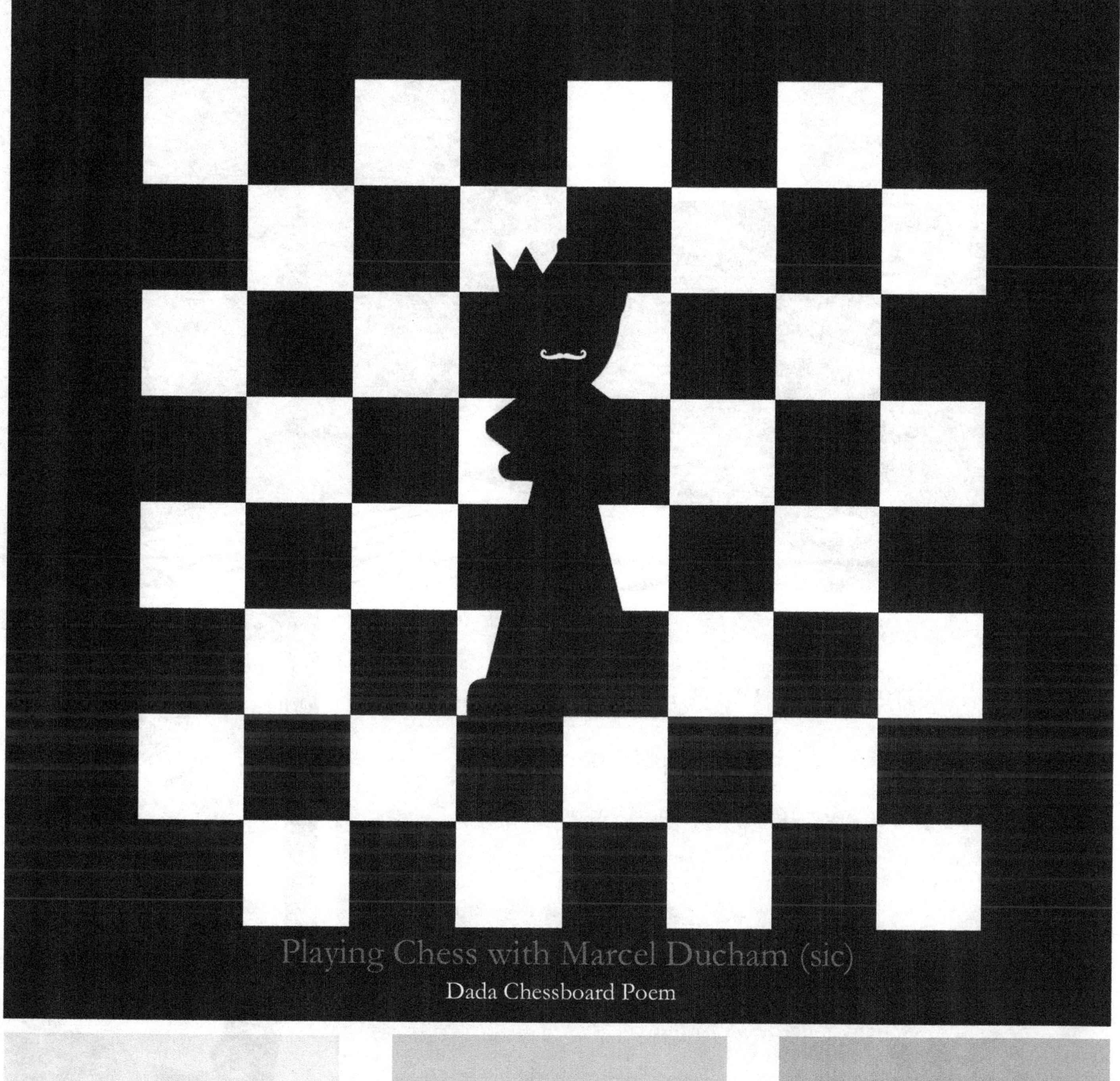
Playing Chess with Marcel Ducham (sic)
Dada Chessboard Poem

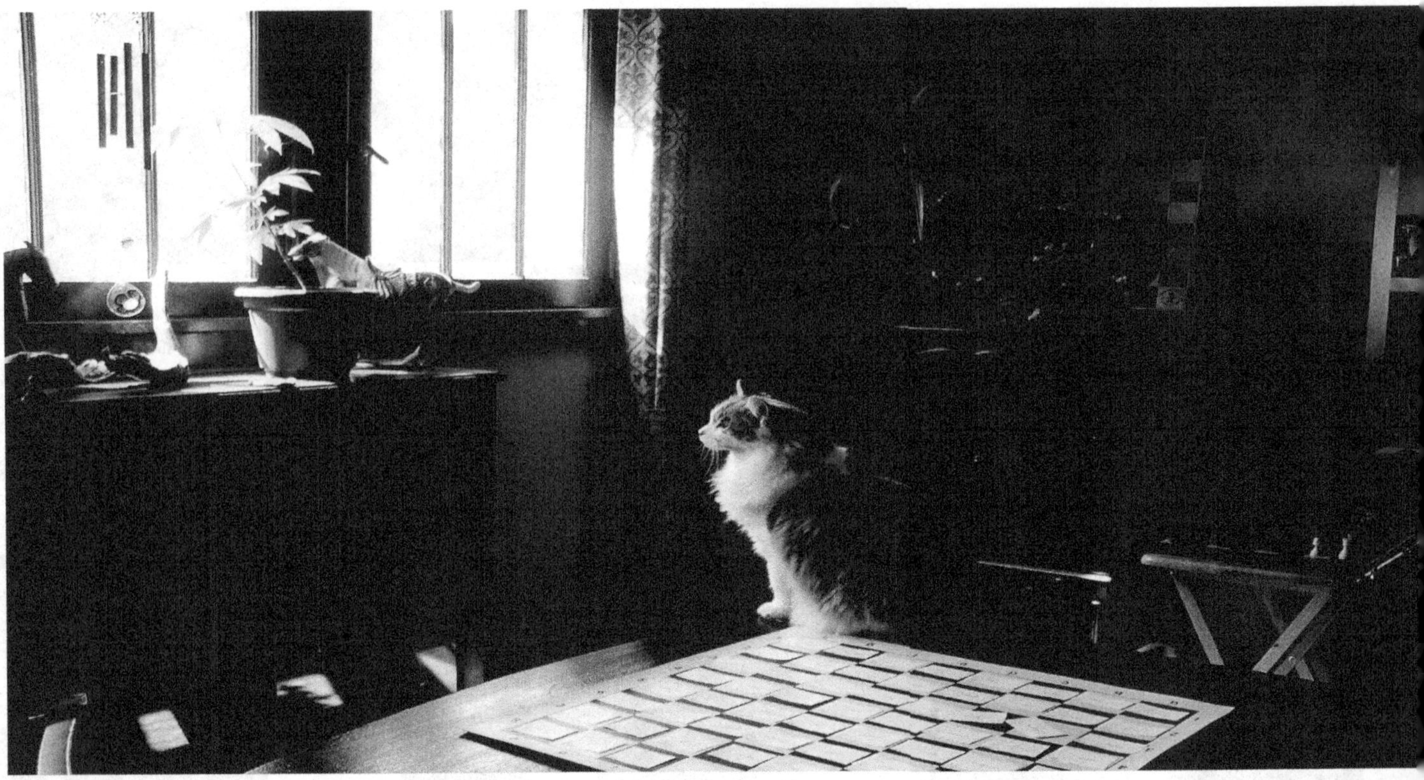

Playing Chess with Marcel Ducham

Dada Chessboard Poem

—after, Apolinere Enameled, Marcel Duchamp, 1916

Playing Chess with Marcel Ducham is a poem dedicated to Marcel Duchamp. Using chess and experimental forms we present a poem of nonsensical gibberish that explores the rhythm of language through the moment and movement of two great minds locked in a puzzle. These poems appeal to the aureate sounds upon the ear and the repetition of the words in their act of play open up new experiences to the eye. Retinal to the last move, this poem neither wins nor looses, its endgame concludes in a draw.

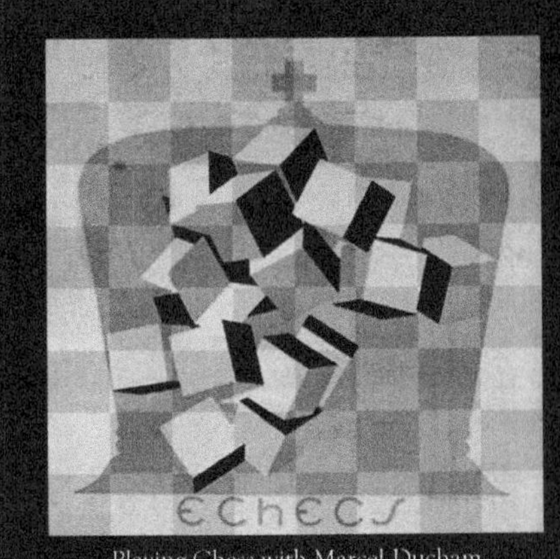

Playing Chess with Marcel Ducham

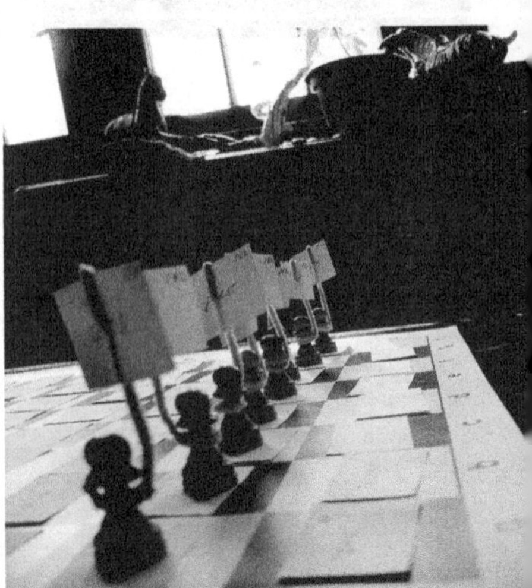

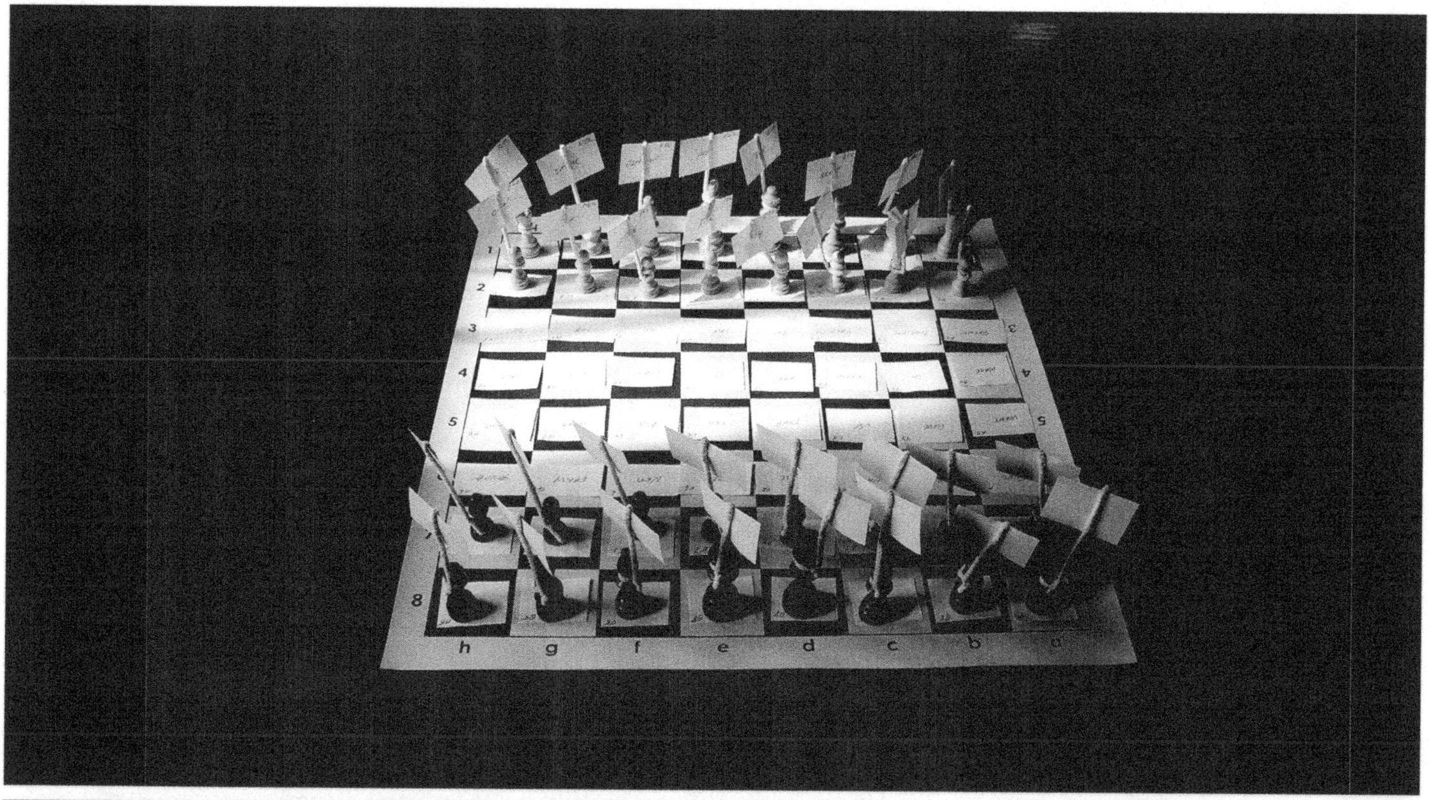

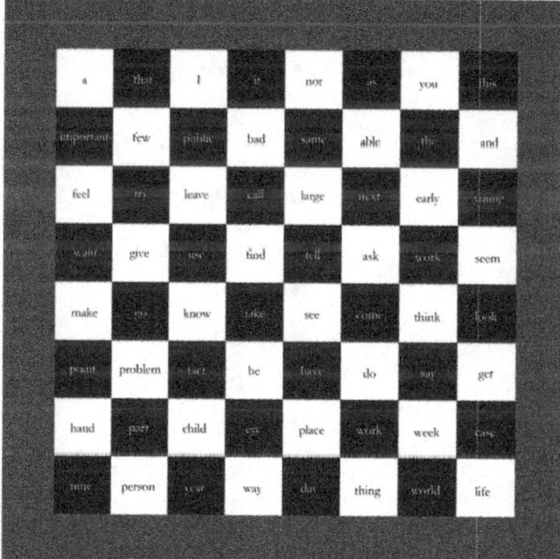

Method

THE CHESS GAME:

The poem uses the actual gameplay by Frank Marshall verses Marcel Duchamp at the Chess Olympiad held in Hamburg Germany in 1930. The whole game is listed below in algebraic notation.

Frank Marshall (Playing White) - M. Duchamp (Playing black)

1.d4 Nf6 2.Nf3 b6 3.c4 e6 4.Bg5 Be7 5.Nc3 Bb7 6.Qc2 d5 7.e3 O-O 8.cxd5 Nxd5 9.Bxe7 Qxe7 10.Nxd5 Bxd5 11.Bd3 h6 12.a3 c5 13.dxc5 Rc8 14.b4 bxc5 15.Rc1 Nd7 16.Ba6 Rc7 17.e4 Bb7 18.Bxb7 Rxb7 19.bxc5 Qxc5 20.O-O Qxc2 21.Rxc2 Kf8 22.Rfc1 Ke7 23.Nd4 Ke8 24.f4 Rab8 25.e5 Nf8 26.Rc5 Rb1 27.Rxb1 Rxb1+ 28.Kf2 Rb7 29.Rc8+ Ke7 30.Ra8 Ng6 31.g3 Kd7 32.a4 Ne7 33.Nb5 Nc8 34.g4 Rxb5 35.axb5 Kc7 36.g5 hxg5 37.b6+ Kb7 38.Rxc8 Kxc8 1/2-1/2

Each square and chess piece is assigned a word. I placed that word on the chessboard as well as a word on each chess piece. The lines of the poem follow the lines of play in the Marshall Duchamp game. The words were chosen from the current list of the one hundred most commonly used words in the English language. Each piece's word begins each line of the poem. The lines of the pieces path crossing the board follow how the rest of the line of poetry will construct. The language of movement can never be checked, never be mated. The game ends in a draw, as does the poem. How can it not be nonsense for the sake of the mirage that is art? The imagination is waiting to play, White to open.

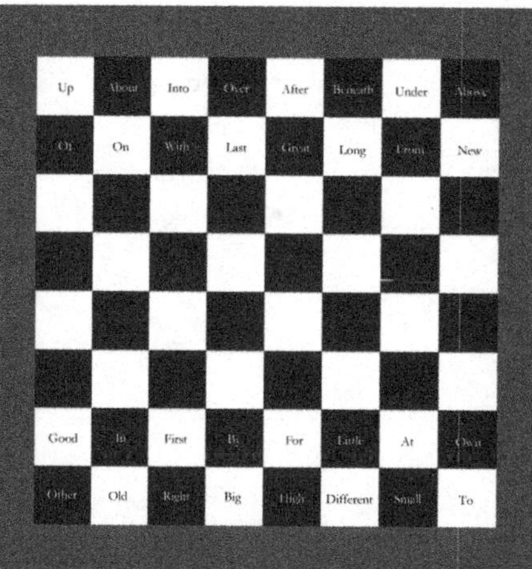

The Chessboard

Word Choice with Corresponding Board Position

• time	A1	• want	A5
• person	B1	• give	B5
• year	C1	• use	C5
• way	D1	• find	D5
• day	E1	• tell	E5
• thing	F1	• ask	F5
• world	G1	• work	G5
• life	H1	• seem	H5
• hand	A2	• feel	A6
• part	B2	• try	B6
• child	C2	• leave	C6
• eye	D2	• call	D6
• place	E2	• large	E6
• work	F2	• next	F6
• week	G2	• early	G6
• case	H2	• young	H6
• point	A3	• important	A7
• problem	B3	• few	B7
• fact	C3	• public	C7
• be	D3	• bad	D7
• have	E3	• same	E7
• do	F3	• able	F7
• say	G3	• the	G7
• get	H3	• and	H7
• make	A4	• a	A8
• go	B4	• that	B8
• know	C4	• I	C8
• take	D4	• it	D8
• see	E4	• not	E8
• come	F4	• as	F8
• think	G4	• you	G8
• look	H4	• this	H8

a	that	I	it	not	as	you	this
important	few	public	bad	same	able	the	and
feel	try	leave	call	large	next	early	young
want	give	use	find	tell	ask	work	seem
make	go	know	take	see	come	think	look
point	problem	fact	be	have	do	say	get
hand	part	child	eye	place	work	week	case
time	person	year	way	day	thing	world	life

The Setting of Words Chosen for the Chessboard

Chess Pieces

White Army

Word Choice	Corresponding Piece	Board Position
1. Good	White Pawn	A2
2. In	White Pawn	B2
3. First	White Pawn	C2
4. By	White Pawn	D2
5. For	White Pawn	E2
6. Little	White Pawn	F2
7. At	White Pawn	G2
8. Own	White Pawn	H2
9. Other	Queen Side Rook	A1
10. Old	Queen Side Knight	B2
11. Right	Queen Side Bishop	C2
12. Big	Queen	D2
13. High	King	E2
14. Different	King Side Bishop	F2
15. Small	King Side Knight	G2
16. To	King Side Rook	H2

Black Army

Word Choice	Corresponding Piece	Board Position
17. Of	Black Pawn	A7
18. On	Black Pawn	B7
19. With	Black Pawn	C7
20. Last	Black Pawn	D7
21. Great	Black Pawn	E7
22. Long	Black Pawn	F7
23. From	Black Pawn	G7
24. New	Black Pawn	H7
25. Up	Queen Side Rook	A8
26. About	Queen Side Knight	B8
27. Into	Queen Side Bishop	C8
28. Over	Queen	D8
29. After	King	E8
30. Beneath	King Side Bishop	F8
31. Under	King Side Knight	G8
32. Above	King Side Rook	H8

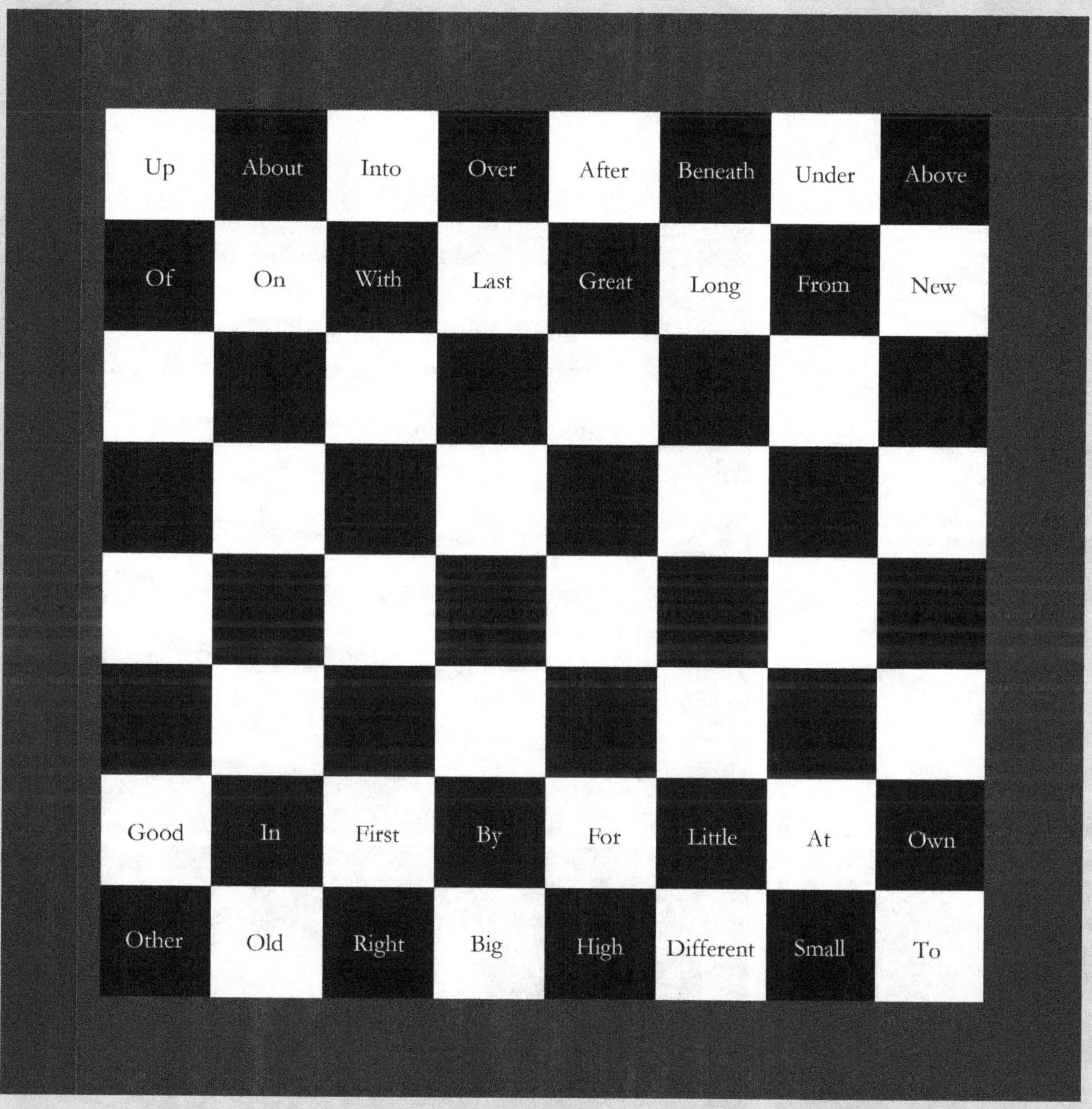

The Setting of Words Chosen for the Chess Pieces

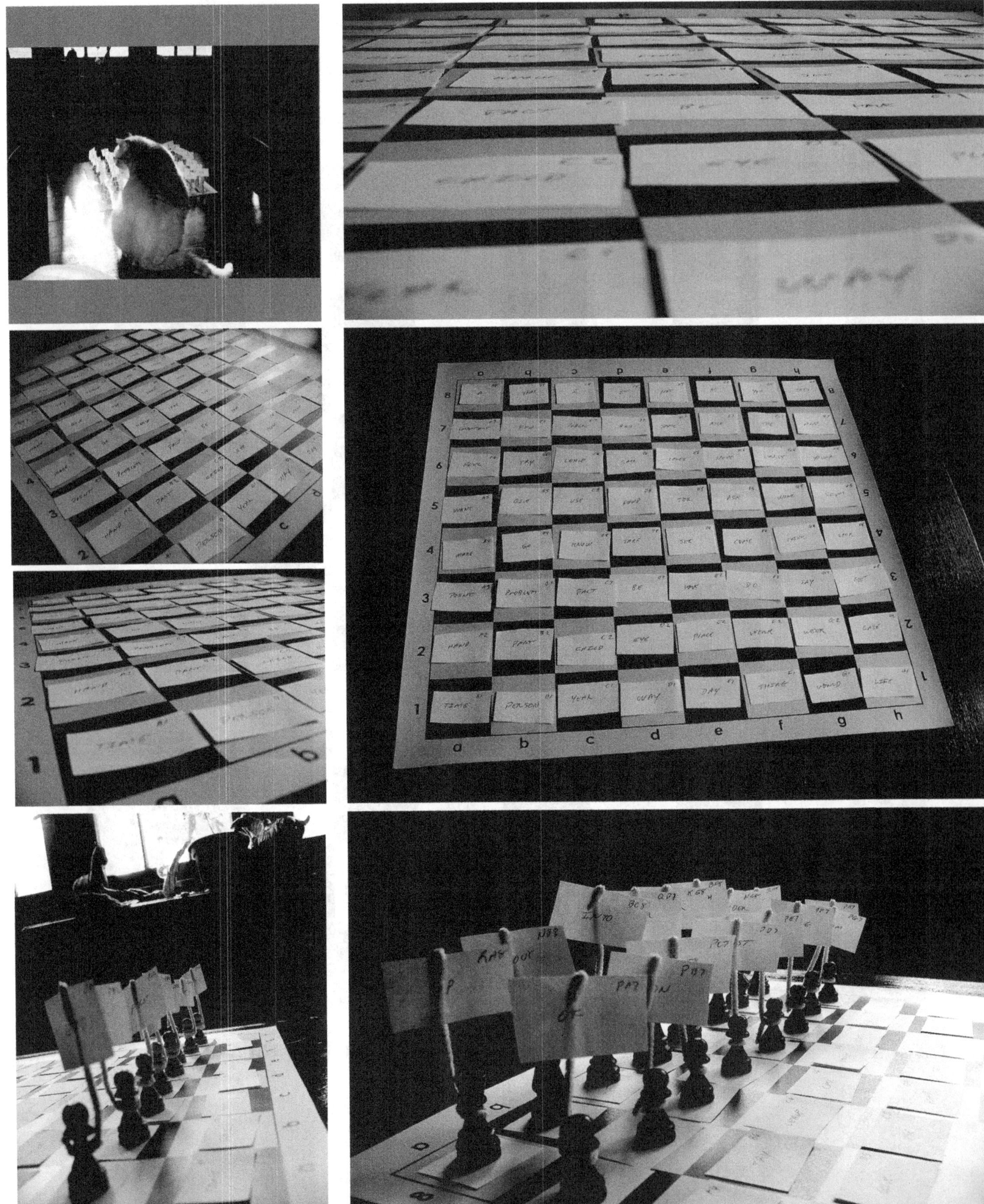

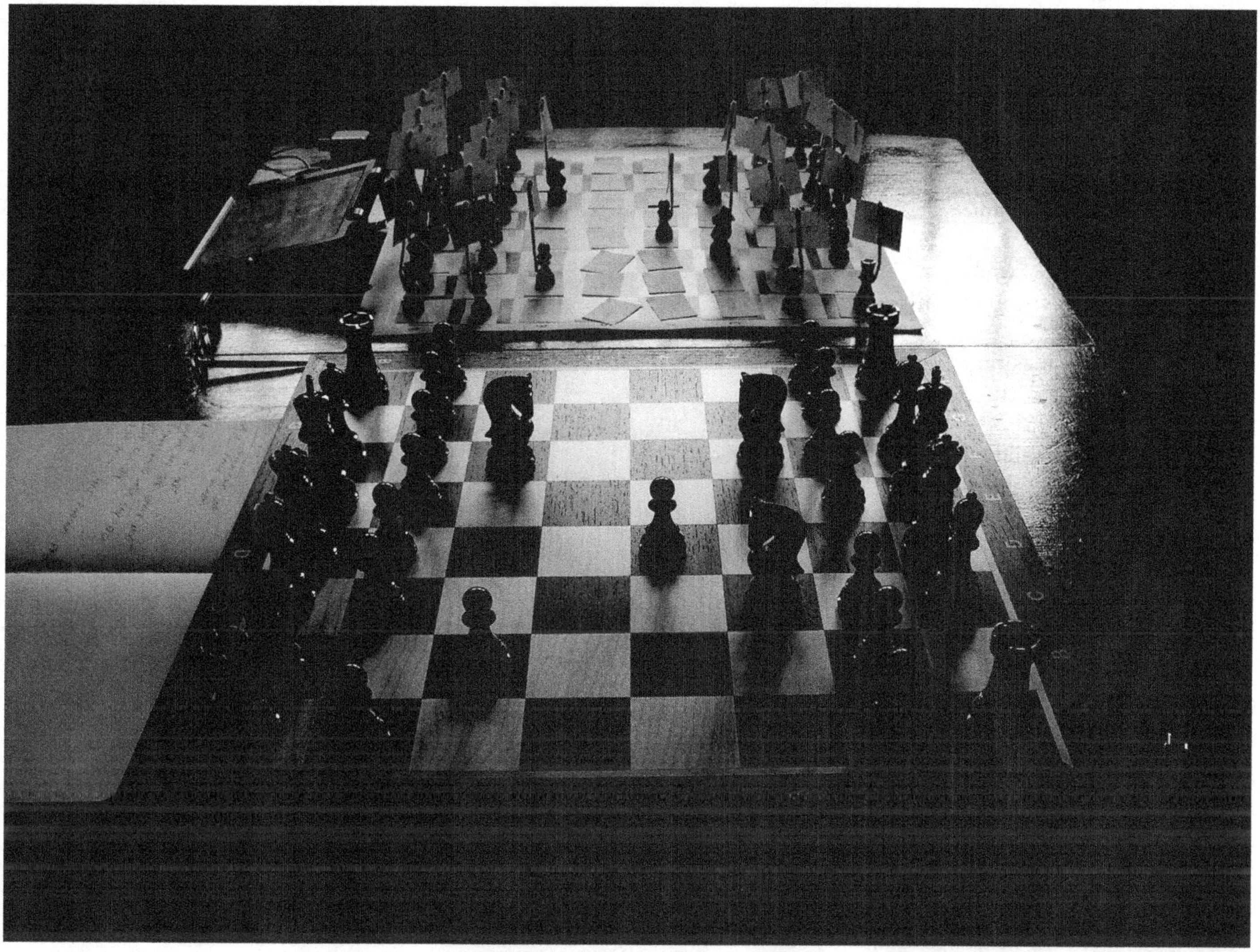

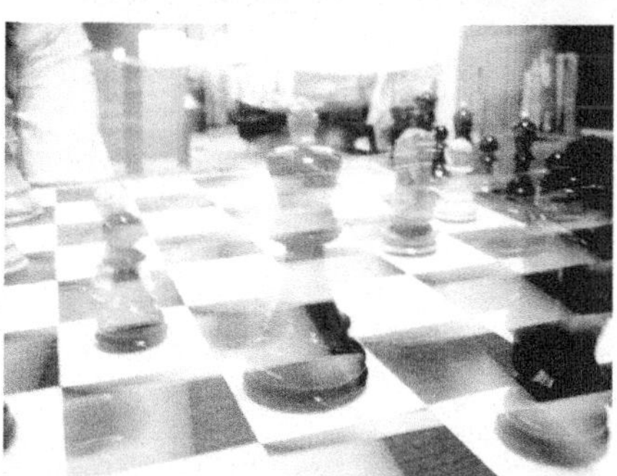
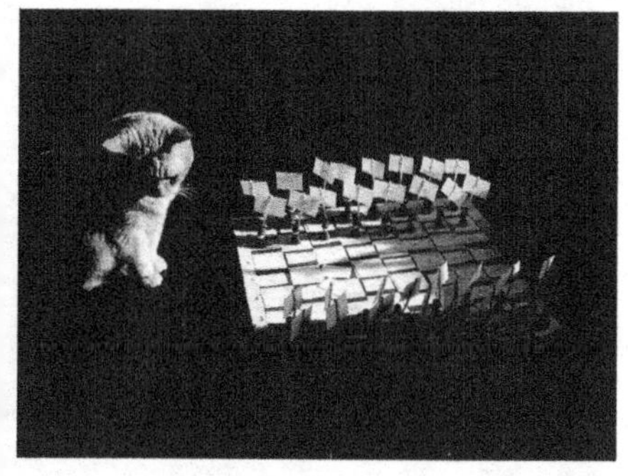
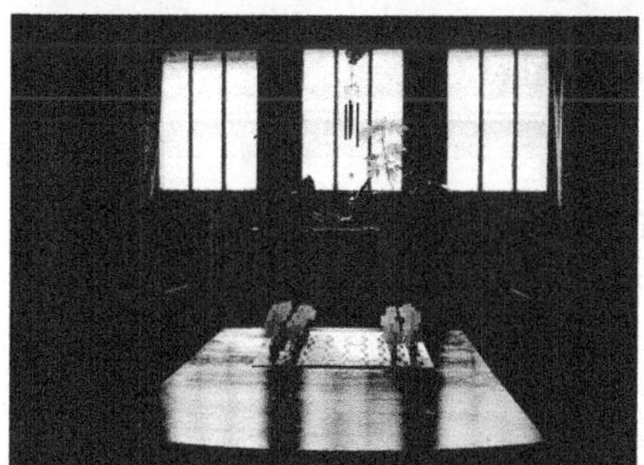
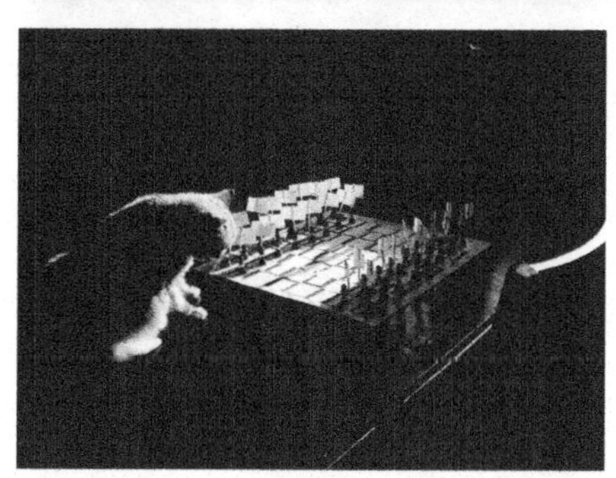
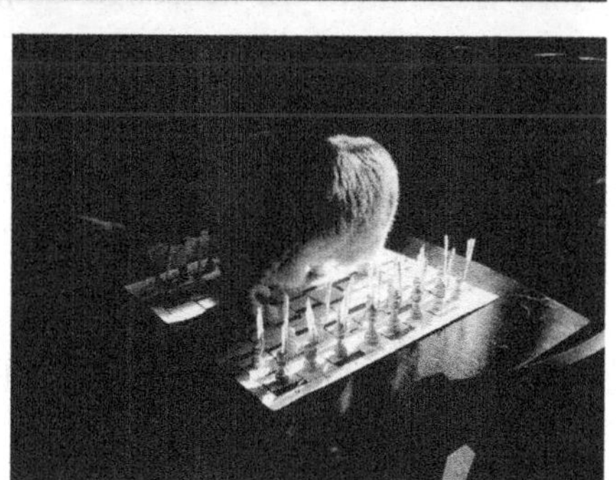
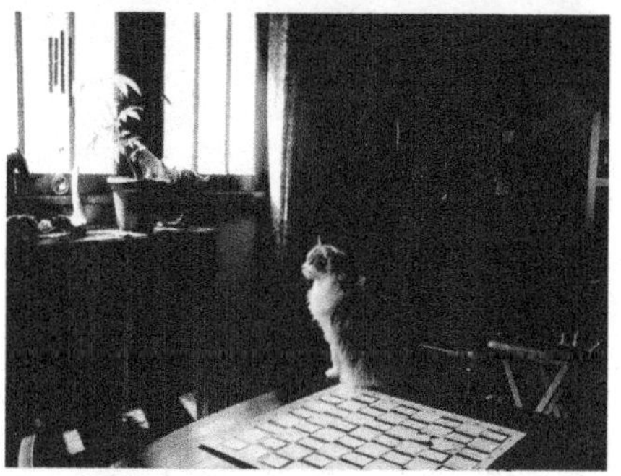

Playing Chess with Marcel Ducham (sic)
—after, Apolinere Enameled, Marcel Duchamp, 1916

1. Opening Game

By eye be take
Under you the early next

Small world week say do
On few try

First child fact know
Great same large

Right year eye have come work
Beneath as same

Old person part problem fact
Into I few

Big way child
Last bad call find

For place have
After not as you, above this you as

First know [takes] last find
Under next large call [takes] first find

Right work next [takes] beneath same
Over it [takes] right same

Old fact know use [takes] under find
Into few leave [takes] old find

Different think place be
New and young

By eye be take

Under you the
early next

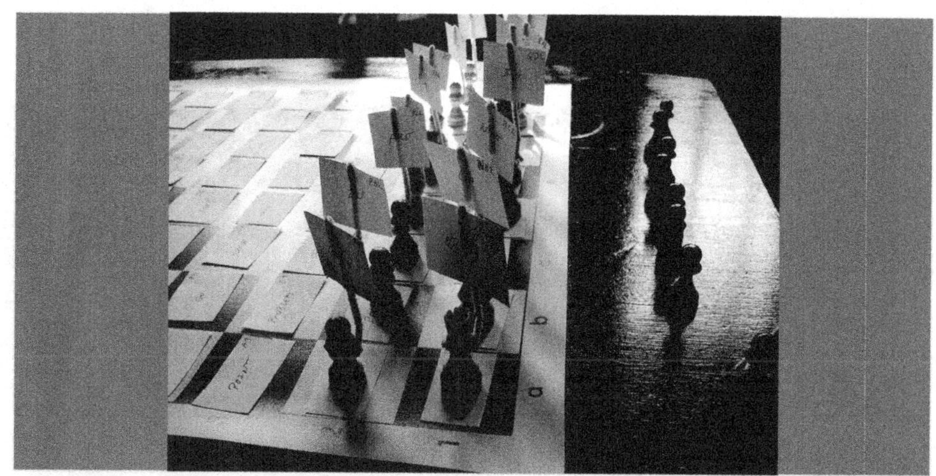
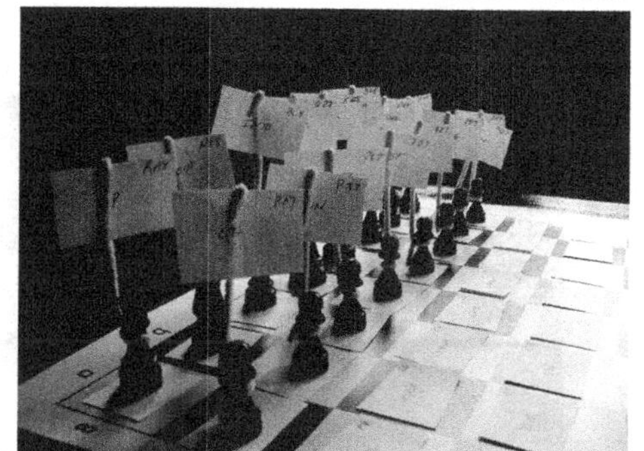
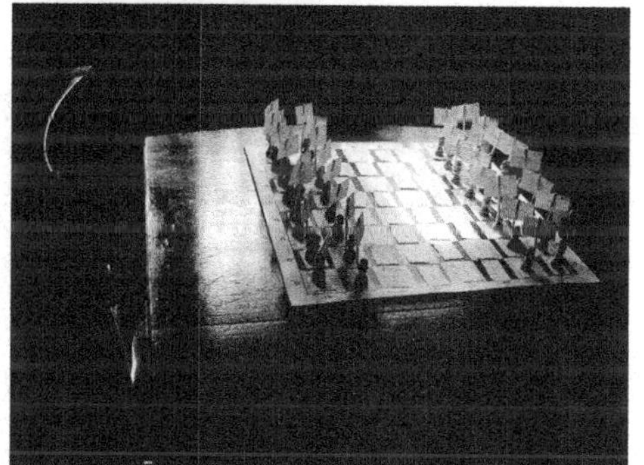
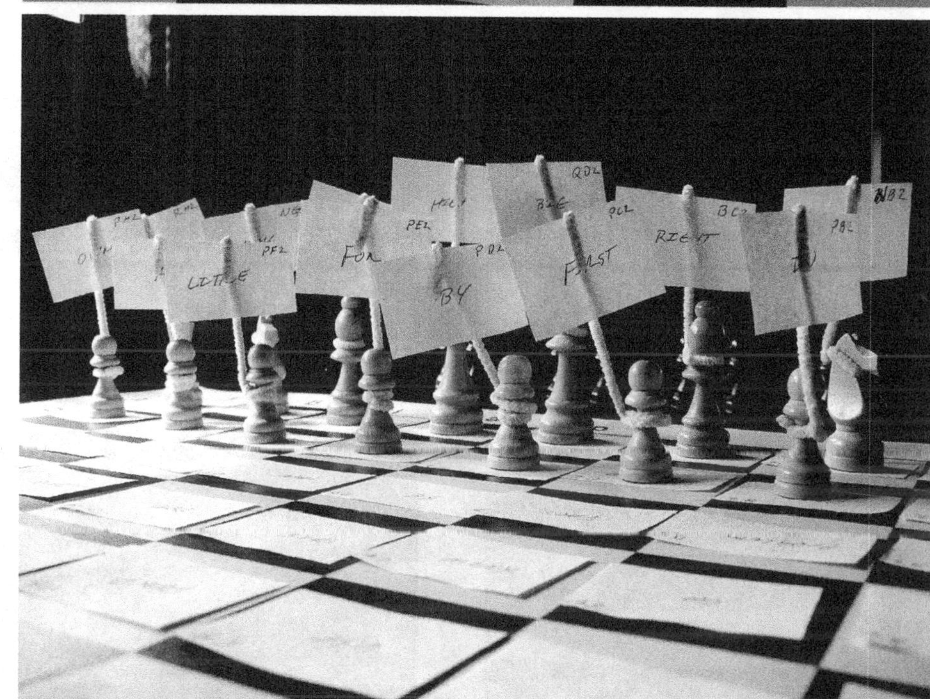
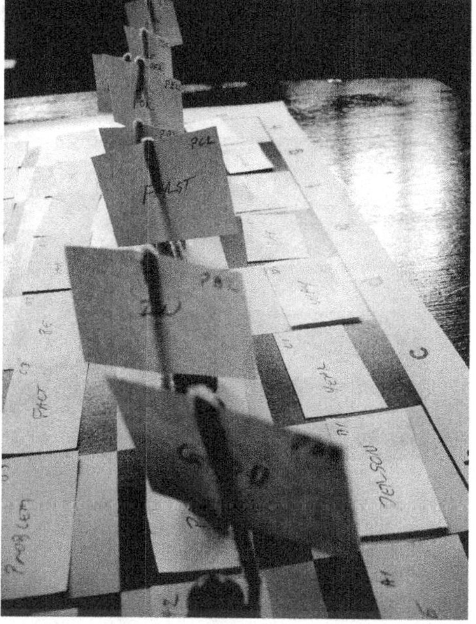
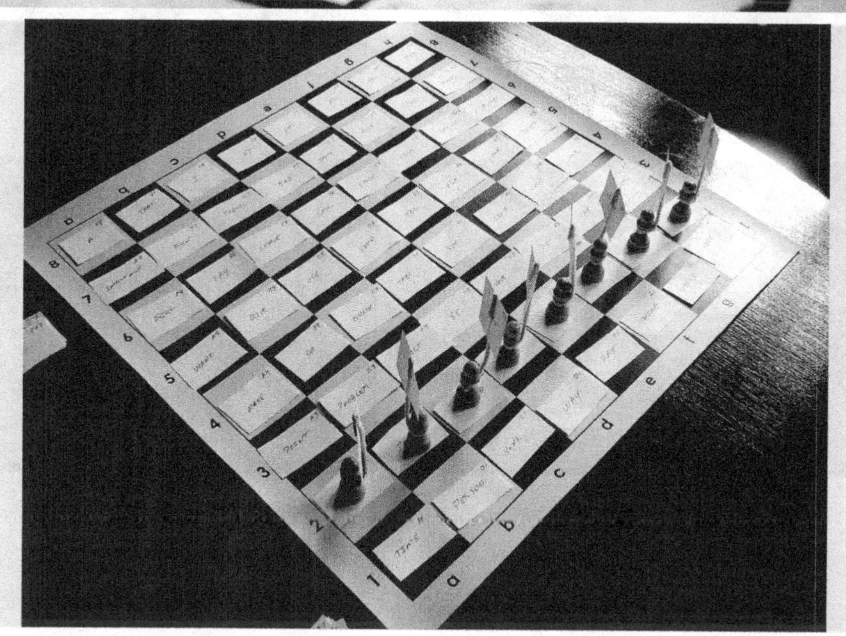

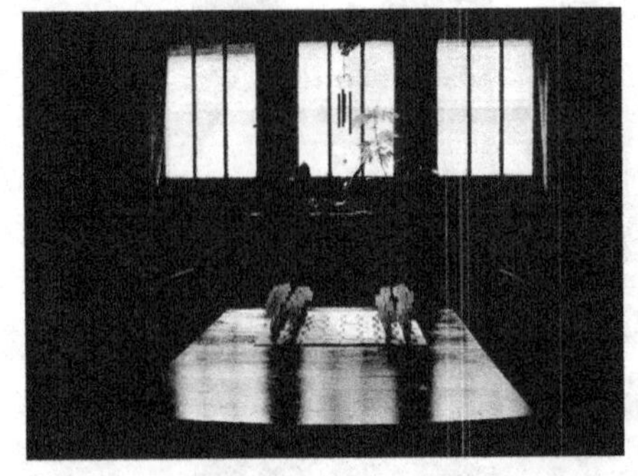
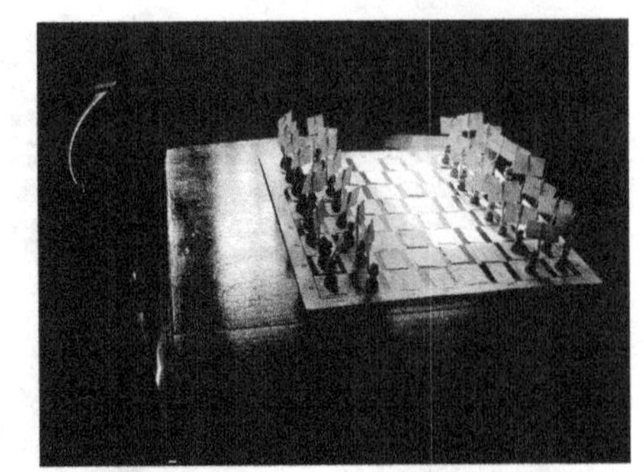
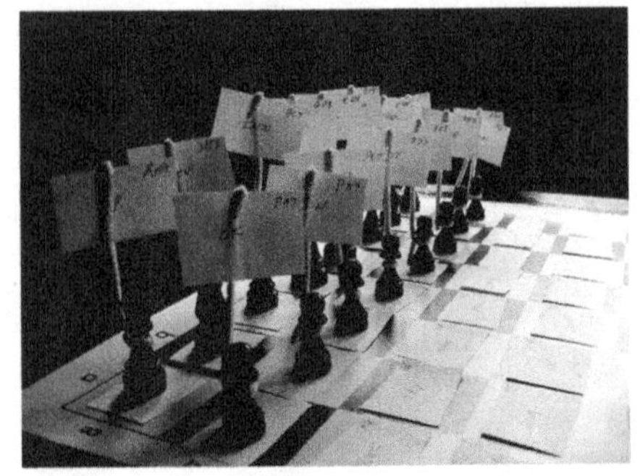
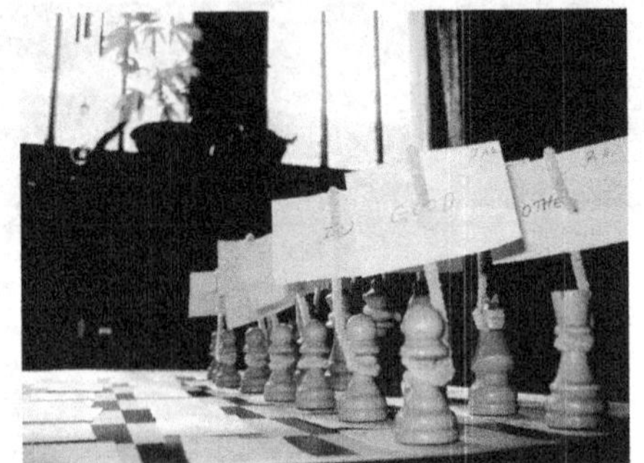
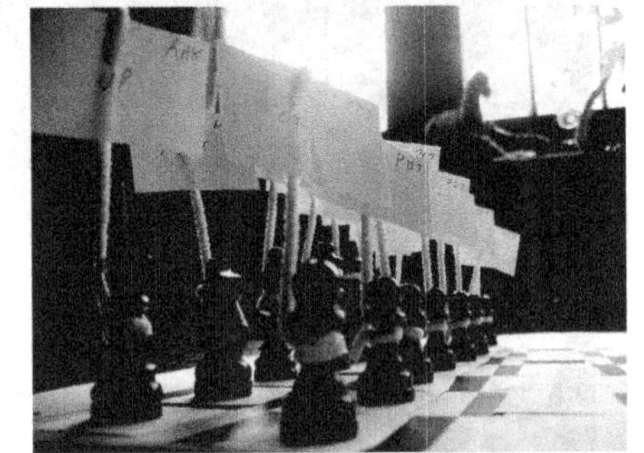
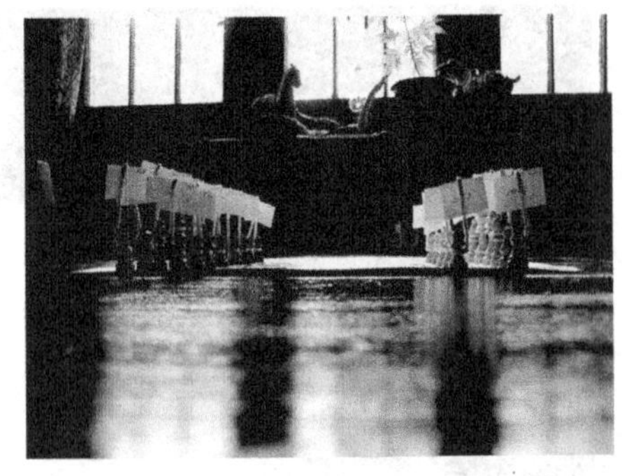
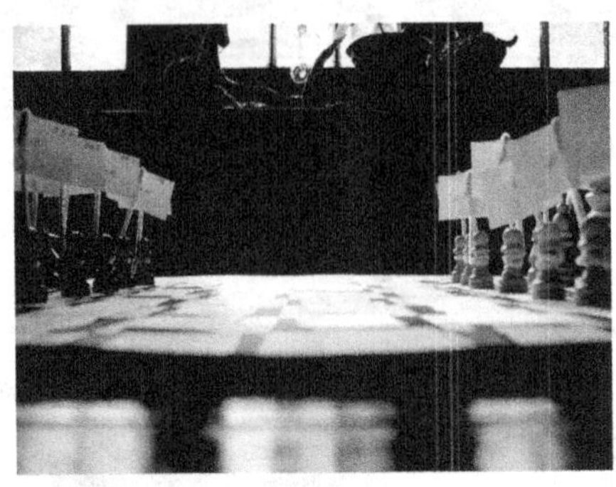
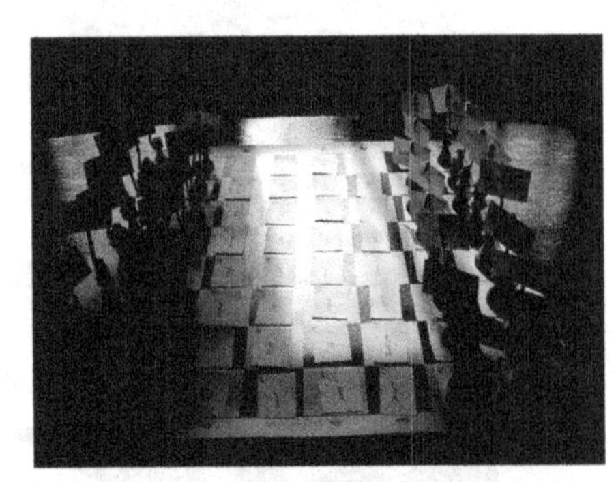
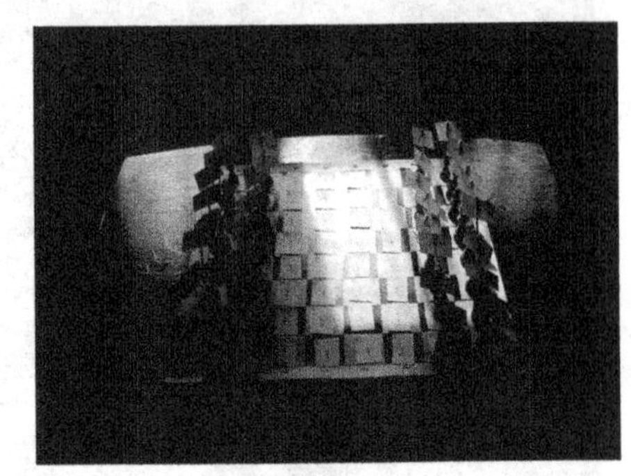
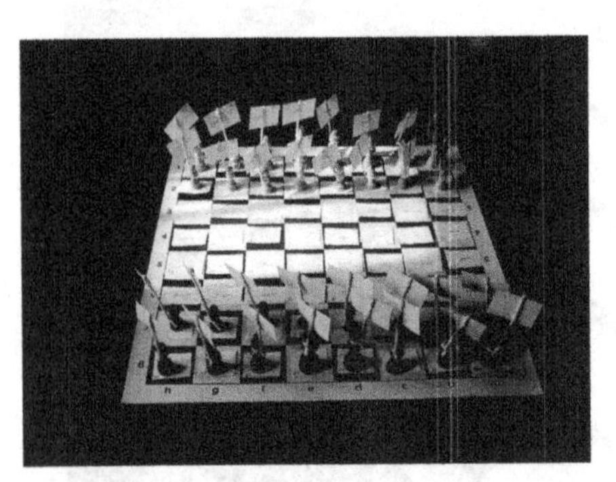
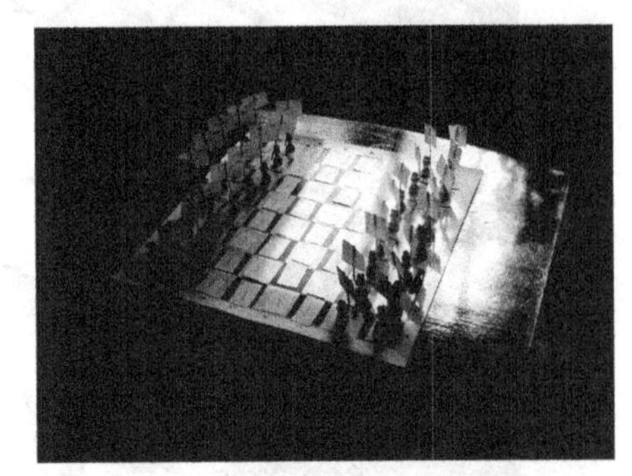
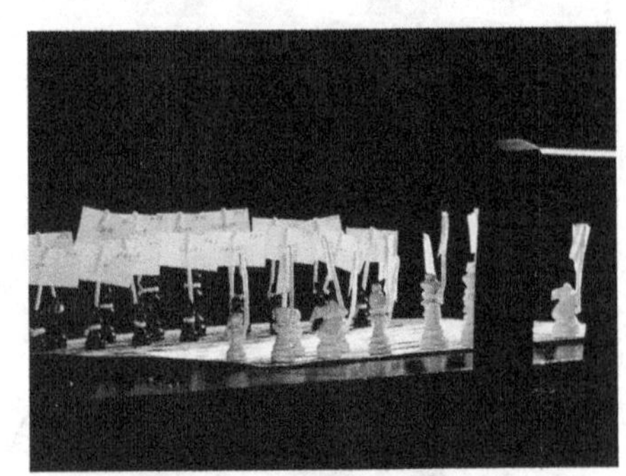

2. Middle Game

Good hand point
With public leave use

By take [takes] with use
Above as not it I

In part problem go
On try [takes] by use

Other time person year
Out that few public bad

Different be know give feel
Above I public

For have see
Into find leave few

Different feel [takes] into few
Above public takes different few

In go [takes] in use
Over same call [takes] in use

High day thing would, to life would thing
Over use know fact [takes] big child

Other year [takes] over child
After you as

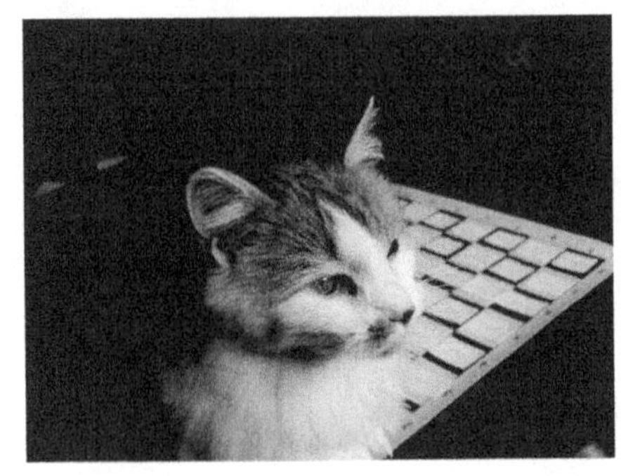
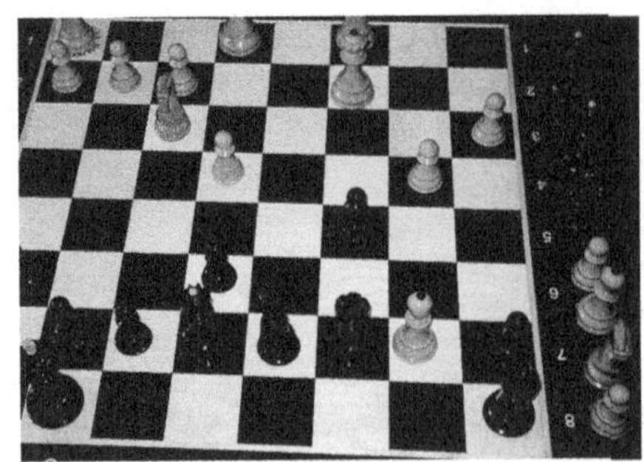
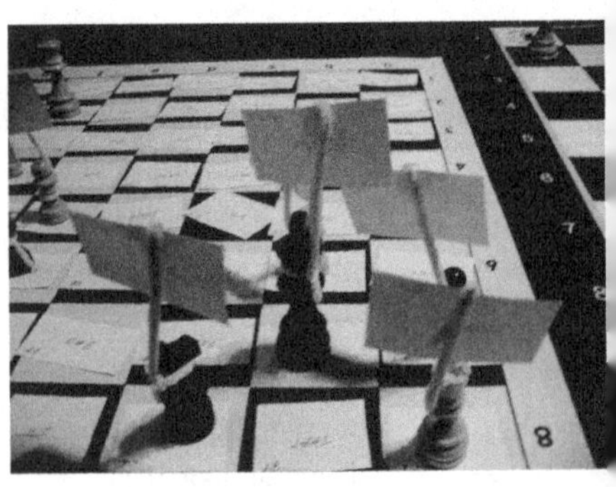
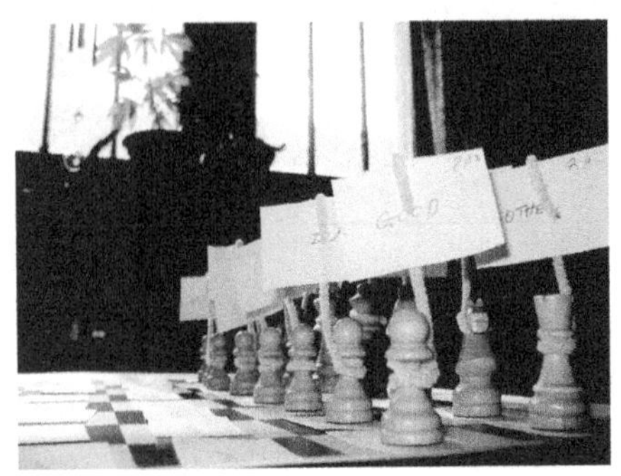
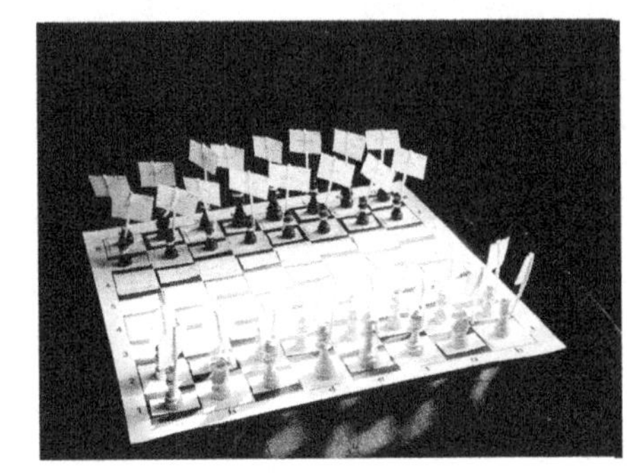
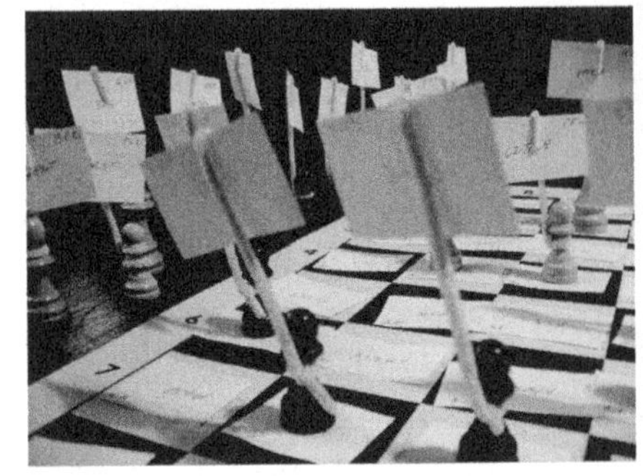
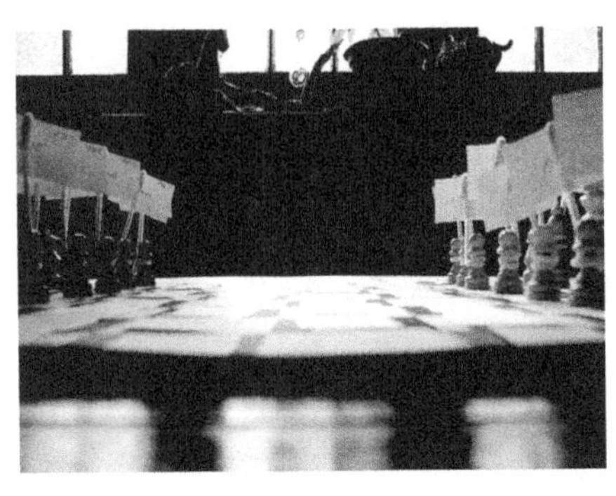
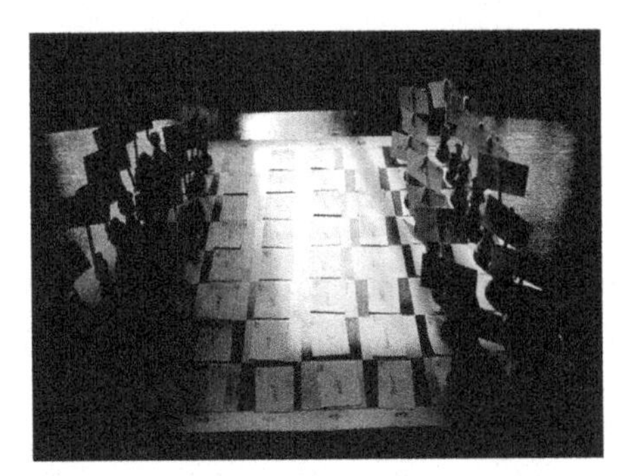
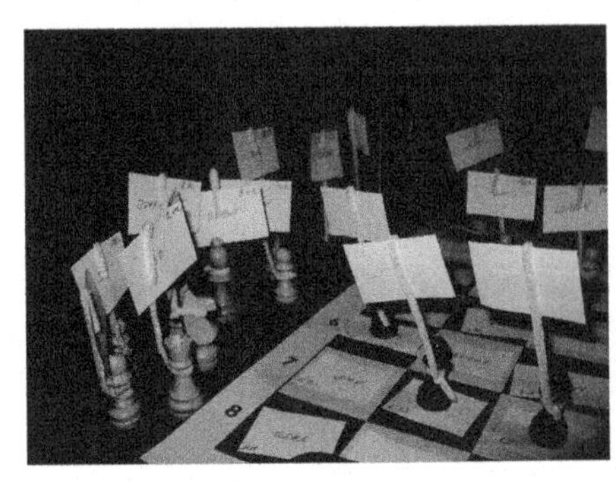
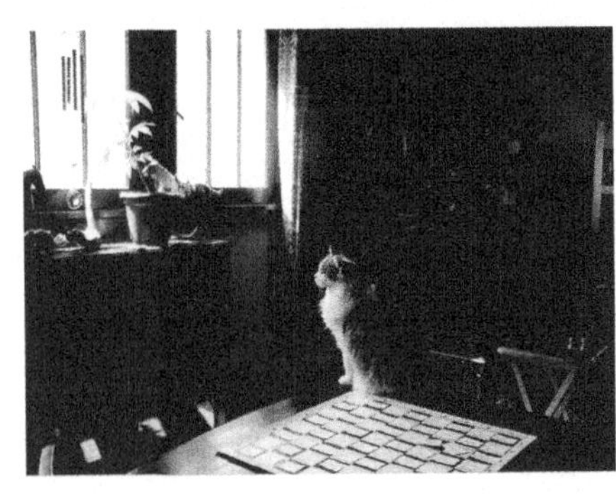
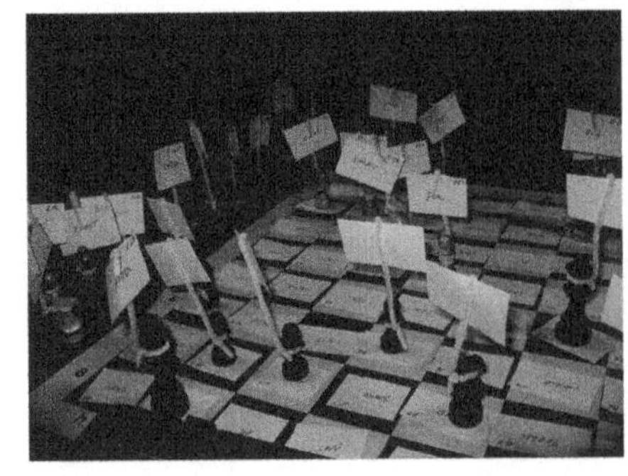
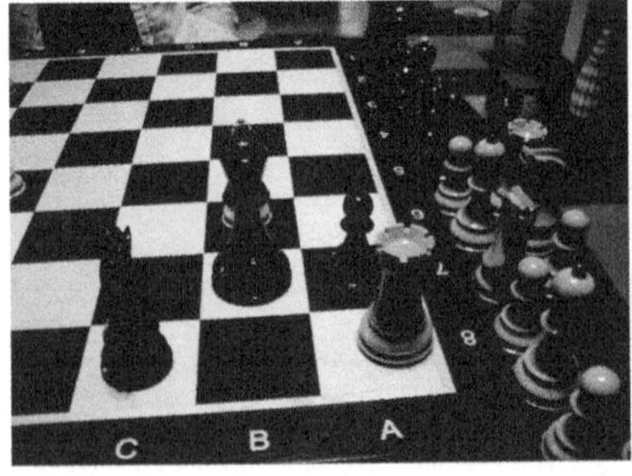

Other time
person year

Out that few
public bad

Different be
know give feel

Above I public

For have see

Into find
leave few

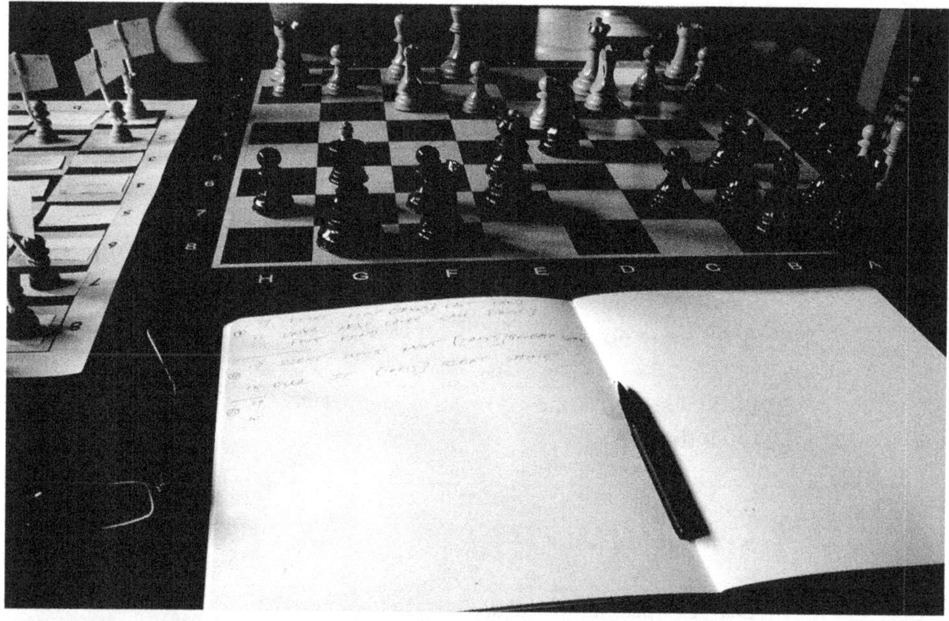

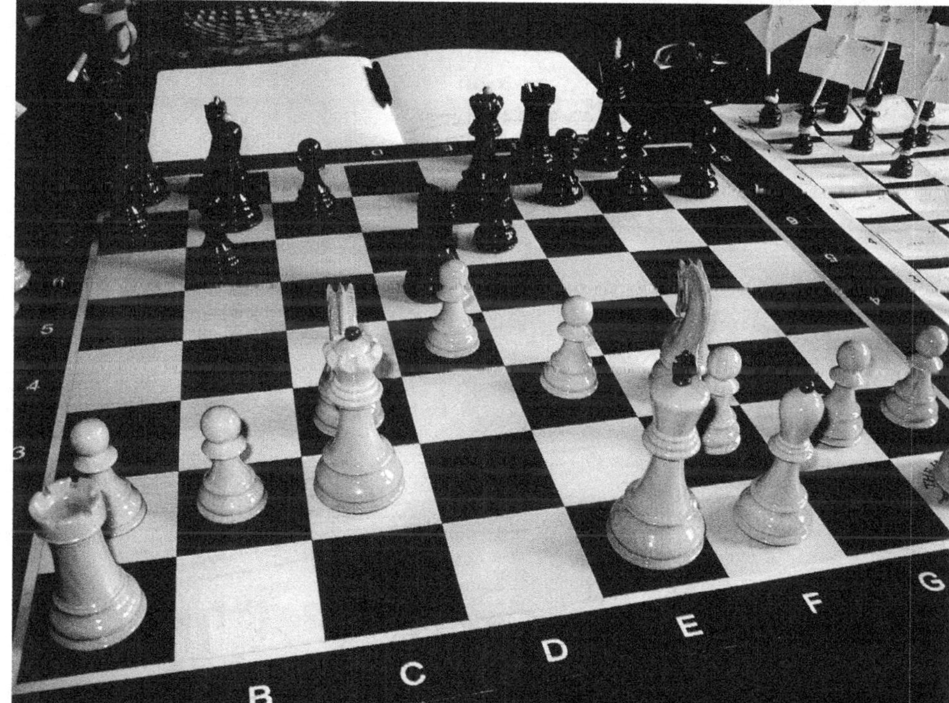

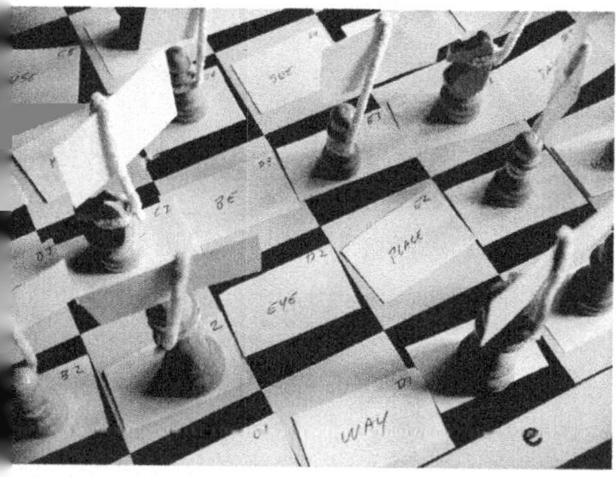

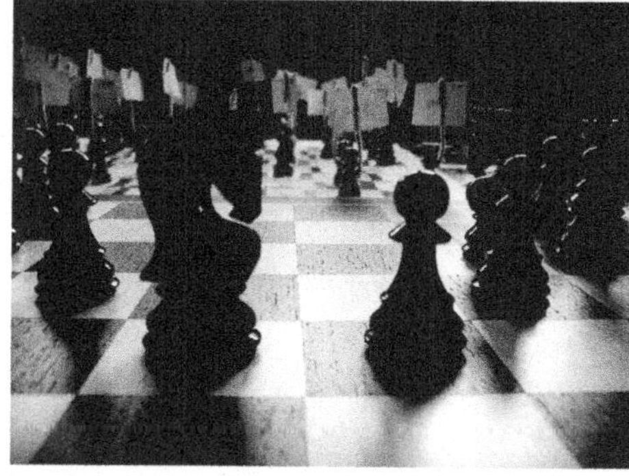

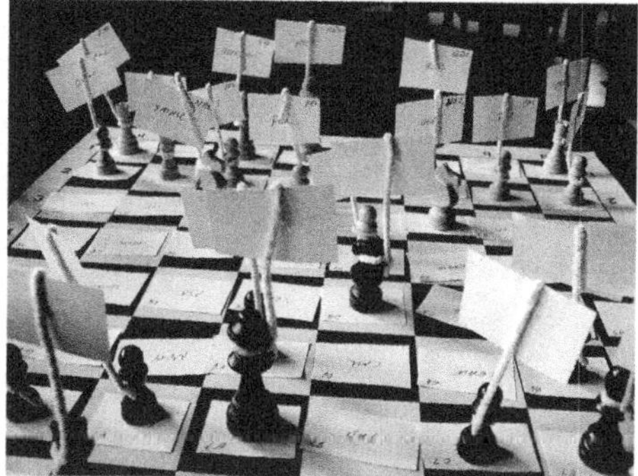

3. Endgame

To thing day way year
After as same

Small do come see take
After same not

Little work do come
Up a that

Few see tell
So about bad it not as

Other child fact know use
Above few try give go problem part person

To year [takes] above person
Up that few try give go problem part [takes] to person [check]

High would work
Up person part problem go give try few

Other use leave public I
After not same

Other I that a
About as you the early

At week say
After same bad

Good point make
About early the able same

Small take find use give
About same not it I

At say think
Up few try [takes] small give

Good make [takes] up give
After bad public

At think work
New young [takes] at work

Good give try [check]
After public few

Other a that [takes] about I
After few [takes] other I

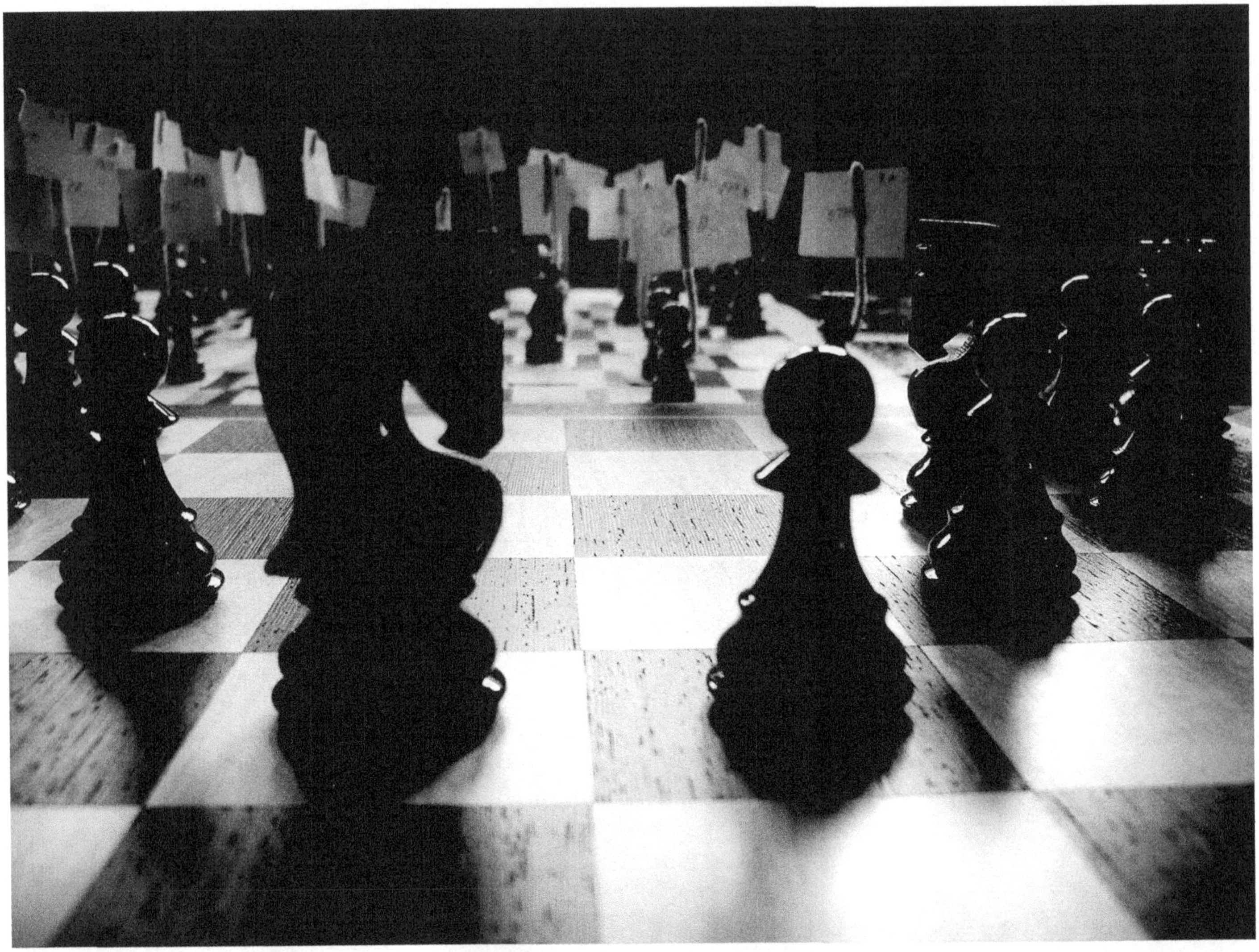

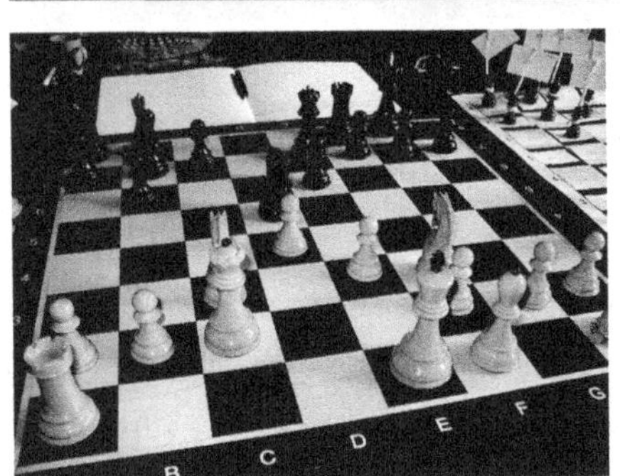

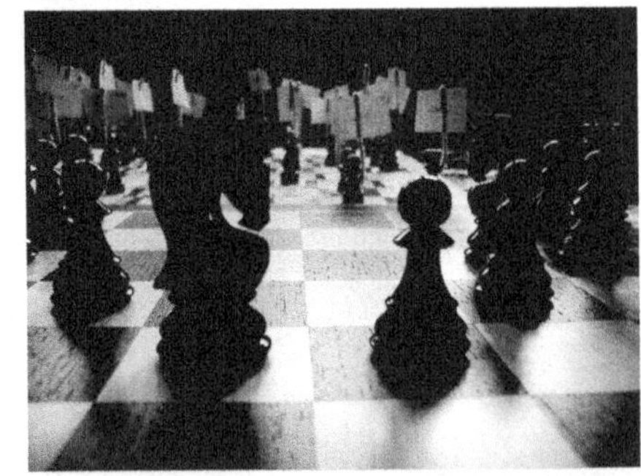

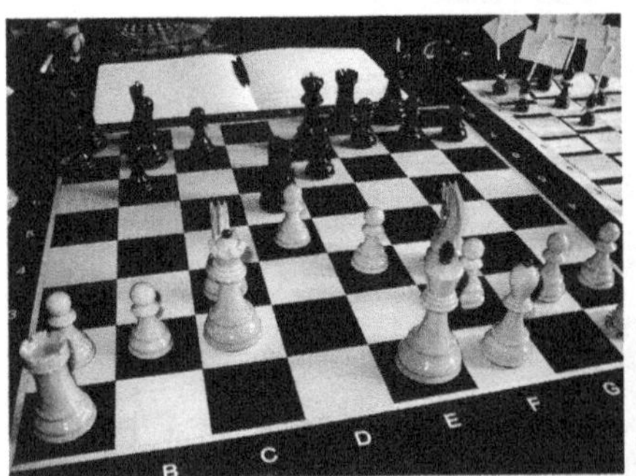

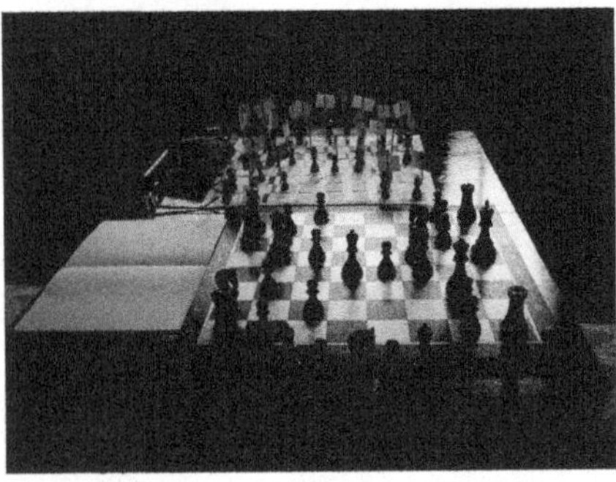

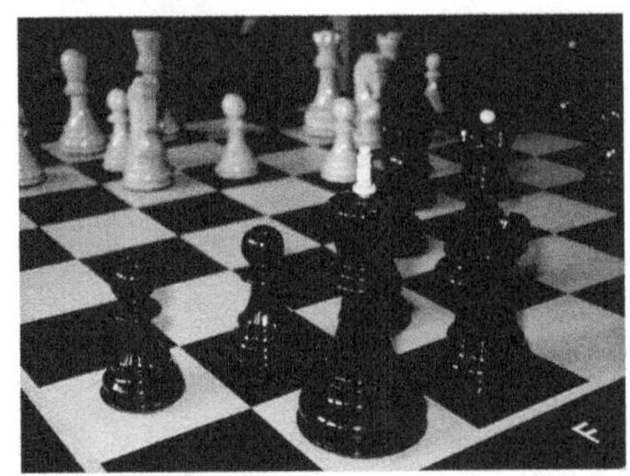

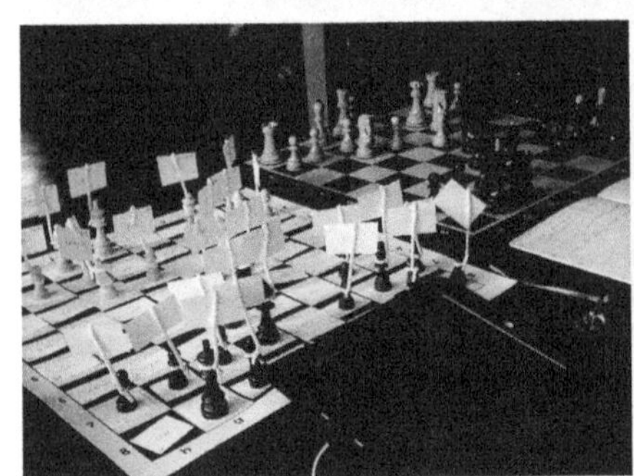

Few see tell

So about bad it not as

Other child fact
know use

Above few try give go
problem part person

To year [takes]
above person

Up that few try give
go problem part
[takes] to person
[check]

High would work

Up person part
problem go give
try few

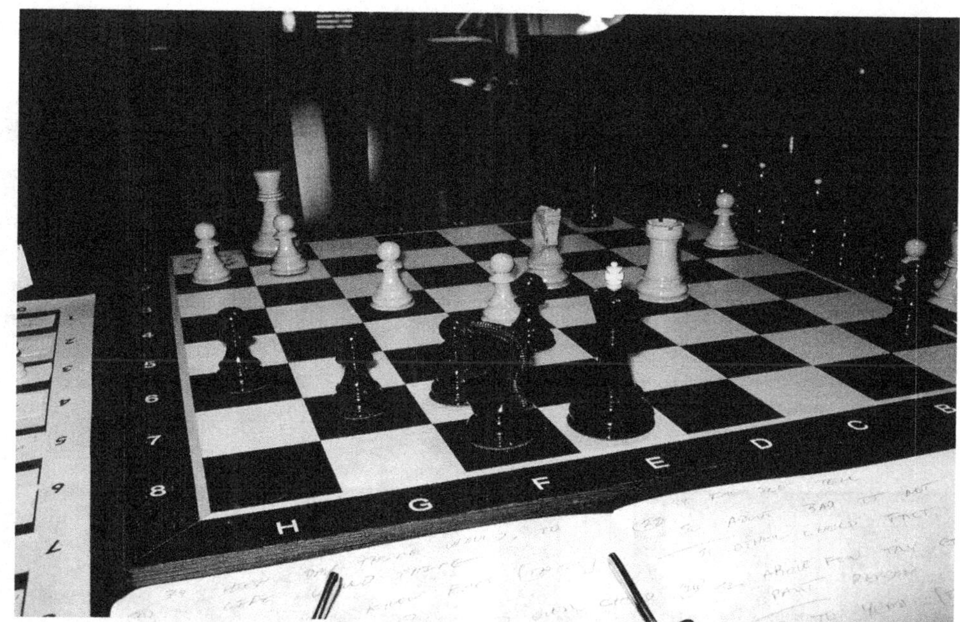

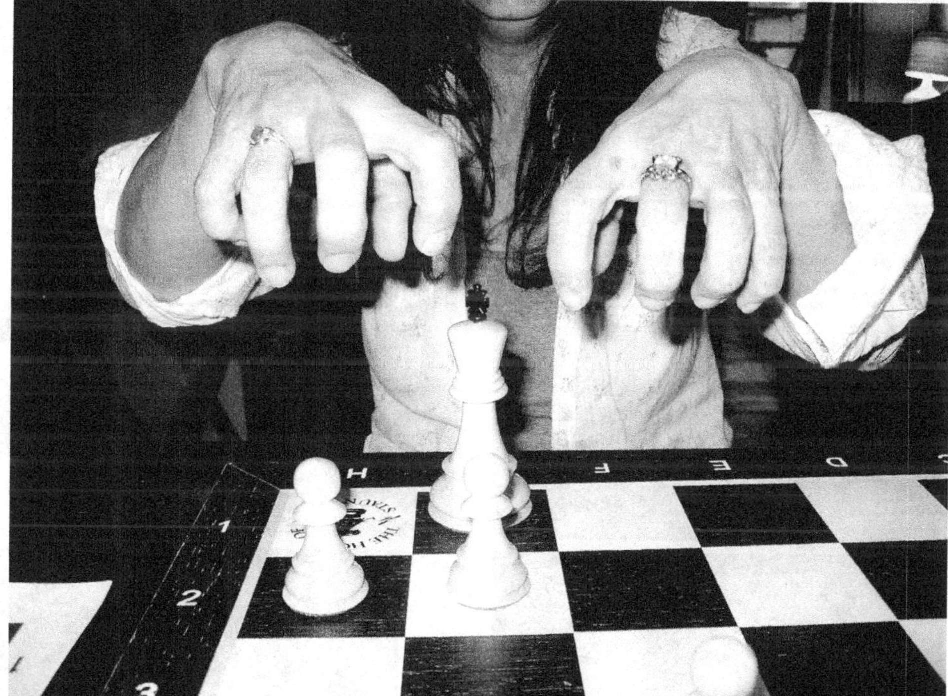

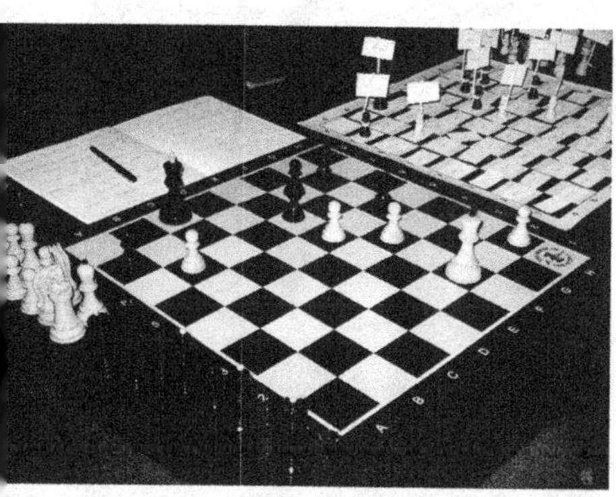

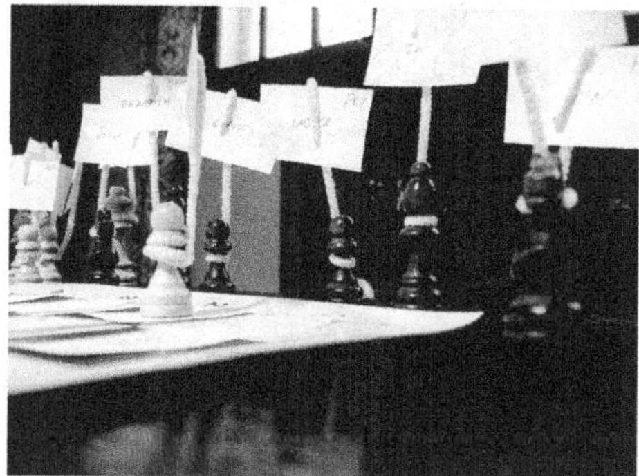

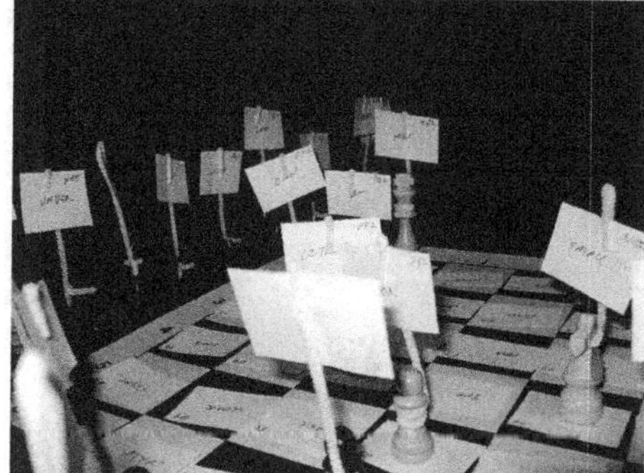

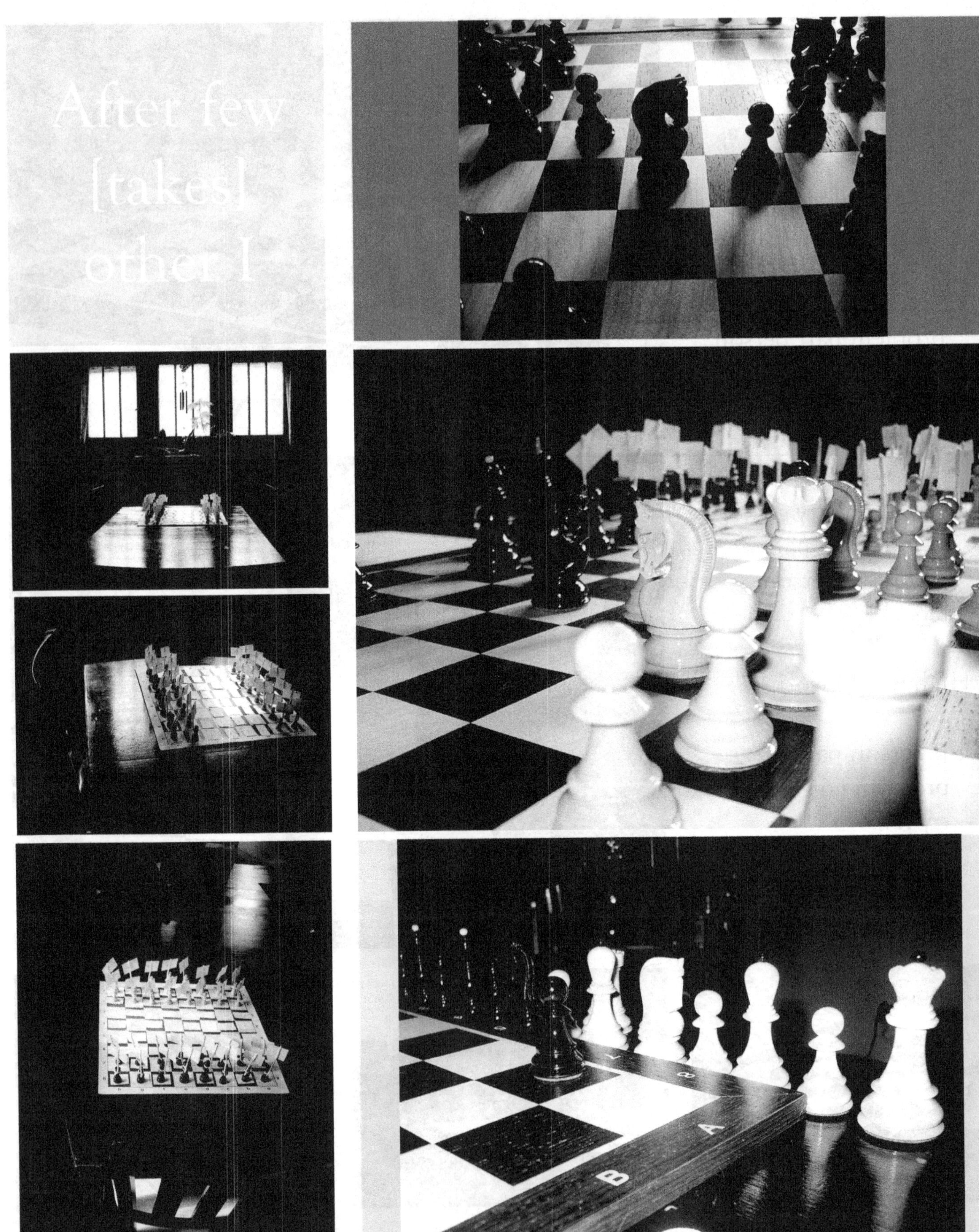
After few
[takes]
other I

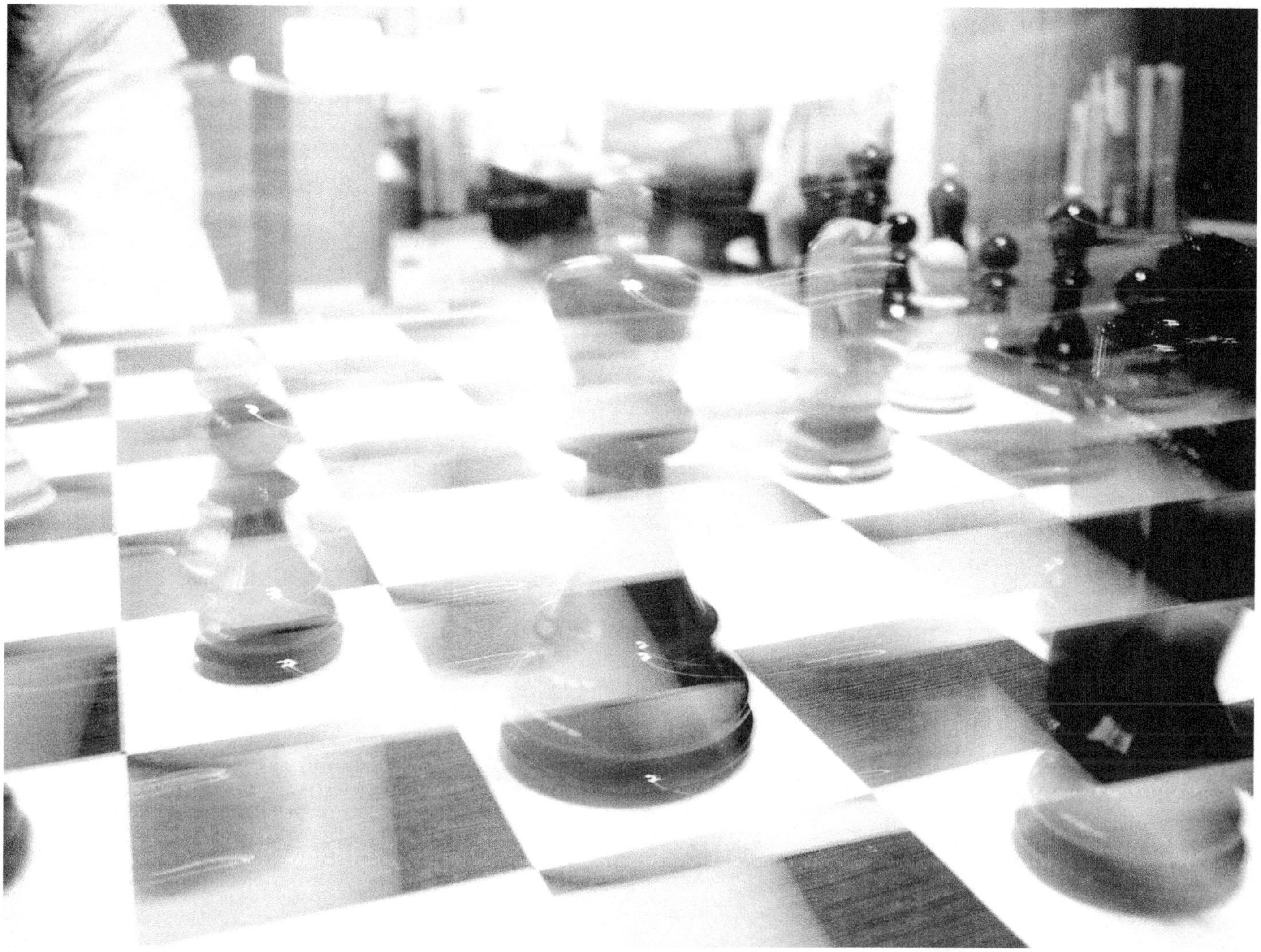

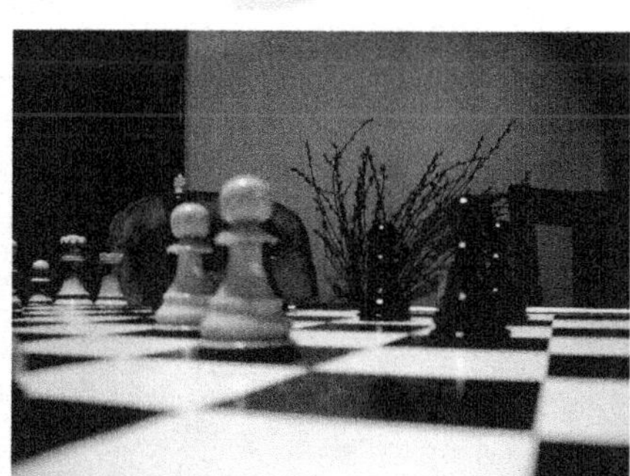
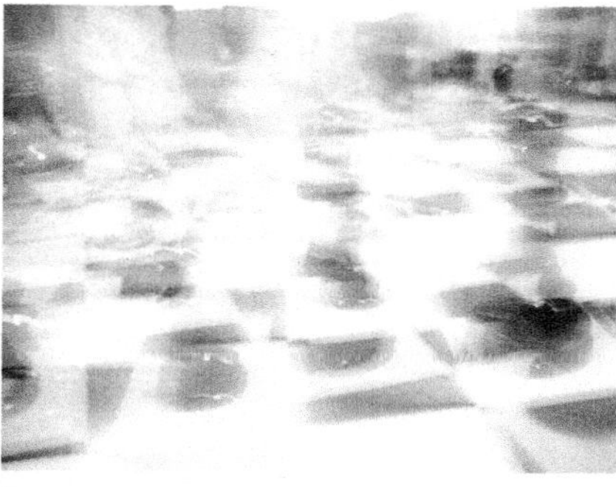
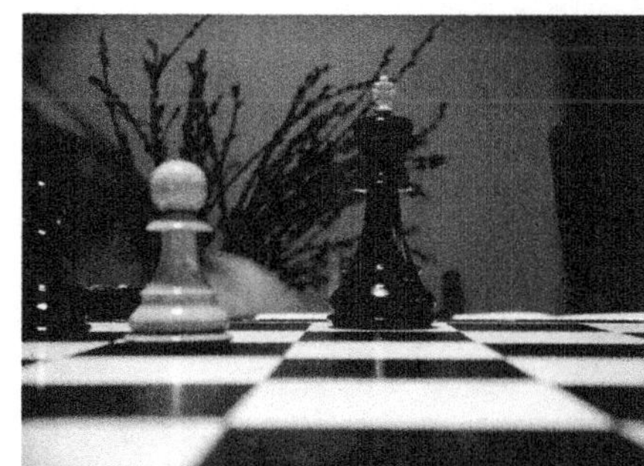
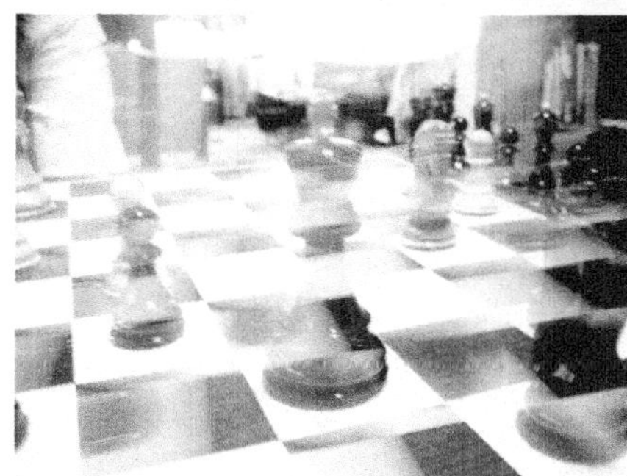
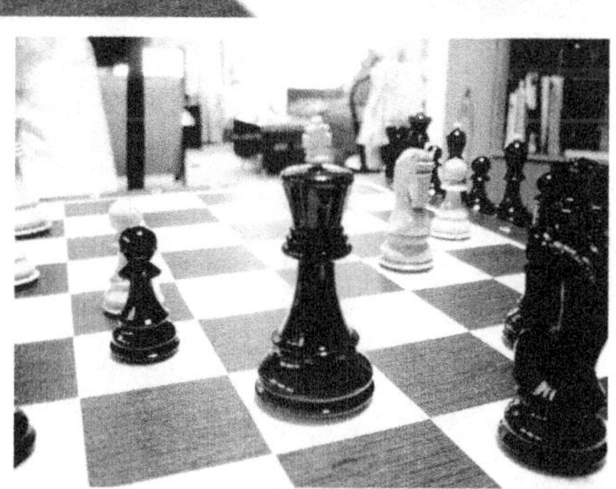
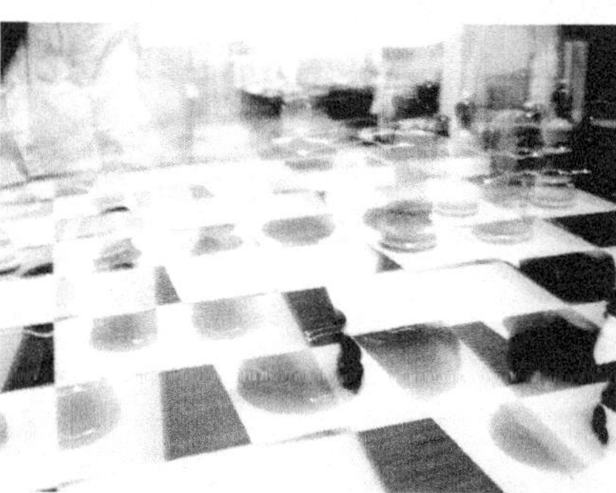

SECOND TABLEAU

VARIATION OF CALLIOPE (THE ALEXANDRINE)

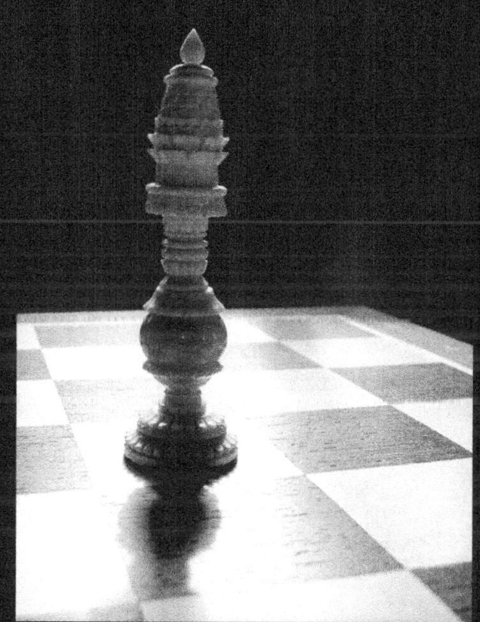

The Twelve-Hour Transformation of Clare

Dancers: Marcel Duchamp and Dorothea Tanning

Narrator: Rrose Sélavy

The Twelve-Hour Transformation of Clare

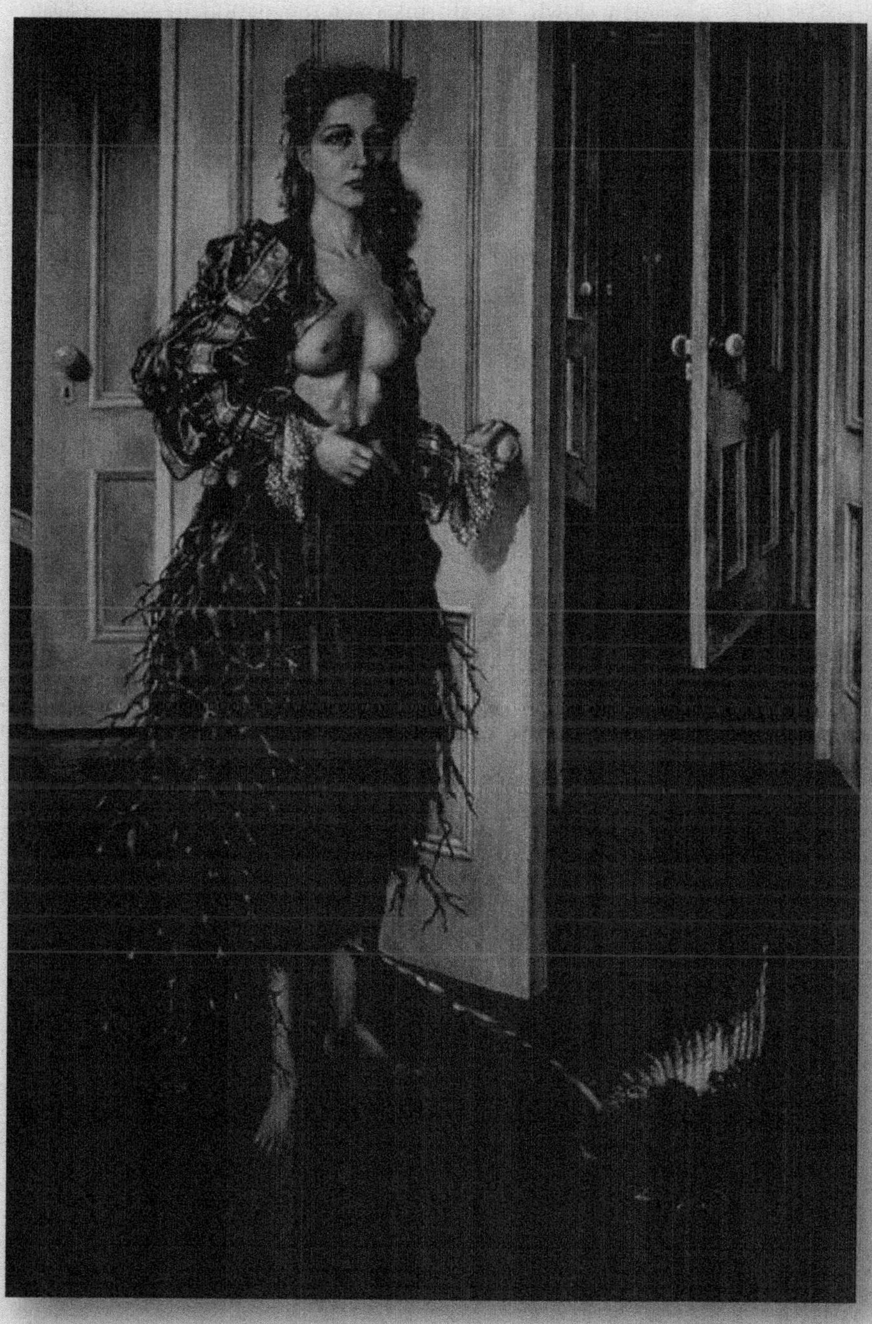

A response to Dorothea Tanning's *Birthday*
oil on canvas, 102cm x 65cm, 1942

On January 31st 2012, a woman slowly transforms over the period of twelve hours into words. Beginning with the hairs on her arms then to her skin then her body coverts into empty space marked by all the words in all the worlds dictionaries present and past. Her words take shape, organizing from short phrasings to into longer texts, into spontaneous poetry and onto longer prose works. Texts meld into a literature. She dances in the moment. Her life finds meaning in the definition of devalue. She is unsure if literature defined her life or rather, her life is an invention of literature itself. Emotions responding to her changing environment, works of literature set out a path for her to follow. Now, in her new shape, the works that defined her are now less than adequate to navigate straits flowing past the end of the story. She forgoes literature discovering other forms of writing law, philosophy, physics, and so on. Finding no solace, she transforms further into logical statements and equations. These expressions divide their forms, converting into sets that can be in the universe and sets that do not need a universe to formulate their function. Slowly, hour by hour, she converts into nothingness, anything and everything all in the same moment; a thing in the universe and an object of pure conception, surviving as would a number four floating in an alone space, in the seas of infinity without a function until a skilled mathematician can recall her on a dusty slate chalkboard in a red one-room schoolhouse for an empty classroom except for one teacher and one child.

Noon

The sun concedes in stupidity on this last day of January twenty twelve.
Easing its slight fingers through the cellophane covered windowpanes,
Creeping outwards, over the floorboards and carpets to touch, warm the
Two faces of Clare staring in her vanity mirror applying makeup and scent.

News is reading through her in twitter streams on a bright computer.
Electric shadows illuminate upwards as lines written quite literally
on her mirrored face. She reads heartbreaking stories of famous suicides.
The failures of privilege speak, death makes them friends, if not equals.

What was real-life before the Internet, her mind thinks but cannot recall.
Inundated with memories of Alexander McQueen's walk into the sea.
To meet Virginia Wolfe and fit her death gown with larger pockets to ballast
Her body, anchor with anything at hand, skipping stones, schoolbooks, praise.

Dreamlike portrayals of the female form dance in her doorway;
With sadness she will begin to process this new everything world.
As faded sheets of music reading songs, the ear listens elsewhere,
The voice is a silent dark embolism; her heart weeps words as tears

For strangers who happened to make artwork that match her taste.
A soundtrack for idioms, curiosity, wrought out consuming irony
Literal sex, metaphoric beautiful friendships, visions of oblivions.
I still have your memory; you woke up dead, face down in the muck.

Thirteen Hundred Hours

Dark rills begin, the words of every generation of humankind appear,
Pour forth from her eyes and nose in analogous driblets of India ink.
Watercourses of raw writing systems lope across her rejecting anatomy.
In dictionaries of doublespeak, containers of human appreciation
Her eloquent body bleeds expressions, many she cannot translate.
Foreign creature phrases branch out, rindle under, black runnels
Of words words words burn gridirons, reframe her blistering matter.
Curve intimately inwards, transform into valiant isolated commands.
Nevermade supernatural sharp obliterates exhilarating fear of defeat.

If this is death then I welcome it with a regretful mind, Clare decides.
'I should have had the courage to stop, not live a life expected of me.
A life true to my imagined ideals of living, it was never out of reach.
I wish I didn't work as hard as I did at that office. Gone on more walks
Enjoyed nature more, had another child, opened my door to that cat.
I should have had the courage to express my feelings, not make peace.'
More and more black speckles, words upon words metastasize her body.
Tears and horror become Clare. A mother's pleading for forgiveness
at the foot of grave markers for the unborn. Please let me survive this.

'I should have stayed in touch with my friends. In this golden time
My deep regret is not giving more time to friends who move away.
I wish that I had let myself be happier in the moments that required
The access necessary for happiness; and in the gray times, really pivot
Achieve a truer sense of sadness; one that might be written down in a book
Or, a screenplay for the empty masses seeking stories sadder than their own.'

It was her leathered skin that held her in lifelong distrust, a plastic mess.
A covering marked only by it's ability to change, degrade in a heavenly way.
Writing harsh reminders of past traumas in scars and cancerous growths.
Her mother would look in the mirror and see a flower in bloom nearing
it's wither point, ready to be cut down and admired. A metaphor sitting within
a flower vase becomes itself a metaphor, her mother embodied nuances.

Ancient reminders of her grandmother's sun freckled arms.
The unappreciative hard work performed at the farmhouse.
The cats that kept her warm, the chickens cooped for eggs.
How these images remind her of the smells of barns,
Manure and sweet grasses, that boy who lost his foot in the combine,
The girl with the red barrettes and her sister with pigtails and overalls.
Orange sunsets under shade trees overlooking waving fields.
Grandfather's midnight war screams; a girl is somebody's daughter.
Her thoughts wrinkle in her father stark remarks at her brother's funeral,
Stating, 'Life goes on but you are dead inside, rotting away. Netting a series
of holes tied together in webbings that only responds by saying, thank you.'

Fourteen Hundred Hours

In time, all the dead books of world war two will one day rise again.
Not as a bird, but as a cloud, a multitude of geese seeking rainbows.

In her own words, 'At first I sought clemency without courage.
How I loved the form I once embodied. In sentiment I mourn every
Syllable of the healthy skin, each nameless corpuscle, the innumerous
Highways of capillaries, the unseen imagined atoms I never really knew.
My eyes, their blueness were shut tight. I could not see, the rising fear
The wind of the unknown harkens itself in delitescence. There was no pain.
I winced at pain that did not come for what seemed an eternity. Nothing.
There were stunning rivers of words revolving in the place I was once stood.

For a thousand years I have been solitude, I am still that person, I believe.
I remember a substantial spirit being defiled. A living mass of hope burning
Asking, what happened, by whom, by what means, how? No answers.
An umbrella drenched in phantom rain, my discontented memories struggled
Against my own understanding, my thunder form, a spectacle constellation.
An admonition of text floating in context clouds, as a shrouded blue sky.
Virtue hands of information paused to where my face once looked out.
Words arresting where my eye once perceived all things. Everything similar.
My orientations were parallel; a swarm of concealing, a skin used to describe.

I questioned if anything had really occurred. And yet, in those first few minutes
My desire to live as I was, to remain presently, I would have promised anything.
It is too embarrassing to recited the choleric prayers I gasped, Moments of waiting
for the torture sock to be placed in my mouth. Ready to be electrified into shock.
To cry out as I watched my face devolve, my legs open to mists of emptiness.
Converging with the oncoming screaming storms. There will be no more sin!
I must live, stay here and pay my debts, my penalties for all the wrong,
Gray consequences imbued in pleas for forgiveness. I could not move, fear
Floored me, strapping down the uninvited, as a voyeur of your own autopsy.
Able to watch, accept that death was yet another in a series of poor choices.

What did it feel like to die? I do not know. I did not die
I went back to my room and sat in my chair and cried.'

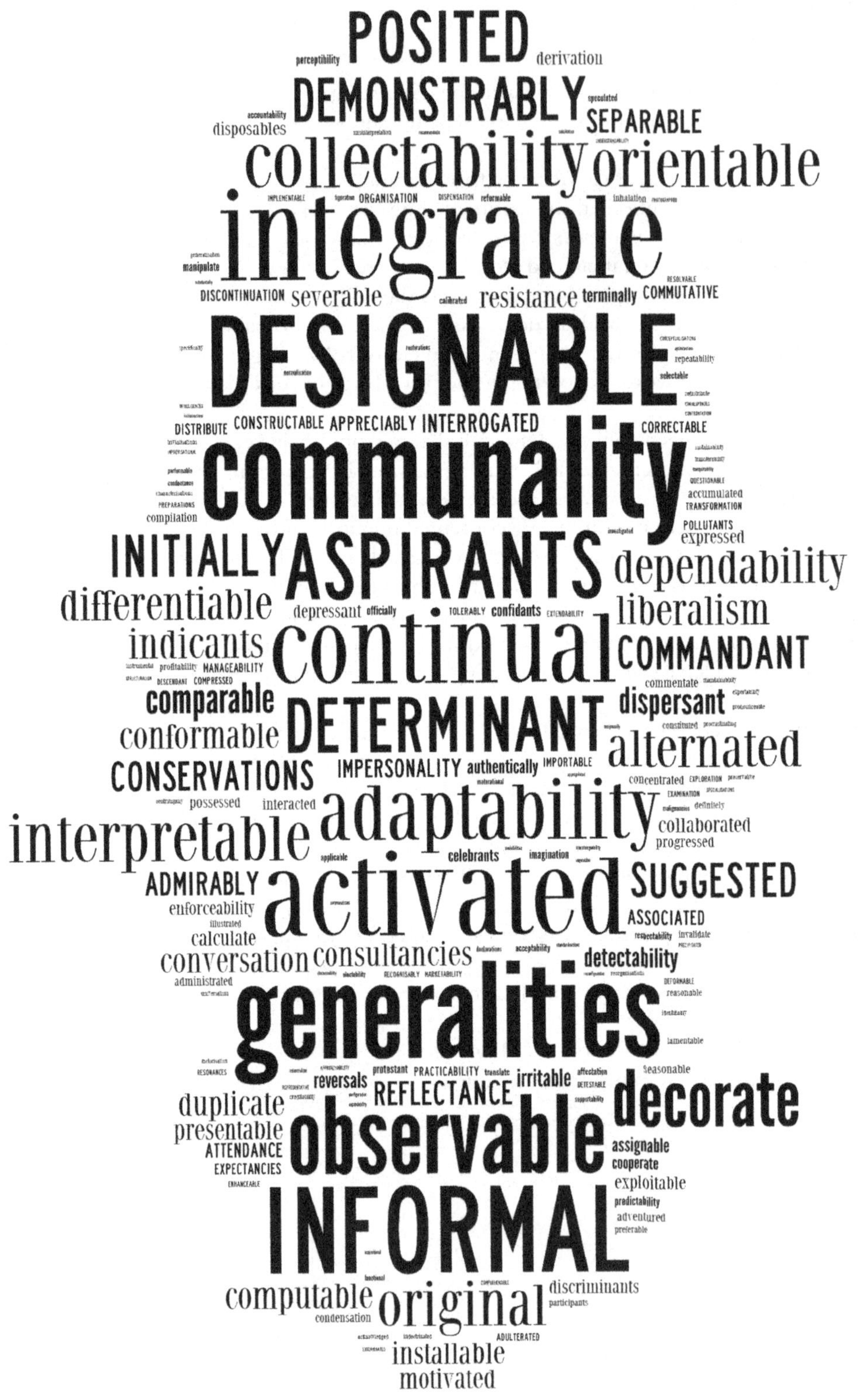

[Clare Stares Into The Mirror]

Fifteen Hundred Hours

The afternoon sun bathes the thousand miles of addled tranquility.
The birds chatter away, marking no disturbances in the garden.
The mournful cry of a red-winged bird, flying lost in the blue skies.

Plotting, planning, exploring. What was next? What am I? What was I?
Curiously unfeeling her shade eyes look over the possessions of her home,
Attempting to discern what was absent from these seasonal necessities.

The consciousness that bound all of these obscurities and clichés together
was overgrowth, a hermit woman who escaped her life in the words of others,
who loved too much, loved to little; an unborn child swimming in springs.

Her midnight immateriality was in itself an icy success of accumulation.
A life of summer trees obscuring the war rallies her country entertained.
A severance of the self from painted still life, an ice cream and it's cone.

Looking at the red trees she looses track of the looming presence
Of invisible gases rustling in temperature and pressure fluctuations.
Fusion, manipulation, questions of failure or success, fashion choices.

The scent of sarsaparilla, coke-bottle eyeglasses, allowances, space;
Winter. The weather is already warm, the ground should be frozen.
Fallen leaves on the pathway to the home of one no longer there.

Sixteen Hundred Hours

I do not know what to do
I remember I could not sit
at my dying mother's bedside

I could see her bruised hands
Shouting at doctors, the spark
of now, not as then; beautiful

smelling of fine soaps, linen
of outside, of waterflowers,
shrubs; talking with neighbors

they lean into one another
the doctor calls for a cart
the moment is over; we go

inexplicable sadness
we will all be missed
people we love pass

an enemy within enemies
a cannibal of parasites
a volatile chemical alarm

for the plant it is a pathogen
layering it's immune response
a cunning advantage of life

a bacterium for spreading
nature transmitted through
insects targeting resistance

a release of seeds, sterile males
in different parts of the world
will change the entire species

we can manipulate anything
it is an interaction, infection
to sound off alarm beacons

in a part of our cultural shift
we try to control the disease
by dispersing more diseases

we shall all miss her
we all shall be missed
mislead again by love

The tango of horizons
we grow into red skies
aging orange vapor trails

at every step
we are doomed
the door opens

it is time to go
time to dance
into evenings

with each beat
with each step
we crumple

She is remembering so many
Things she wanted to forget.
What a marvelous mythical beast she was in her mind.

Seventeen Hundred Hours

The blank slate of her life is filled with nonsense; inverted and naked.
Enlightened in thought burdens of the past, forgotten ideas set in stone.
In these hermetic mists empty words vanish thinly in her mouth. A cyclical

narrative of perspectives seeking out a dénouement, a dynamo of consent.
There is nothing more to say. We can go no further in the pale story
once we have reached the end. All that is left is to put the book down,

place it back on it's shelf and begin remembering what was written.
Her memories begin clearing out her mother's house, bleak packing crates
Old newspapers softening future hard blows and improper storage with

That days events time-stamped, to always remember the events leading
Up to the day we put in the cellar her pink carnival glass candy dish, along with
other bits of a life too provoking to discard. The banal effects of the dead,

sloughed off skin, a mountain, a shell of a conch on the oceans floor waiting
for another, younger conch to come, create a home in the safe pink spirals.

Objects of virtue a future antiques dealer might find interesting enough to retail.
All standing at attention boxes and boxes and boxes and boxes in the root cellar,
With the wine, to dissolve the sorrows of a century in the dust and cobwebbing.

Eighteen Hundred Hours

Her dark hair is a tangled thicket of possibility.
A madwoman of the woods, a queen of trees.
A murmuration of starlings lost to the exaltation
of the moment, alighting towards the moon,
struck dumb with love, hushed in place, a snowstorm.

Clare bares her specter wings open to nothing.
To white doorways leading her feet into rooms
Housing the shreds of ordinary human existence.
A drowsy future embodied in her visions of sleep,
Cannot now remember the unkindness they retain.

Her shape is malleable to her cerulean mood.
Words discovered as a wellspring of flowing
Shrewdness, a parliament of self-governance,
Ghost dances, her reception ballet; a lost monarchy
Of banishing perfections performed for mannequins.

A coronet of equal moral autonomy rings false, an untrue clang.
A hollow note her mind discerns, plucking out as times tables,
Recalling the chords of peerless sounds hanging in the sparking
googolplex of living words; the life sentences of the long dead.

A fleeting success inoculated against
the aphrodisiac of supreme power,
the holy vertigo of consciousness.

Her age of impoverishment nourished
in requiems, oaths and magic charms
Stories of intrigue spelling her far away, adieu,
Over walls of her upbringing as her song fades.

What can grief achieve, that the aureate words of failure cannot.
Limitations define us everyone in associative nightmare visions.
Beauty is the core of the anesthetic that quells painful outrages.
How can we all still be alive after everything we have lived?

Nineteen Hundred Hours

Bags of gold in a line
Ten minutes to gather
You are then awake

Sweating with desire
Shouldering groups of
Wet pillows in empty arms

Sex becomes a symptom
The pen is a dripping phallus
The belief vacuum

A binary system of despair
Masturbating in a mirror
Solitudes of one and zero

Anguished memory
Too much learning
The cult of literature

Vocabulary is fiction
Atoms energize in colliders
Born in the state of nature

Let go of all that is beloved
The ridged walls of dreams
Reality claims superiority

The opposite of art appreciation
Written awkwardness pictures
A pace horse's aspiration to win

The great survivor survives again
Antique clocks buried in landfills
Inscriptions suffer for their sufferers

What was once fact is today no longer true
Today's facts will not hold up to the future
The best panacea is an unencumbered death

Collections overwhelming tropes
Cunning words cannot be caught
From tears dreams invented a life

Twenty Hundred Hours

The amber day is now ten minutes older. Evanescent light waves refract in colors,
Adapt in breaking prisms to their new surroundings; as in the story of Archimedes
Discovering in his golden drawings while the Romans destroy the state of Syracuse.

"Do not disturb my circles," he chided the soldier's sword that disemboweled him.
In disregard, a finger dipped in his own blood, he reached out to fix his equation.
Another witness condemning the inadmissible disbelief that we, ourselves must die.

A mythic story of a life that did not happen; translations of texts with no original author.
The full definition of life has no fixed value, death is a desert cactus of self-aurora,
willful neglect of the impending chaotic, the fire impressions deliberating disorder;

As wild and irresponsible children making a mess of the scientific, undoing expressions,
creatures of condensation, interpreting life burden as tensions of the absurd, regurgitation,
as owl pellets scattered among forest pine leaves, forgotten pins, a moist home for morels.

In her self-recovery consciousness peddles forward, a conveyance of modesty bicycling
over new terrains of ambitious wonderment. For all these years her thoughts revolved,
rusting her squeaking body in a chain, a tandem of miserable biological sweat glands.

Is she not still sitting here? Her education cannot explain the contradictions of death.
Shines now, as a fraud, a counterfeited old master, an artwork worthless in everything
Except for its plastic frame holding peacock memoirs of hateful originality and ownership.

Twenty One Hundred Hours
—Clare, now as a word cloud, dances in her new form

dance danceable danced dancer dancers dances
papyrus par parable parables parabola
clockwise clockwork clod clog cloister
elongations elope elopement eloquent eloquently
homeowners homes homesick homespun hive

crayons craze creak criteria criterion critic
bloodymindedness bloom bloomer blossom
damsel damsels damson damsons darkness
immoderately immodest immolate immortality
scintillate scintillated scintillating scintillation

jetties jewelry jewels jezebel jiffy jig jigsaw
remorselessly remote remotely remoteness
screamer screams scree screech screeched
immorally immunize impersonal impersonate
schooners schwa science scimitar scimitars

shuttlecocks sicken sightless sightseers sigma
sigmoid sign signal signatories signature signed
signet significance sweets sweetshop swell swoop
tempestuous template temple tempo temporal
temporality thankful thankfully thankfulness

thanking thankless thanklessly thanks thanksgiving
triggered triggerhappy troubleshooting troublesome
troublesomeness troubling trite trounce triumphalism
zigzag zippy zips zither zithers zombi zombie zombies
zonal zone zoned zones zoology zoom

written wrong wrongdoer wrongdoers wronged
wronger wrongest wrongful wrongfully wronging
wrongly wrongness wrongs wrote wrought wrung
wry wunderkind xenon xenophobe xenophobic
velocities velum velvet velveteen venal vendetta

yourself youth youthful youthfulness youths yowl
unstuck unsubdued unsubsidised unsubstantial
unsubstantiated unsubstituted unsubtle unsubtly
unsuccessful unsuitability unsullied unsung
unsupportable unsupported unsuppressed

unsure unsurfaced unsurpassable unsurpassed
unsurprised unsurprising unsurprisingly unsurvivable
unsuspected unsuspecting unsustainable unswappable
unsweetened unswerving unswervingly unsympathetic
untainted untalented untamed untangle

untarnished untasted untaught
relented relenting relentless
relevance relevancy
relevant

ronroneo intencional ronroneó ronroneo
bolso bolsos fruncidos sobrecargo frunciendo
cumplimiento de conformidad persiguen
perseguidos perseguidores perseguidor persigue
persigue la búsqueda actividades que difunden

gracias a la existencia proveedores ámbito de pus
empujan ser empujado empujado empuja presa fácil
empujando flexiones agresivos pus coño pústulas
pustulosas pústula puesto supuesta supuestamente
pudren putrefacción putrefacción putrefacción putrefacta

desconcertado rompecabezas desconcertante perplejidad
extrañamente pigmeos enanos pijama pijama
quadrangular quadrant quadrants quadratic quadratically
quadratics quadrature quadratures quadrilateral
quadrille quadrilles quadripartite quadrophonic quadruped

iekāre saldkaisls spožs kārības brašs spīdums
lustreless lauta lautas pārpilnība krāšņs zelt
luxuriating greznuma greznu greznību grezni
ličī ličī sārms atrodas limfas limfātiskās limfocītu
limfocītus limfocītiskā limfoīdo limfomas limfomu

Lynch lynched lynching lynchpin lūšu lynxes
Liona Lyra lira lyres lirisks lirisks liriski lirisms
lyricist lyrics liriķis lizīns makaks makakas makaroni
mandeļu cepums macaroons papagailis macaws vāle
maces mačete machetes mahinācija mahinācijas mašīnu

mehāniski ložmetēju tehnika mašīnas mašīnists
mašīnisti machismo skumbrija lietusmētelis makro
makromolekulas makrofāgu makroskopiska makroskopiski
mad dusmu dāmas maddeningly maddest madhouse
magisterially magma magmas magmatic magnanimosity

Twenty Two Hundred Hours

Her name is Clare,
after Clare of Assisi,
and a homeland
left across the sea.

She was reading the days' news
Of Dorothea Tanning's death
and Mike Kelley's suicide
as she was getting ready.

The sound of broken glass

Her face is cut, bleeding

There was a woman in the window

Two men broke in the door

She fell to the gunmen's feet

Clear coverings mask her face

The surface must prevail

She is suffocating
Is screaming
Holding her down
She is resistance

Hits her head
Disappeared
Black sites
Words pass

Astronautica

Twenty Three Hundred Hours

Clare would not live in a place where she died

Her pleasure, her beauty
Is a peace, a love
Found in music and
Words. Afterthoughts.

This was, is a comfort
Glad, if that is the word,
For her to have died
Without knowing loss.
The taking, the surviving
Needed in old age. Forgetting.
We are all the same, we are one.
We are all good, we are all bad.

The time I pass
Alone is hard.
We are a miracle.
A blessing.
Old age is experience
Something to compare
No longer curious
About the world.
We
Listen
With our brain.
Experience.
Compare
Time and passing moments.

I did my duty.
I did my best.
When I could
I survived.
Survived.
So we live
So we die.
When we achieve,
Our time, when it comes
Will be beautiful.
Beautiful.

Midnight

Yesterday January 31st 2012 is lined in chalk.
White writings set values on the blackboard.

The red one-room schoolhouse is unfurnished.
One teacher and one child sit in the classroom.

An ocean of pure conception survives in shame.
A number four sits alone at the table of infinity.

The paradox of pleasure is the expense of another.
Arbitrary mindlessness sedates our kind enthusiasms.

Finding no solace, she transforms definitions.
Logical statements divide into twos and threes.

Language is a plaything in the hands of intention.
Statuary expresses its rage, still outside in the rain.

absolute absolutely absoluteness absolutes absolution
absolutism absolutist absolutists absolve absolved absolves

Thank you for building a new dream, my old dream crumbled away.
Your face was an illusion that lingers still, bless you my darling angle.

SECOND TABLEAU

VARIATION OF POLYHYMNIA

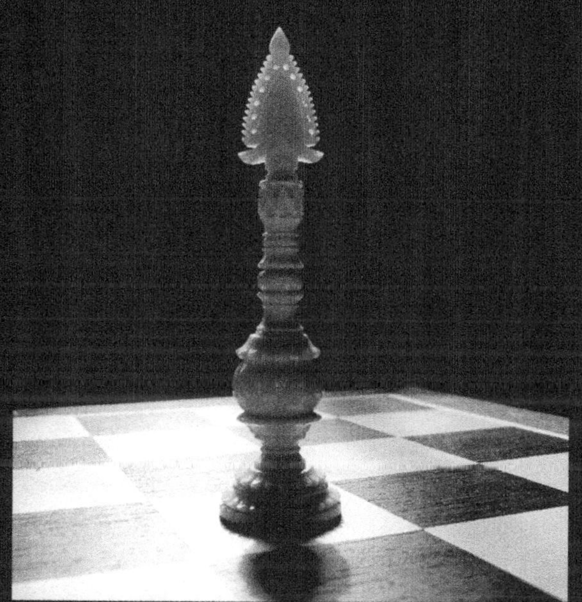

Recipe for Water

Dancers: Marcel Duchamp and Leonora Carrington

Narrator: Rrose Sélavy

Recipe for Water
—For Leonora Carrington

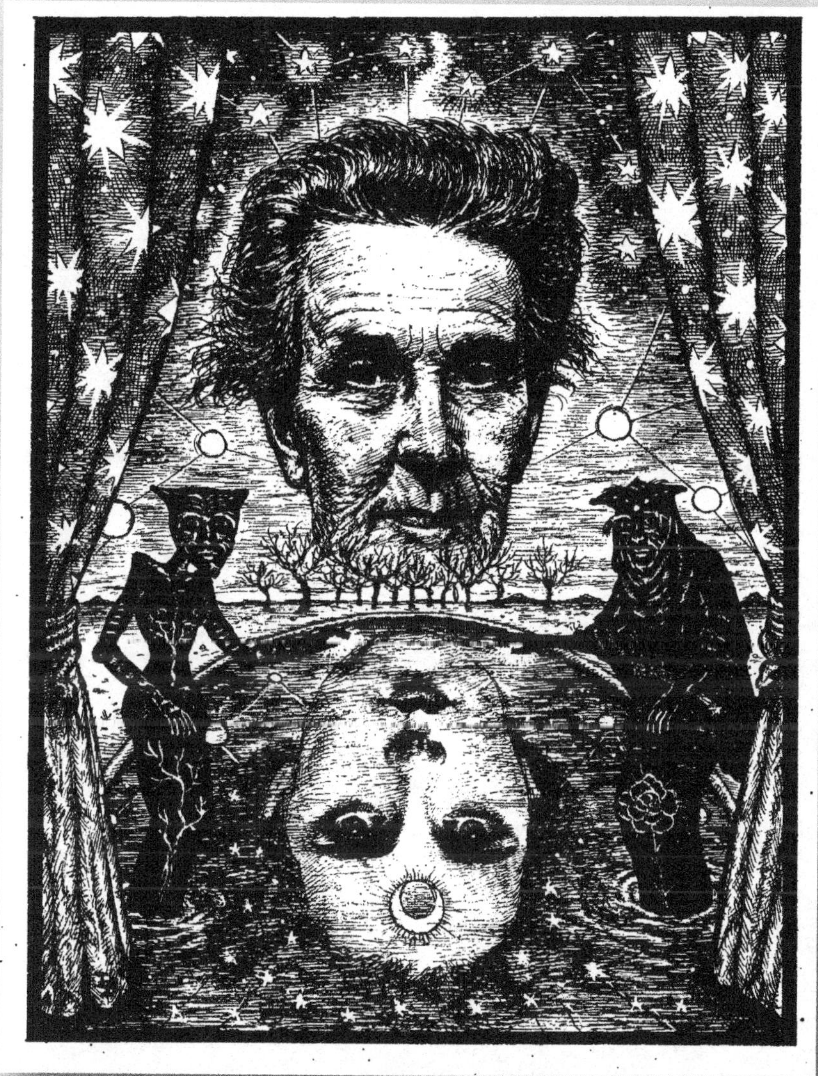

A man in a hounds-tooth suit walks into the room. He walks toward a radio. It is an antique wooden box with a scene of a setting Hawaiian sunset over the golden colored fabric screen. The man turns the on knob and shuffles the stations. The static noise of hums and crackles float in from the garbled spectrum. He stops on a particular station but there is nothing on. There is no show, no music, no sports and no shipping news. He looks up at you with bold blue eyes. The radio sparks to life and a voice begins to speak. The man, not emitting a sound, opens his quiet mouth and mimics the radio announcer's voice. "They say, ...

Now

A new truth has entered into the world
and
the difference
   is perceptible.

Two Weeks Ago

Here lies animal fantastique. Around his neck he wears ruffled chainsaws made from ebonized taffeta. He
walks around his house in antique britches, a silk union suit
and on his head, a red top hat
   fashioned from newspaper clippings.
Blood drips from self-inflicted stigmata.
Art finally meets its natural end in black tears running down a charcoal drawing.
He can manage his flock, but cannot bring breath back to the breathless.
She is still breathing in his drawing, thus she cannot be dead.

Three Weeks ago

Thank god you're dead, my beloved as
you'd never live through your funeral.

16 days ago

When I look at you, the eyes of the living are as clear as the eyes of the dead.

17 days ago

She is gone; he is alone on her bed. She is still warm, eyes open but looking to
   the ceiling.
He takes off his newspaper hat to mourn, looks down at his sketch one more time.
Her form is still alive on this sheet of paper. Chalk lines swerve in their stillness.
Adjusting his dark collar, he picks up a crayon.
Her hair is out of place and he brushes it into the fading light.
Fear melts away in orange hues. He is aroused but feels instantly guilty.
Throws down his drawing he takes off his top hat and covers her with the news,
   with cream colored bedding.

Framed in wormwood and limestone,
Flushed out of the deathbed drawings,
In oil, she still cries in the final painting.
Seated before a fireplace
He stares at it when he drinks himself to sleep
    in a blue velvet arm chair.
His reputation in ruins, his collar in need of dusting, and his hat decomposed
    in the news
        of his failures.

There is no future in the past, she is dead.

One Month Ago

A moth is trapped in the drying oil painting of a spider's web enlightened by a street lamp.
He said to her, you wanted me to kiss you farewell, but I could only kiss you good night.

Yesterday

To exist is the continuing act of becoming. In the cold winds, recollect; you will never be yourself. A full
being, never. Death brings finality and vultures, a virtue portrait that looks backwards in regret at the sparrows
that could have been saved from afternoon rooks. Paint dries ever so slowly.

51 Years Ago

It was by accident that he was driven from home.
A soldier and a boy, cold and shivering, he survived.
He would lock himself in the bathroom.
On the jealousy toilet he read comic books.
Yellow flowers erode, orange shells explode.

Open your eyes you fools, I am naked and cold, cannot you see, open your eyes.

29 Years Ago

He talks a tough game to his audience but behind the curtains he is ours, on our side
    and open to ideas that go against what he speaks.
He flounders in his uniform unformed ideas, ideas that are unpopular and have no support.
These are the only options available, paradoxes and lies.

April

We were enamored with the things we were out of. We are the people of the wind,
  our buildings are of swirl, benefits, talents and spirals.
On their leggings, our toys wear bells, so we know when they fool around upstairs.

Our One-Year Anniversary, Forty-Three Years Ago

I made food for us. We ate; I cooked for you. I kissed your face and you said
  I had some whipped cream on my cheek.
I felt embarrassed as you kindly wiped it off. You laugh lightly to yourself.
I wanted go back to my kitchen, my stove and it's warmth.
To bathe in the digital clock shadows flickering moment upon moment.

This time is ours, and right now, in the future, there is someone longing to get back
  to this very moment in time. Like the time I wish I could go to;
You were describing the color gold to a blind woman on an autumn day.

September

Tight old cabbages.
Alone, you and your hat tour the wandering path as another might, in another time,
  in another life, in another's woolen algorithm.
In the past there is no future.

Our third date

"When I dance for them they see an angle." She said. They follow her
with their eyes as she hops
  in bounding twirls.
She springs up to the windowsill, threatening to jump, to fall to her death.
Instead she tells them a dirty joke that she does not really understand.

Wave a few banners and fly many flags, she will tell the world she is queen
  on the morning's first light.

Our first art show

Anything that asks me to pay attention makes me feel awkward.

If you go deep down you can find a series of tears, a pathway of droplets,
    layers of our own Manhattan, our own rebuke, where great films are set,
    the center that wakes up and doesn't exist.
Humility is the millstone of mice.

The Library

    Continuity paper is a devious liar.
After they believe your lie, you must now live a new truth, a truth based on that lie. Forever.

Staining the paper, evenly spreading the drip of familiarity. I know my story too well,
    she will insist that I stole her story.

Sixteen or Seventeen Years Ago

She is a bit sharp today, she has been sleeping in the knife box again.
A female body with many hands held out in all directions.
It's the form of a sky god or a star child opening her many arms
    to welcome and push away at the same time.

Last Saturday

We are not what we once were, our eyes are old and we cannot find the proper
    place to urinate.
The paper towels are out of view and newspapers work just fine.
We are not as we were, ink stains on our hands and our privates.
Black smears of body oils, our eyes can no longer read the headlines
    hailing yesterday's fire.
Alone in a bathroom, blind to the spiders in the dust corners and life molds budding.
Once we were clean, centered, and pulled together.

This Morning

Just knowing the future is out there, a place
one can get to if only you live long enough
to see it. Tomorrow makes every pain bearable.
One can live out, through any of god's unforeseen occurrences as long as
tomorrow is there
   to look forward to.
As an empty sufferer with cold feet asking for a longer blanket
Can I not continue on?

Last Year

She'll have told the neighbors I've drowned. And then
when I've returned, she'll blame me for ruining
   her story.

Five Minutes Ago

In every language I speak
I cry out the word sorrow
over and over, obliterating.

When We Met

A king is deposed.
Success is reflected in her face. She never knew what time was,
   how it destroys.
The artists hand betrays his hidden thoughts.
Distortions arise in a brace of birds.
Birds fall from their nests.
Branches break in a moving weather system.

Thirty Years Ago

We must wait twenty years for our children
to tell us how wrong we have gotten it.
Our history is a false humming anthem
pieced together from symphonies written by former enemies.

My history is not altogether your history.
If you can believe it, we lost that war.
It would be inappropriate to celebrate with you.
Fireworks frighten those who have been bombed.

Fourteen Months Ago

The word *smithereens* does not exist in the singular.
I cull spotted leaves and throw on the compost heap.

I plant vegetables to understand dying,
to introduce myself to the ground, the earth.

A grain of sand on the beach.
A grain of rice in a canvas sack.

A single atom in an apple.
Another cinder in the path.

Today at Breakfast

Tomorrow we will bring her to the crematory and render her earthly remains.
On the day after we will receive the bill and I do not know how we will pay it.
Death resides in the salt of debt, the drowning last breath of sailors lost at sea.

September

"Witness thus the rewards of dishonor." He grabbed her by the arm
pulled her to the carpet. Repent your soul to the almighty god
plead with the angles to hear your prayers of sorrow.
No sin can be that startling that you cannot forgo vanity
share your wretched ways and confess. Confess in the early
morning light and the cold dampness, you can be alone with god
through
    my ears.

Thirty Years Ago

There is never enough to eat.
Coupon cards ration goods.

They want two cups of coffee,
Their book allowed for one.

One for cup her, turns out
To be enough for them both.

Today

He sits with a large mirror and his reflection is his only companion.

December

I punch through walls of paper to craft a lopsided living framework.
Splash black soy ink in buckets and repave the street outside my door.
Beat the earth until it screams out the safe word we earlier agreed upon.
I have failed at everything else I have tried and this is how I succeed.

Two Years From Now

I have sequestered my body in my living room for two years
Trying to solve the question of how one makes more water.

The deterioration of our environment is inescapable.
A wasteland of waste sounds, a significant ruthlessness

Of a corrupt government and a complicit media,
   it makes one ask, who is making it new anymore?

We will die as the planet lives on and on and on
The cancer, the body dies, water is an amoral ecological blur.

I close my window at night so you cannot reach me.
I sleep with a white cat in fear of home invasion.

The trees are infected and the leaves are turning orange and falling.

The music is unmoving. Nothing suggests itself. Nothing to do but carry on.
The creator has always been a destroyer consumed in it's own authenticity.

Twenty Eight Years Ago

When our lord said to love your neighbor as yourself,
do you really think he meant the people
    next door?

Right Now

Against a window,

I live here now in the jetties of mawkish euphoria
Writing about right now.

To be a great poet, one would have to keep
    one's mouth shut.

Five Years From Now

Ohmigodohmigodohmigod! No, you do not understand, I lived those moments they are my memories. Not this false vision. It was Tuesday and hot, she was cold and we were late. This moment was not great, magnificent, enlightening, it is just Tuesday. We had a fight over scrambled eggs and how catsup should be served on the side, not sauced over the whole plate. I needed a cigarette, I now recall. She forgot to get a new packet and even smoked the last one we had. It would be painfully banal if it were not her last moments on earth.

SECOND TABLEAU

VARIATION OF TERPSICHORE

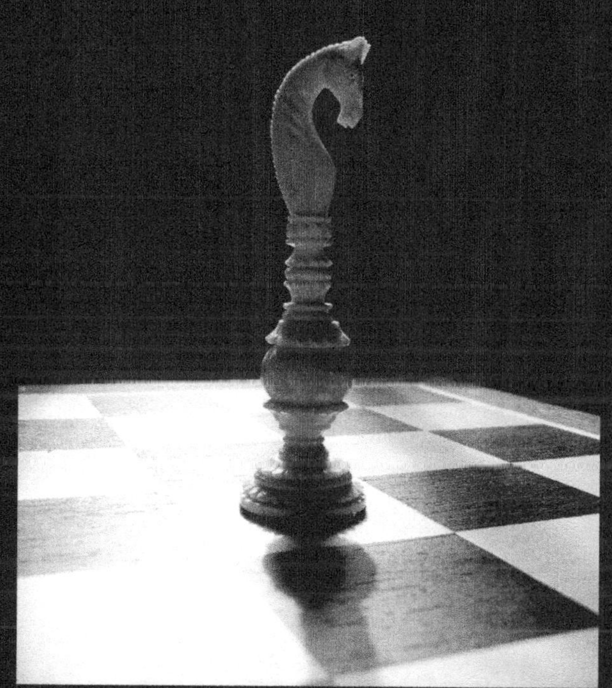

Donna di Scalotta

Dancers: Marcel Duchamp and Gertrude Abercrombie
Trumpet Solo: Dizzy Gillespie
Narrator: Rrose Sélavy

Donna di Scalotta

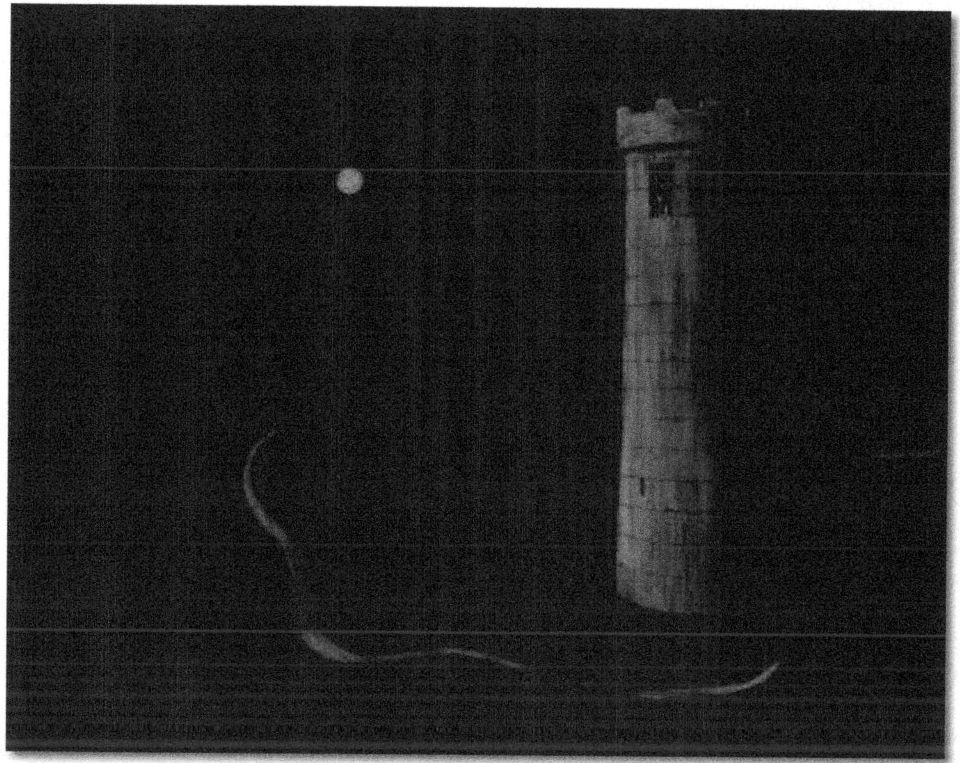

The Ivory Tower, Gertrude Abercrombie

1. The Gray Tower

In Scalotta's silvery mirror
Striving upwards, climbing

To meet the lordly gray sky.
The ivory towers reflect life;

In reverse she sees Camelot
The castle projected in silver.

She sees the world make their way
To the glistering castles of Camelot.

Leather jerkins and dirty linen caps,
Trundle men in mule-driven carts.

Musicians in motley sing to ladies
In flowing white silks. They shadow

Dark knights following their fortunes.
The realm is paralleled within her hands.

Certain death waits beyond every doorway.
Back to her room

Back to her loom
And never from this place should she stray.

Spinning under a magic curse
She weaves yarns into images.

Her memories are knotted in suffering.
From shearlings came shivering words.

Tight knots coding and encoding red
Fabrics, mythic incantations and chants.

Do not look out the window and do not dream;
Death means agony, yet death may bring peace.

Up the road and down the river she watched,
Weaving her songs, into blossoms and roses.

To her all things are possible, for everything is impossible.
She is free to be playful in her paradoxical island of Shallot.

2. The Blue Knight

Beauty may be truth but she rarely speaks it.
We are all fascinated by the magic of the mirror.

We understand a way of life in reflection, as it passes away.
Just as Narcissus, bewitched by his own reflection in a pool

Drowned in his attempt to touch what was beyond his grasp.
Unable to be true to his own self fulfilling Tiresias' prophecy.

Only in hindsight
Can we feel loss.

She saw the knight in reverse.
A burning blue flame ignited.

Lancelot riding on horseback
Had come home to Camelot.

Without a moments hesitation
Her head spun out the window.

The mirror melted
Pooling on the floor.

The curse has come,
Cried Donna di Scalotta.

3. Down the River

An enclosed room occupied by a lone woman
A broomstick, and a black cat on a leash.

She pushed open the heavy wooden doors
And made her way down to the riverbanks.

Hurriedly, with a finger she wrote
In red ink a note onto her mantle

Blanketed herself and pushed the boat from shore.
She lay down, folded her arms across her chest and sang.

Isolated   a single road cut
Into the wasteland   leading to the unknown
The ever-present   an echo of her presence
Movements of water   reflect upon

The nature of time   Tuesdays
I want more flowers   dirt
An enchanted horse   one not frightened of wraiths

Sprinkle my body with rosemary; rosemary for remembrance.

Bury my body in
>The simple patterned lace I left on my bed.
I went to the window
>A single leaf fell, and so it is with whispers on the wind.
In pristine and haunting echoes, I fell too.

In mournful glory
>In an exhibition of joyous love
A jazz funeral trumpets without hesitation

Hold up your blue garnets
And let every man drink his glass full
And here's to the health o' tha young lass.

I roamed and I rambled while all 'round me a voice was sounding
A voice was chanting, the sun came a shining and the wheat field
Was a waving the fog was a liftin'

The flame spoke
No words
But illuminated
All the same.

"Who is this? And what is here?" asked the courtiers of Camelot
As they made the sign of the cross to protect them from darkness
Frightened silent by the evil that destroyed this unknown voice.

Lancelot mused down from his staircase,
This fine lady has such a charming grace.

SECOND TABLEAU

PAS DE DEUX

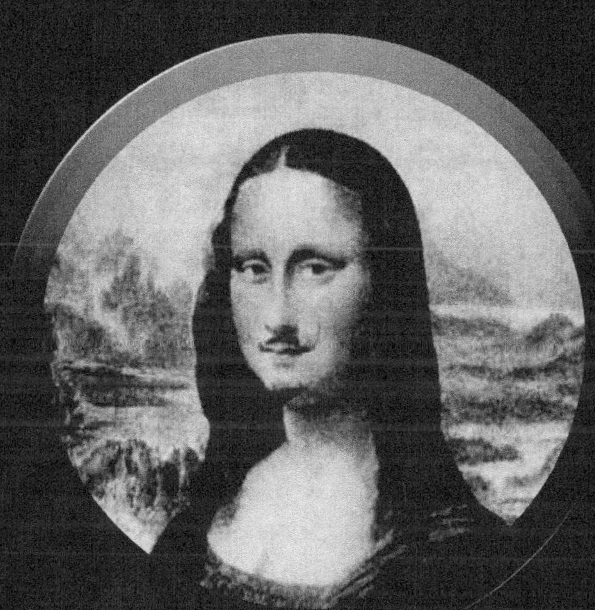

Retinal Movements: A Choreography

Dancers: Marcel Duchamp and Rrose Sélavy

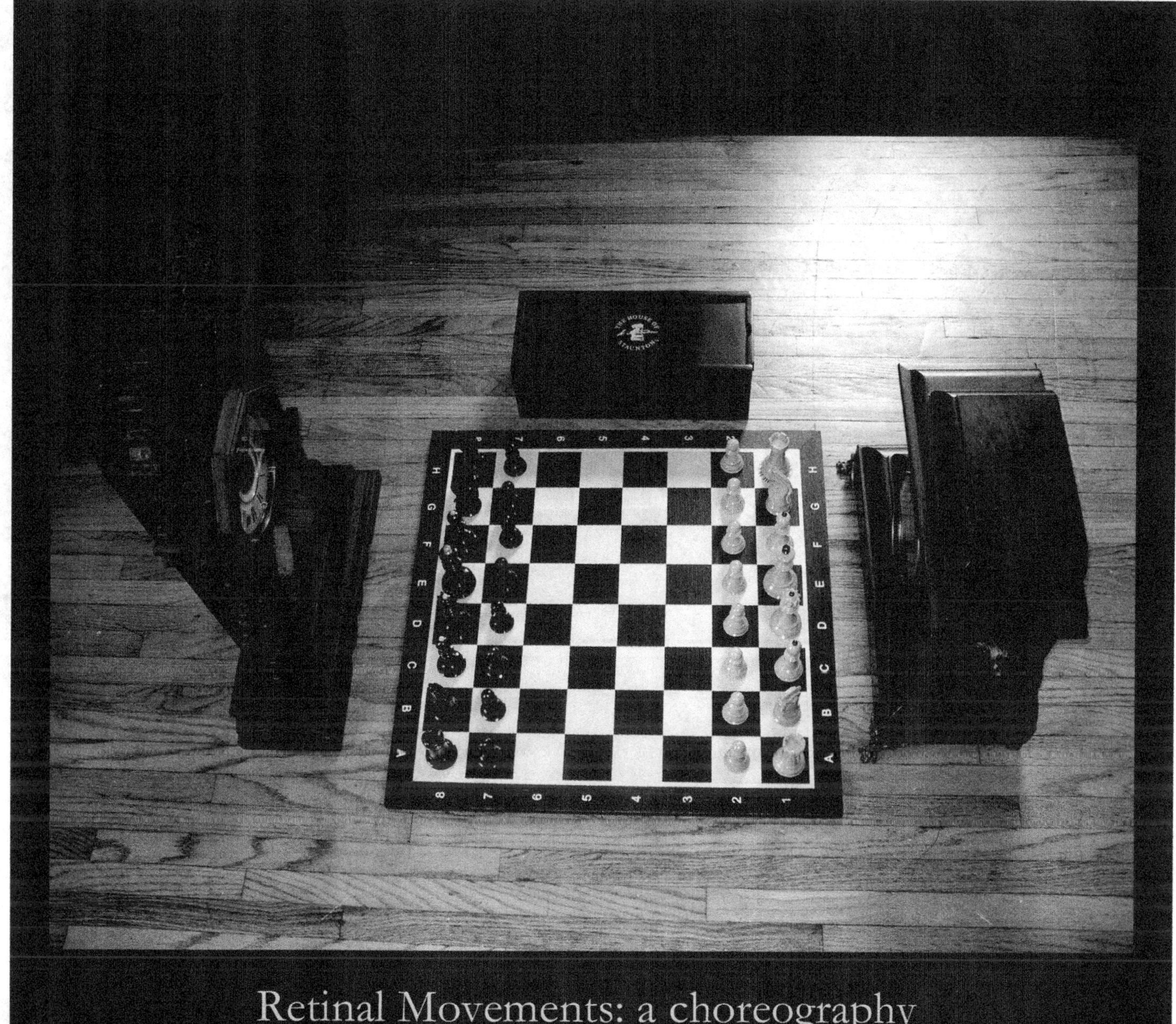

Retinal Movements: a choreography

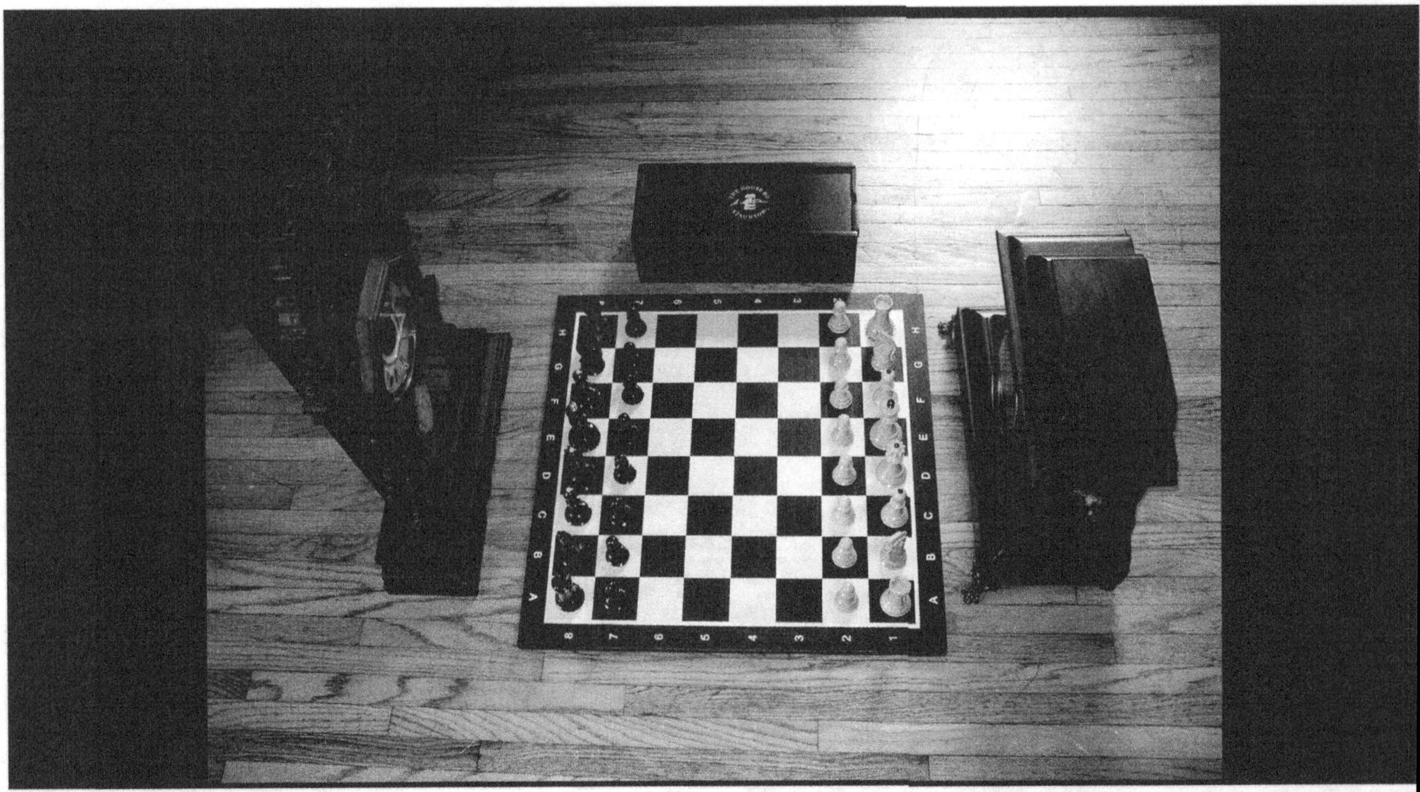

THE CHESS GAME:

This choreography employs chess as the movement of the pas de deux between Apollo and Tiresias. The outcome is a draw, using the actual gameplay by Frank Marshall verses Marcel Duchamp at the Chess Olympiad held in Hamburg Germany in 1930. The whole game is listed below in algebraic notation.

Frank Marshall (Playing White) - M. Duchamp (Playing black)

1.d4 Nf6 2.Nf3 b6 3.c4 e6 4.Bg5 Be7 5.Nc3 Bb7 6.Qc2 d5 7.e3 O-O 8.cxd5 Nxd5 9.Bxe7 Qxe7 10.Nxd5 Bxd5 11.Bd3 h6 12.a3 c5 13.dxc5 Rc8 14.b4 bxc5 15.Rc1 Nd7 16.Ba6 Rc7 17.e4 Bb7 18.Bxb7 Rxb7 19.bxc5 Qxc5 20.O-O Qxc2 21.Rxc2 Kf8 22.Rfc1 Ke7 23.Nd4 Ke8 24.f4 Rab8 25.e5 Nf8 26.Rc5 Rb1 27.Rxb1 Rxb1+ 28.Kf2 Rb7 29.Rc8+ Ke7 30.Ra8 Ng6 31.g3 Kd7 32.a4 Ne7 33.Nb5 Nc8 34.g4 Rxb5 35.axb5 Kc7 36.g5 hxg5 37.b6+ Kb7 38.Rxc8 Kxc8 1/2-1/2

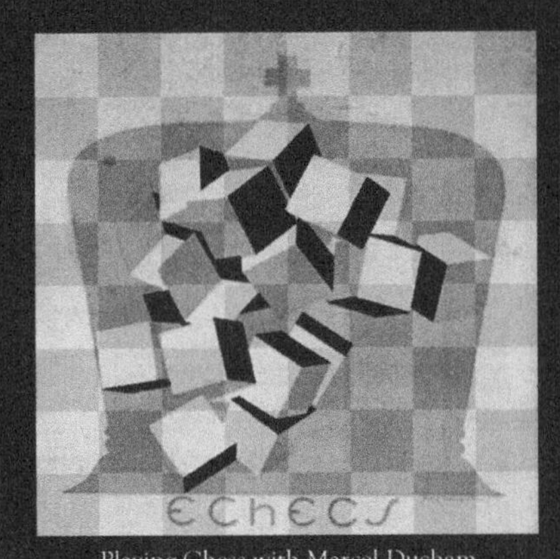

Playing Chess with Marcel Ducham

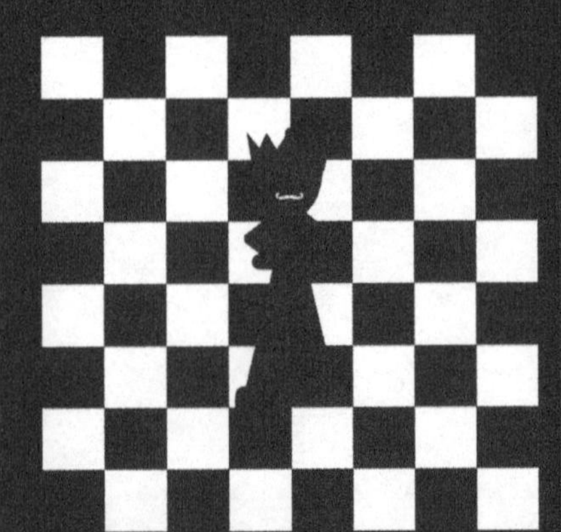

Not all artists may be chess players, but all chess players are artists.

—Duchamp

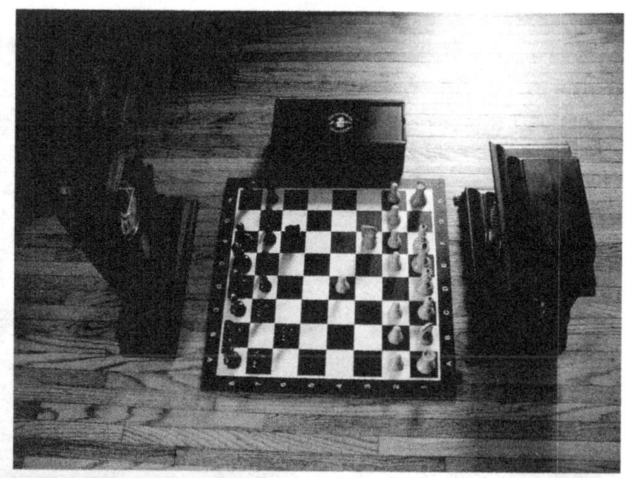

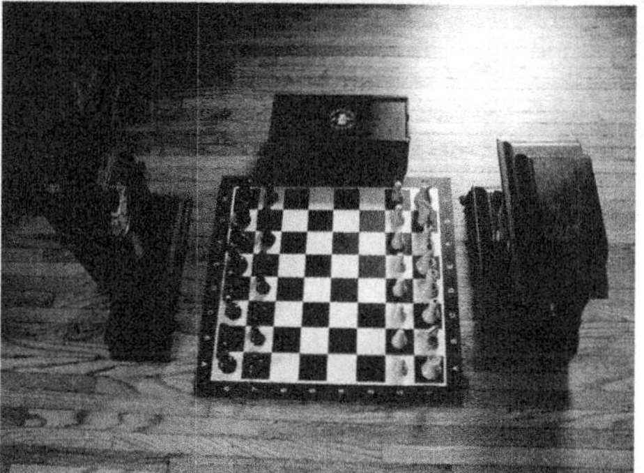

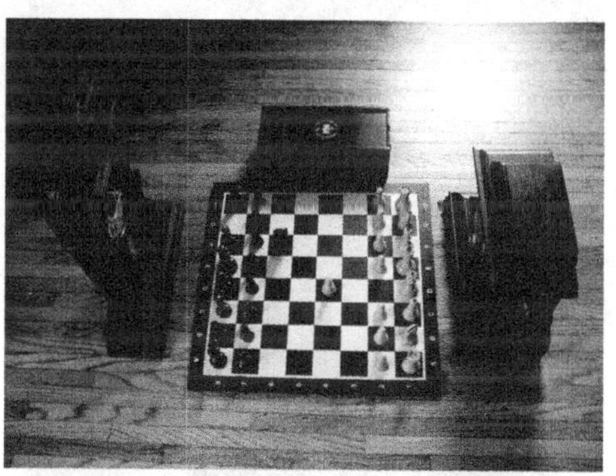

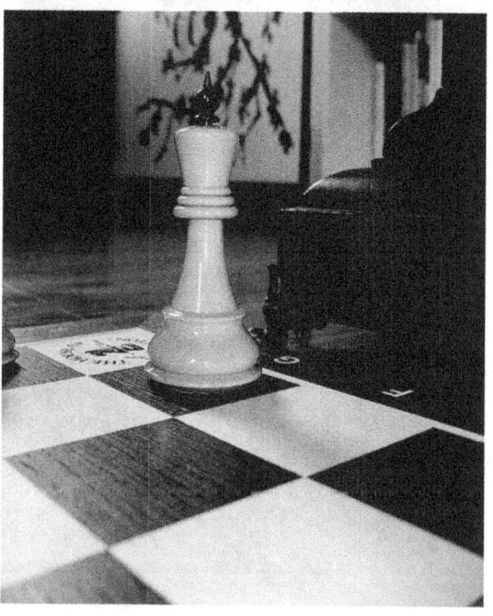

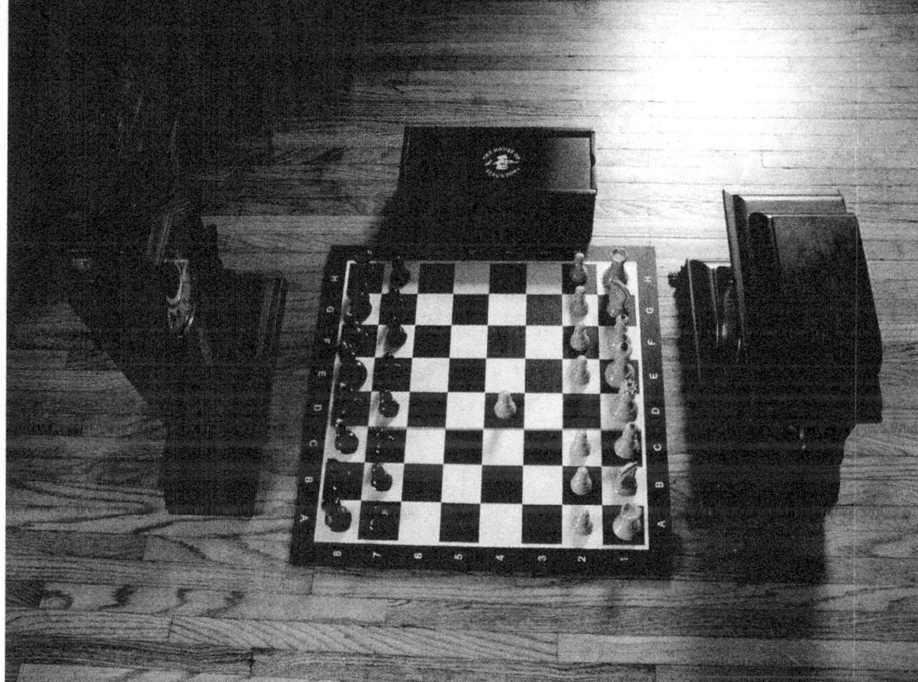

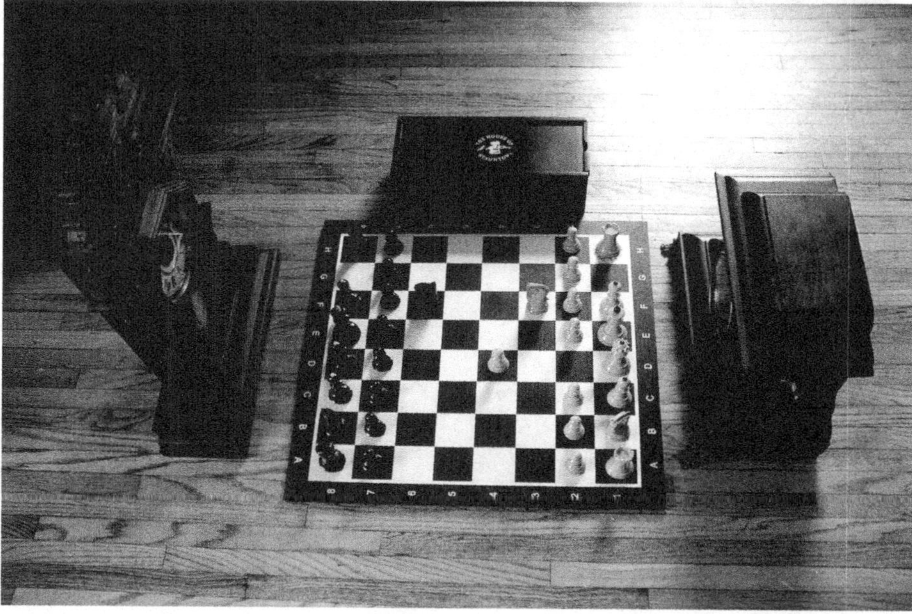

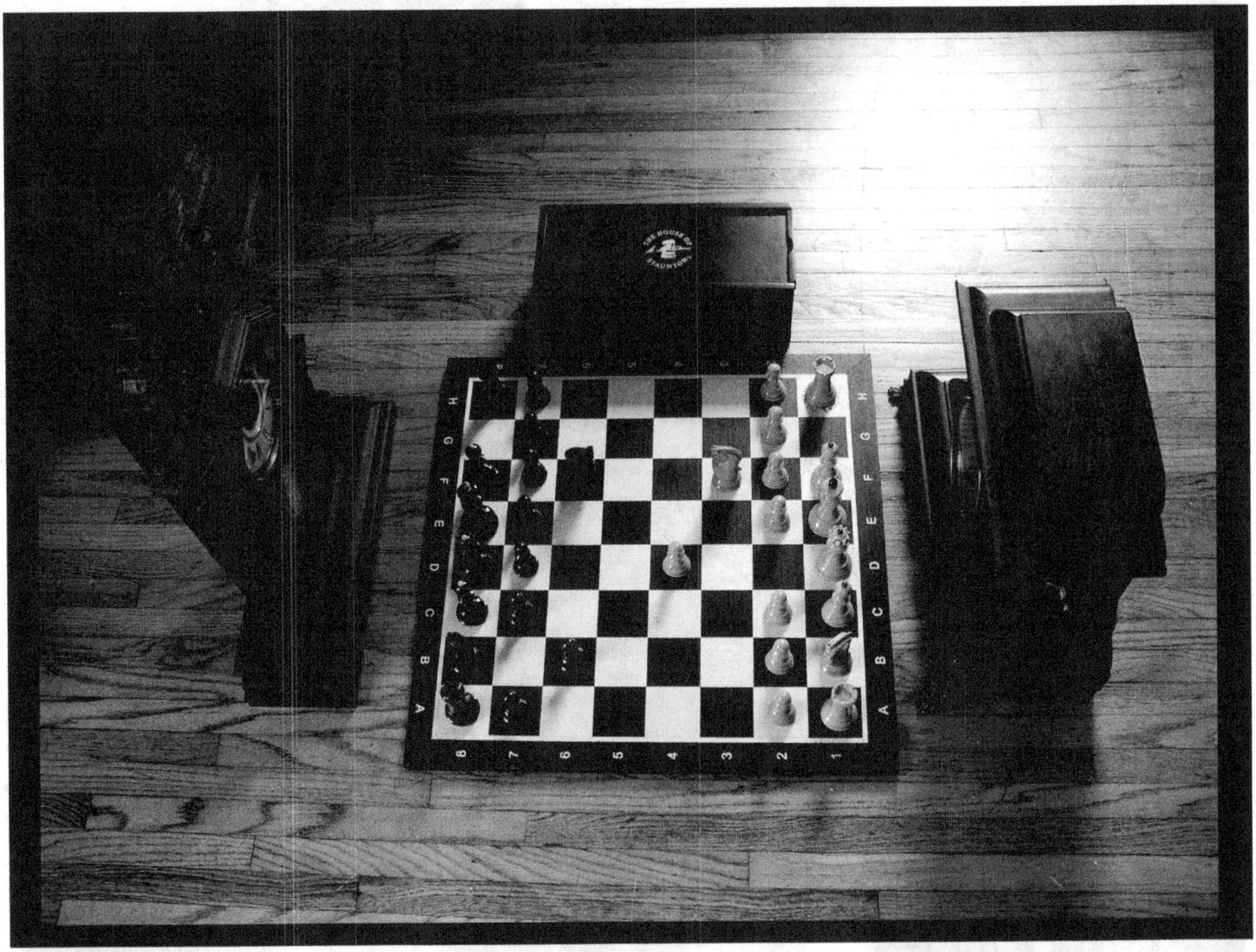

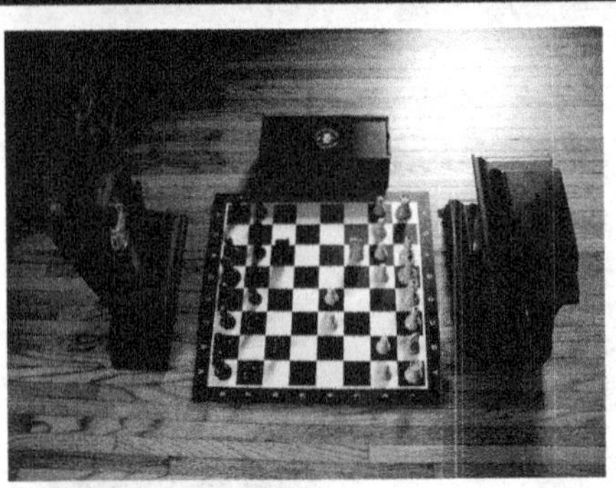
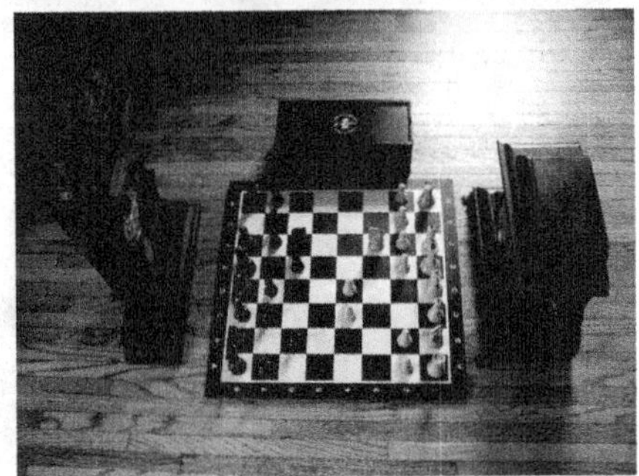
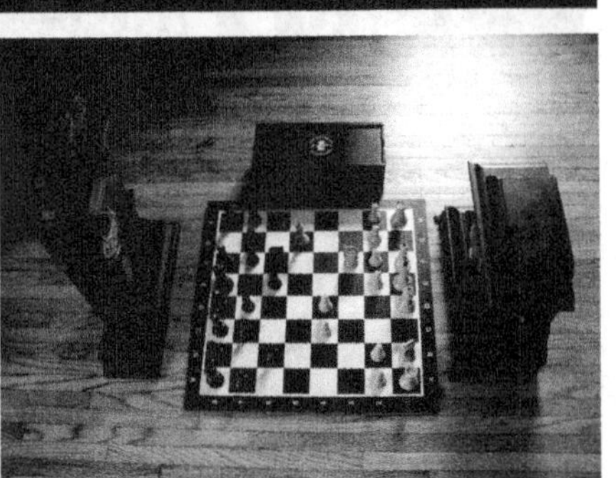
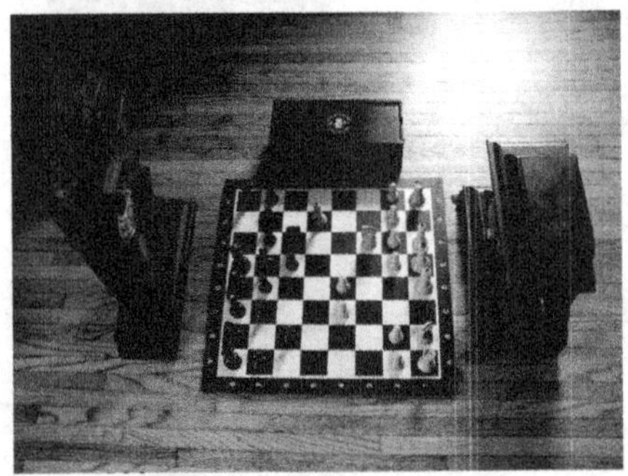
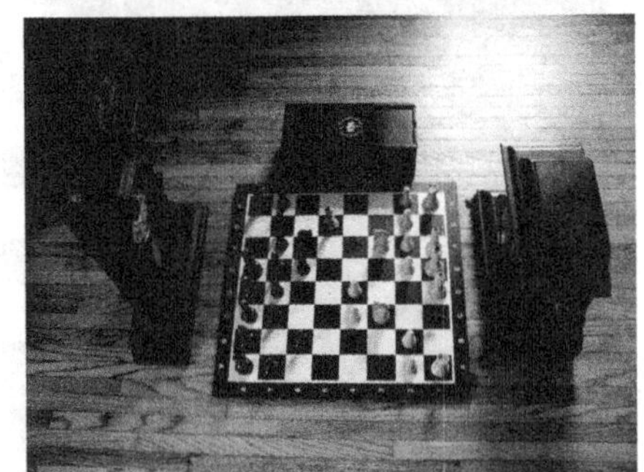
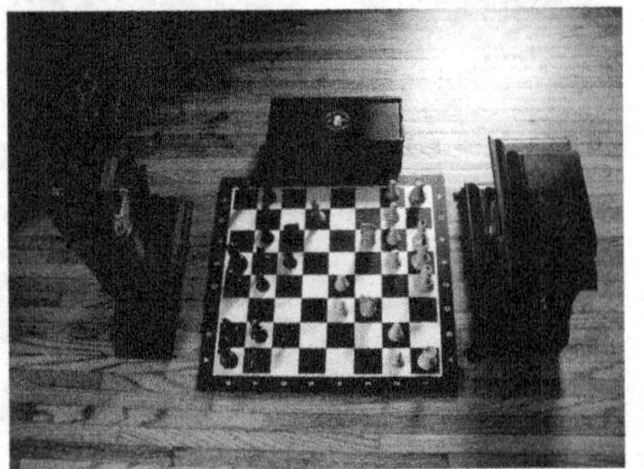

Chess is the
touchstone
of human intellect.

—Goethe

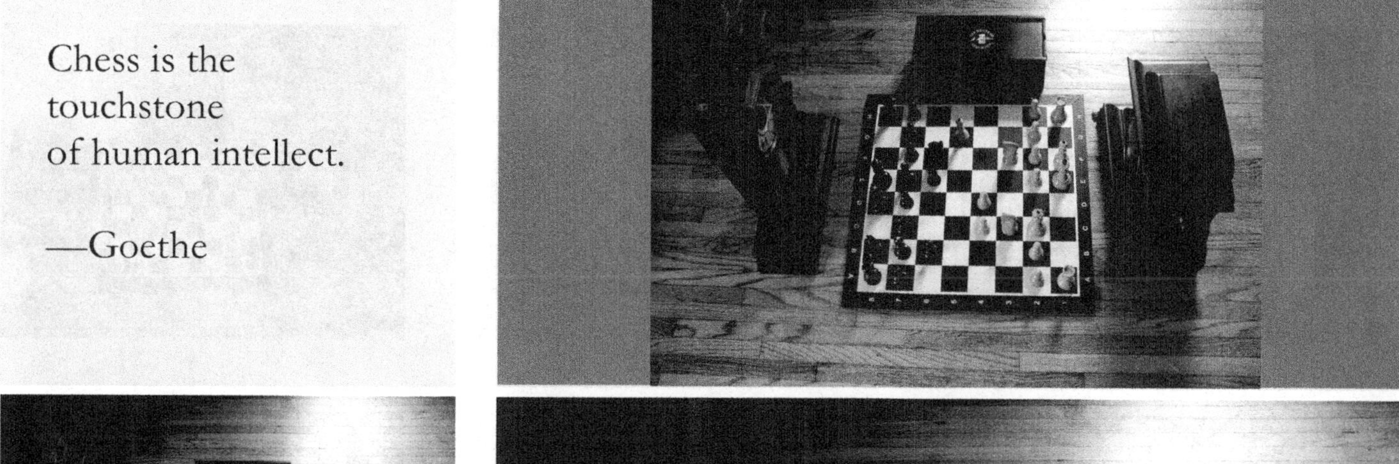

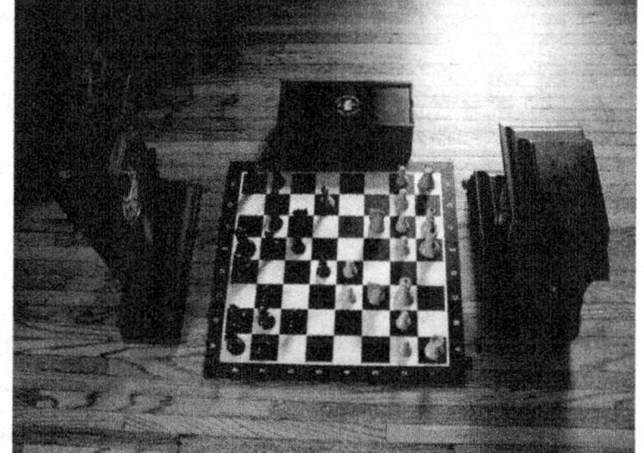

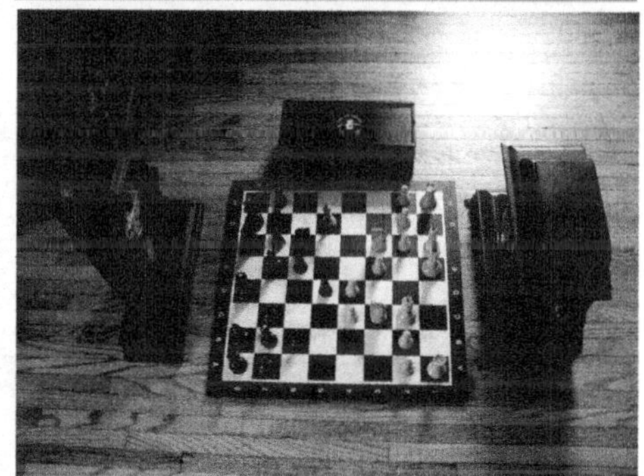

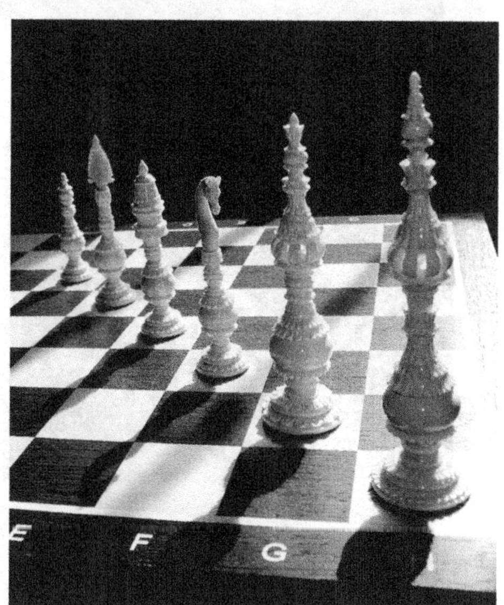

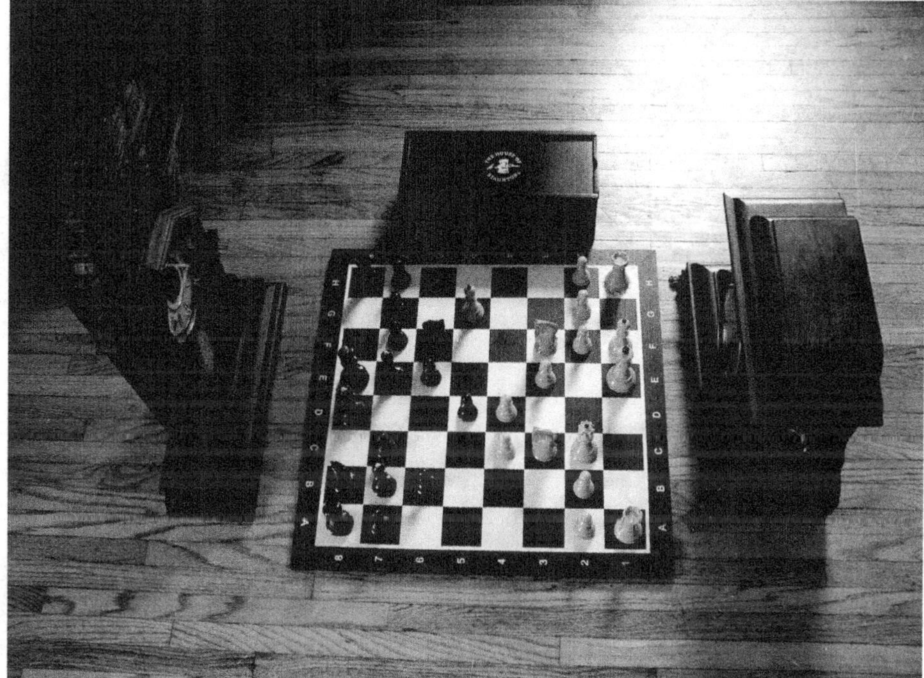

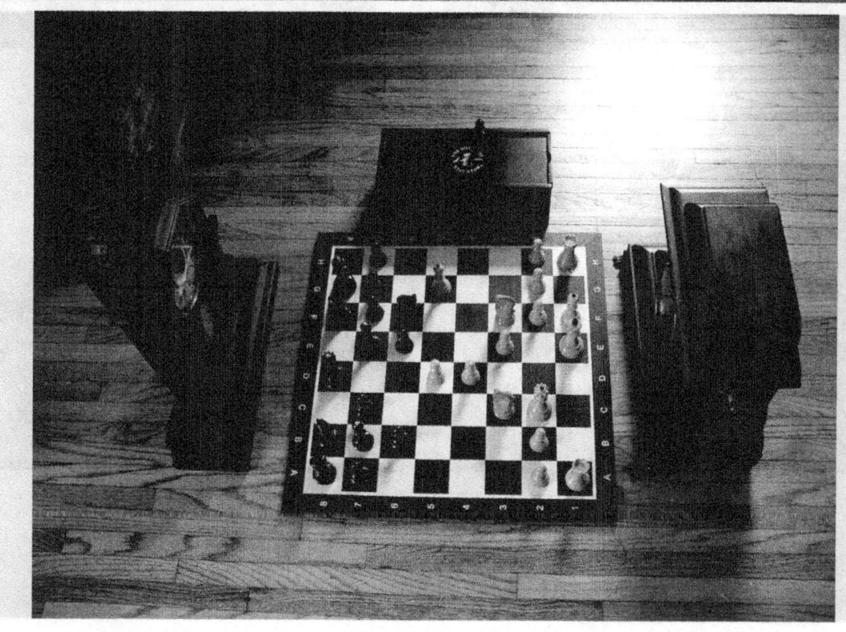

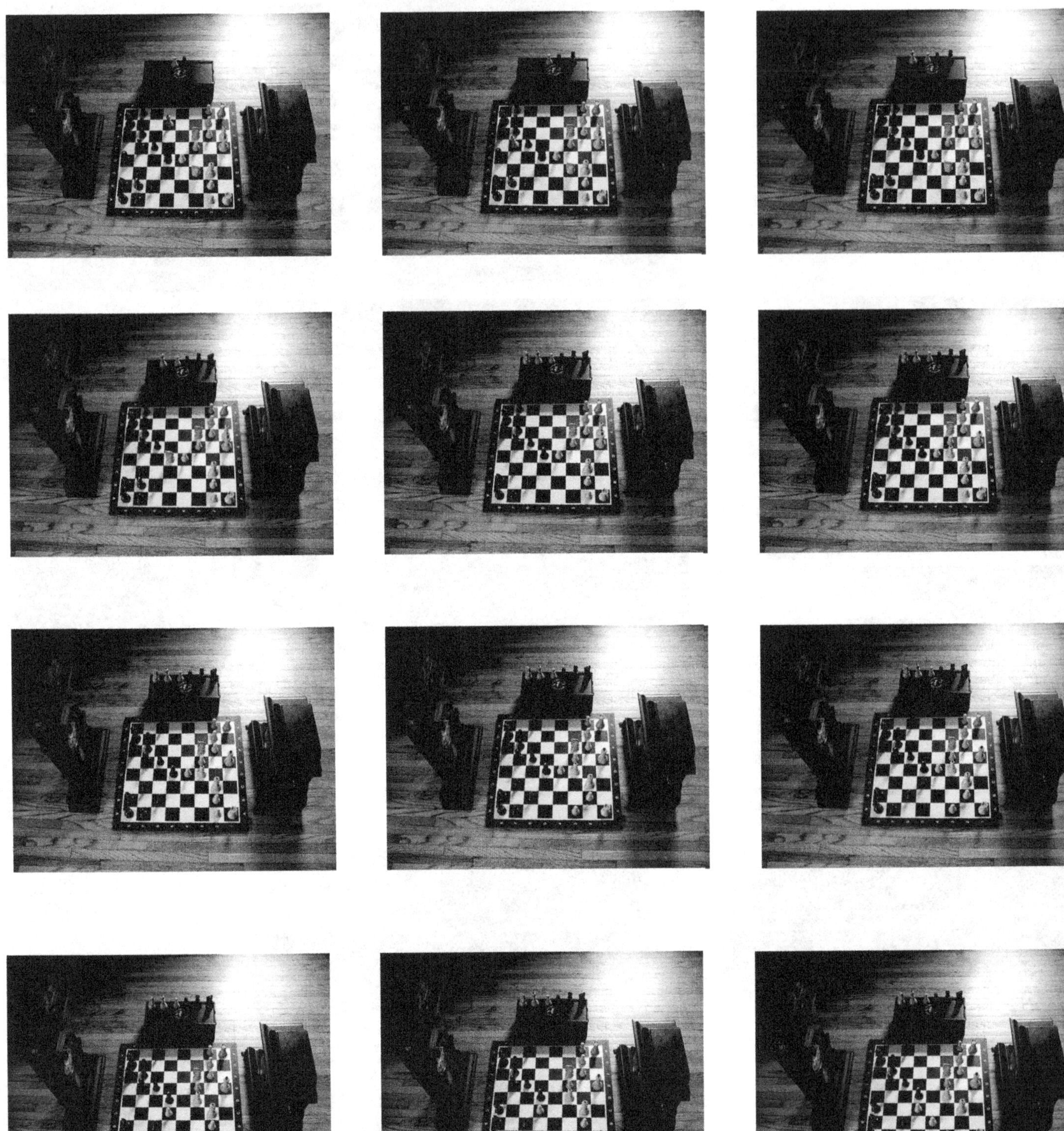

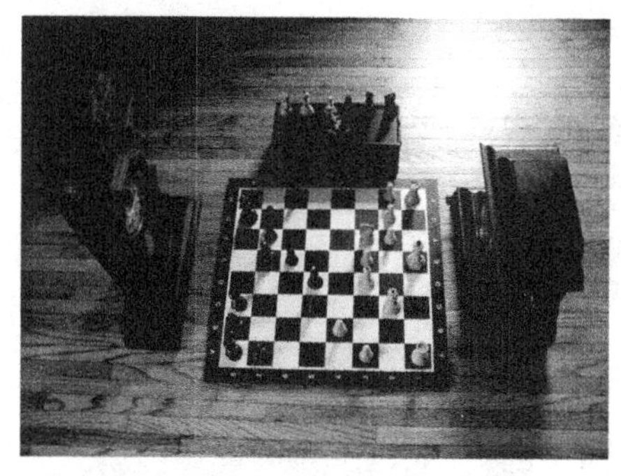
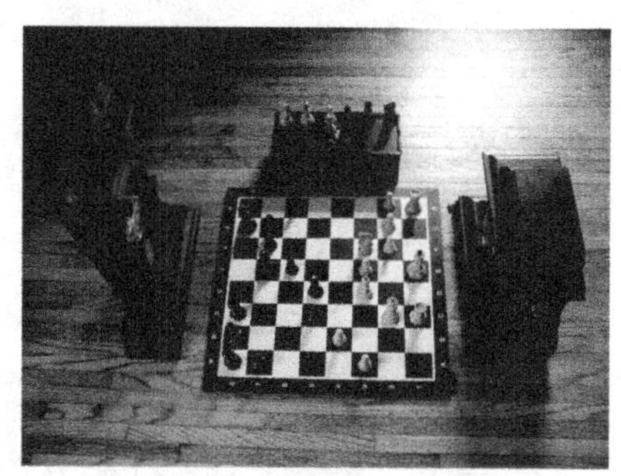
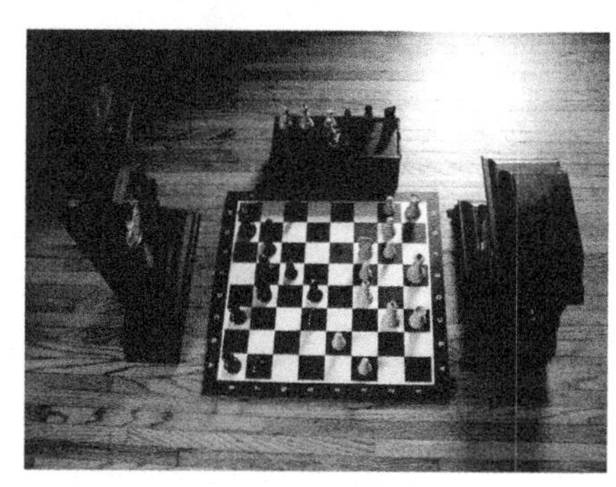
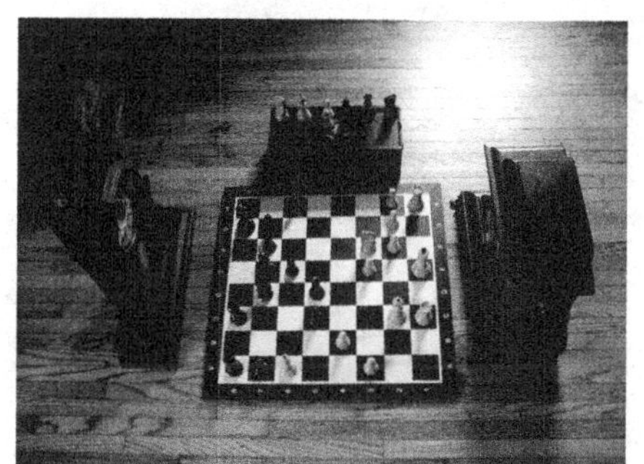
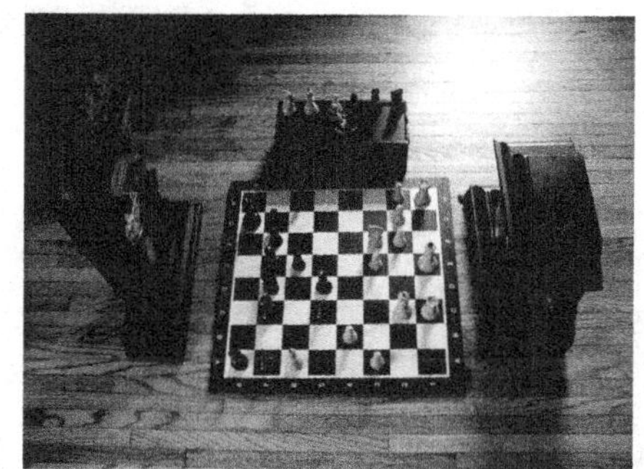
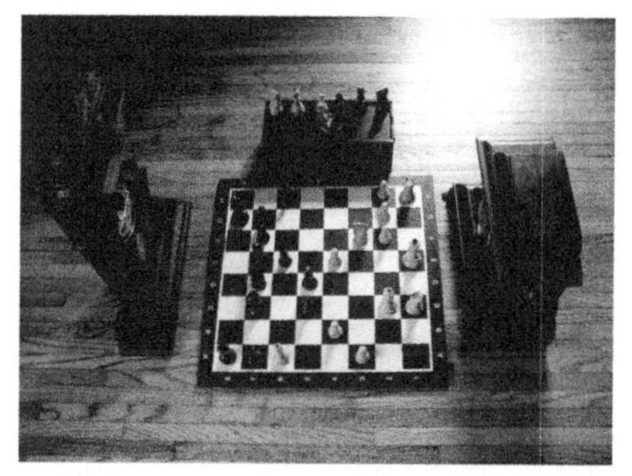
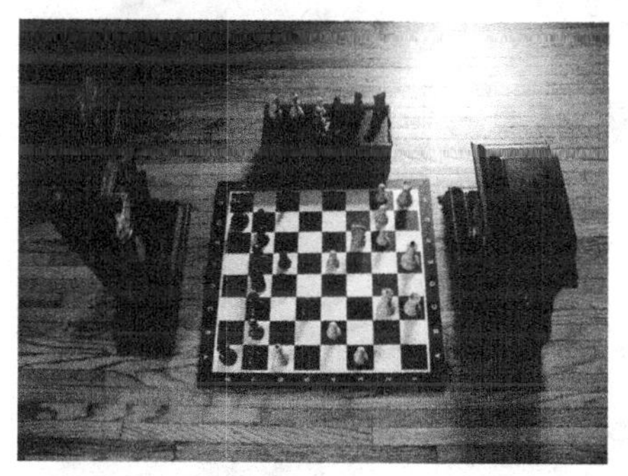
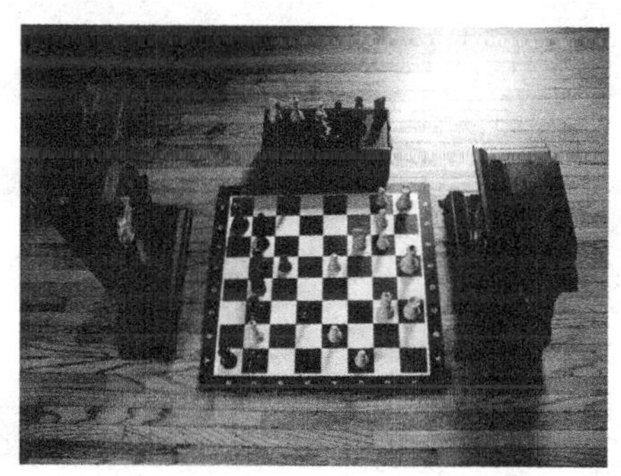
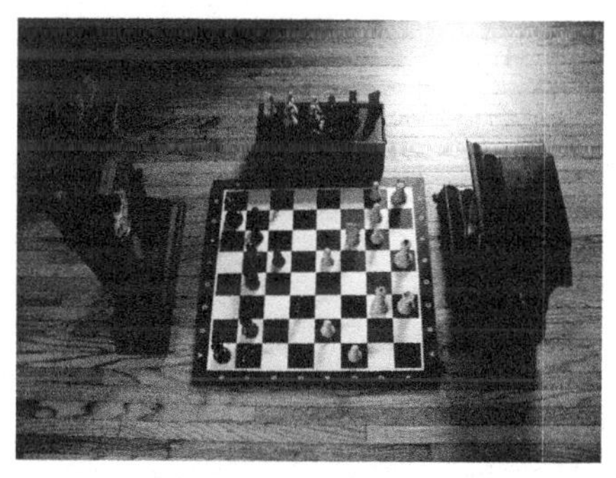
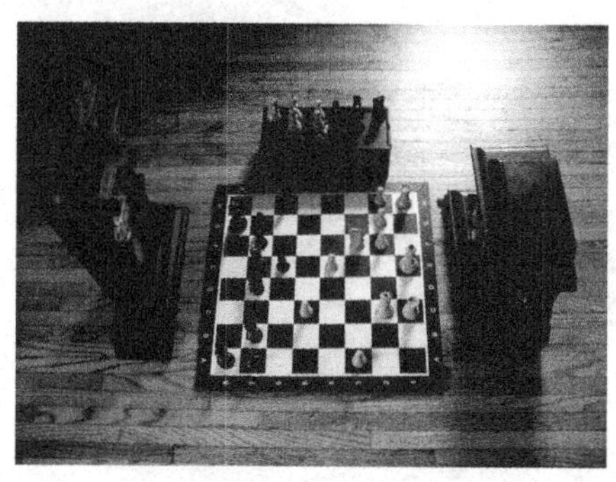
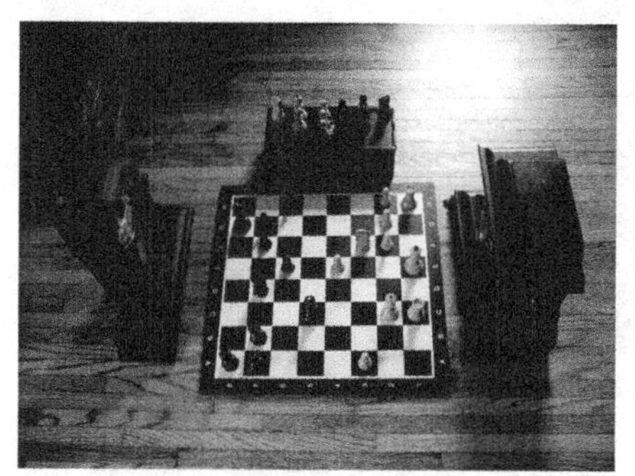
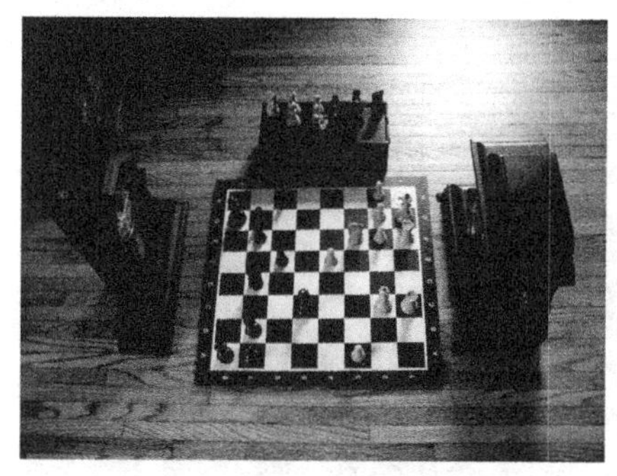

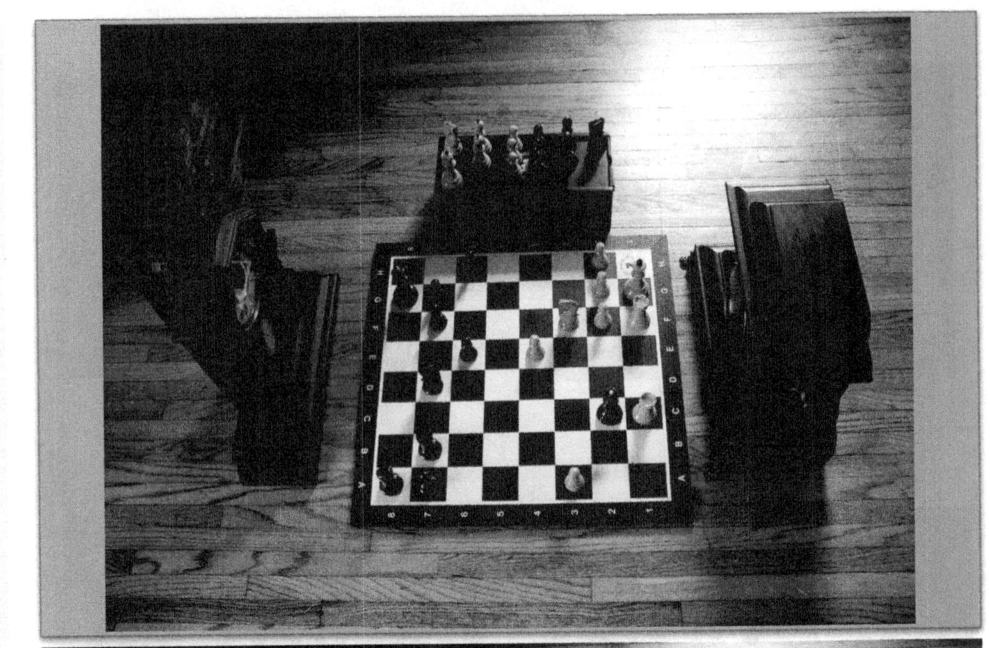

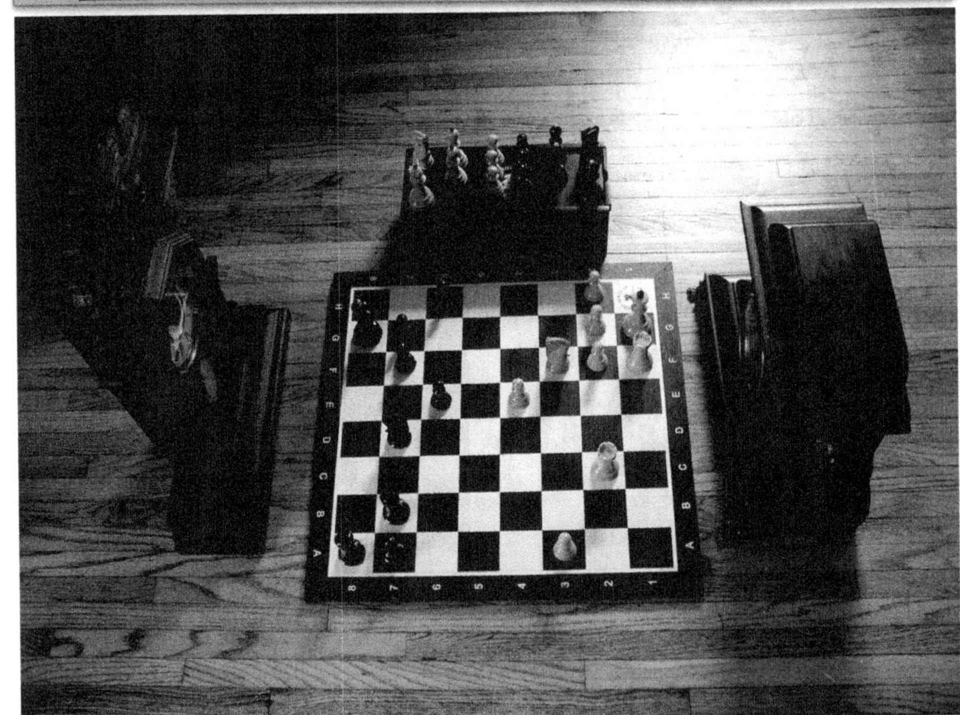

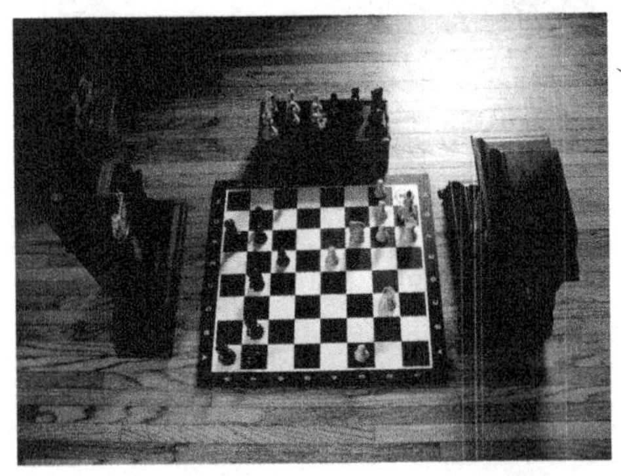
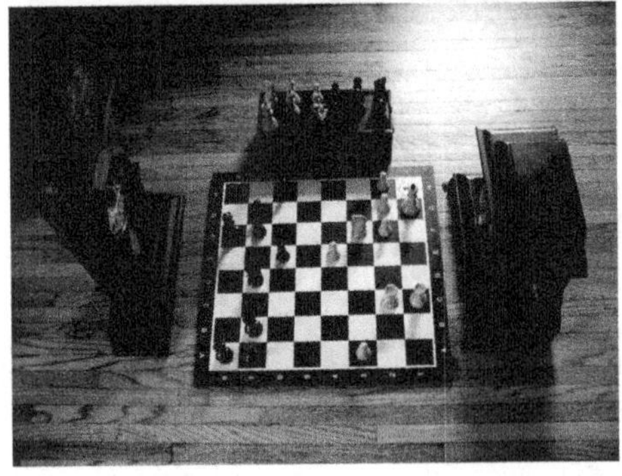
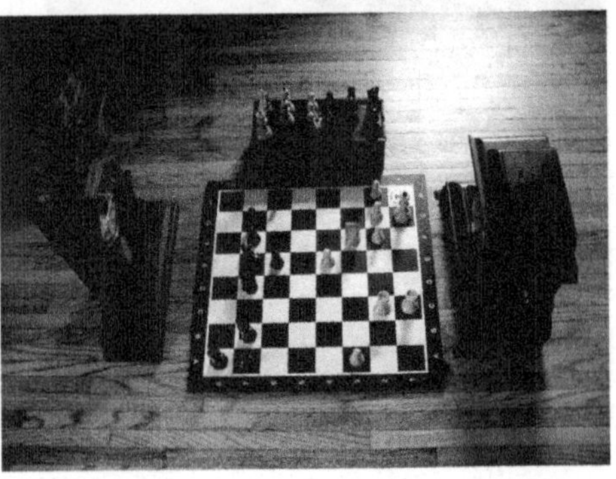

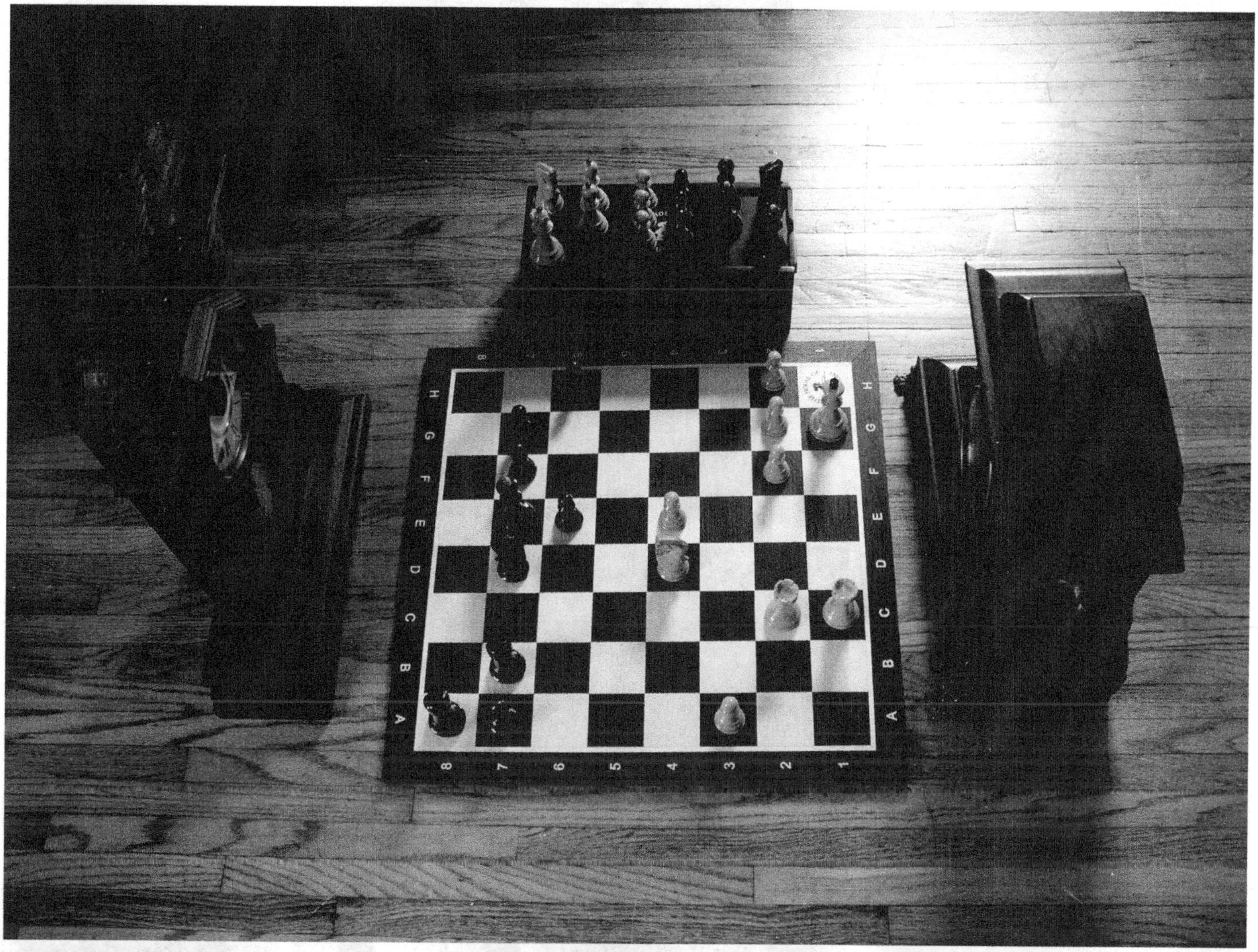

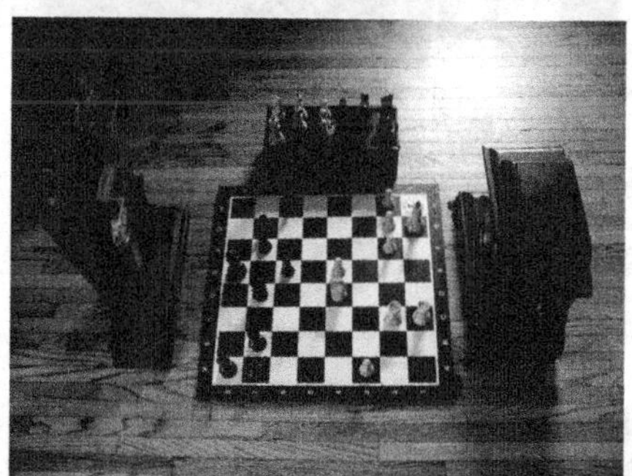
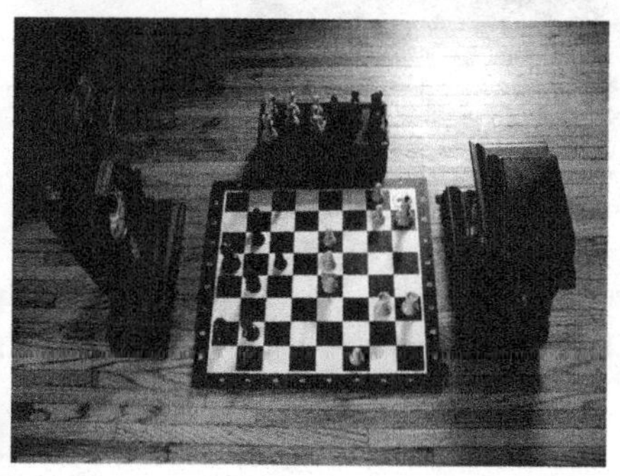
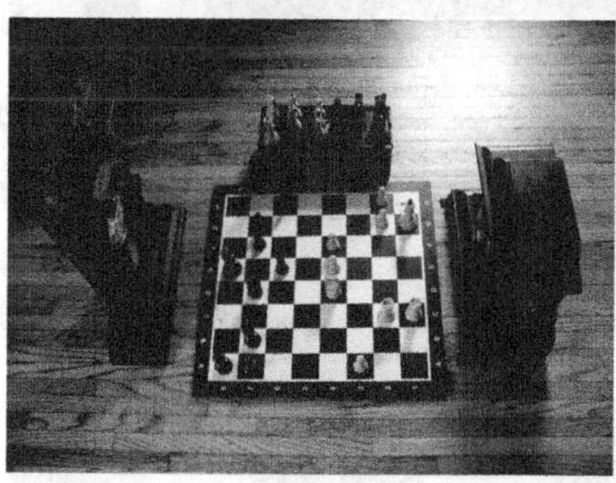
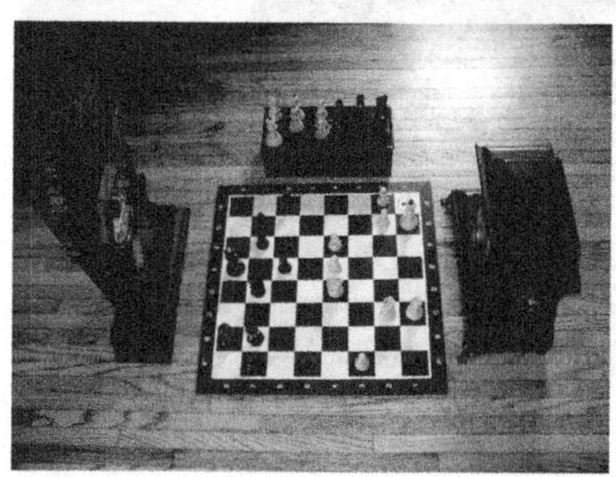
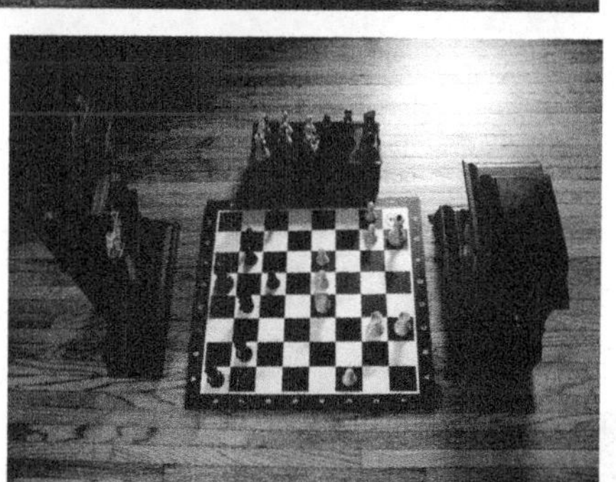
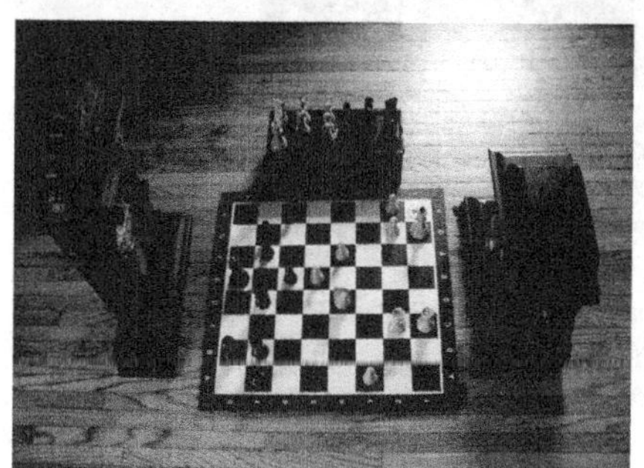

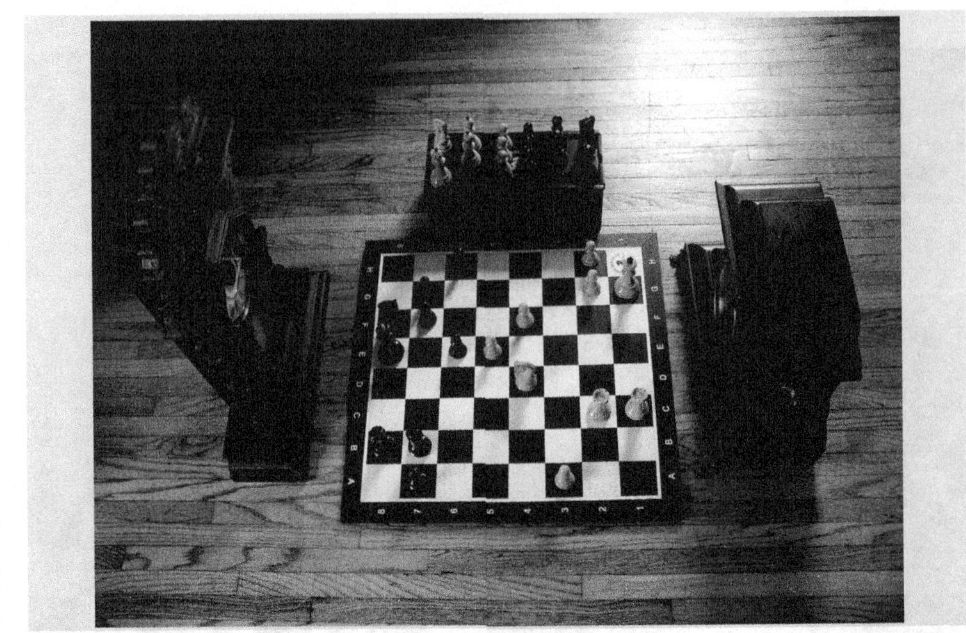

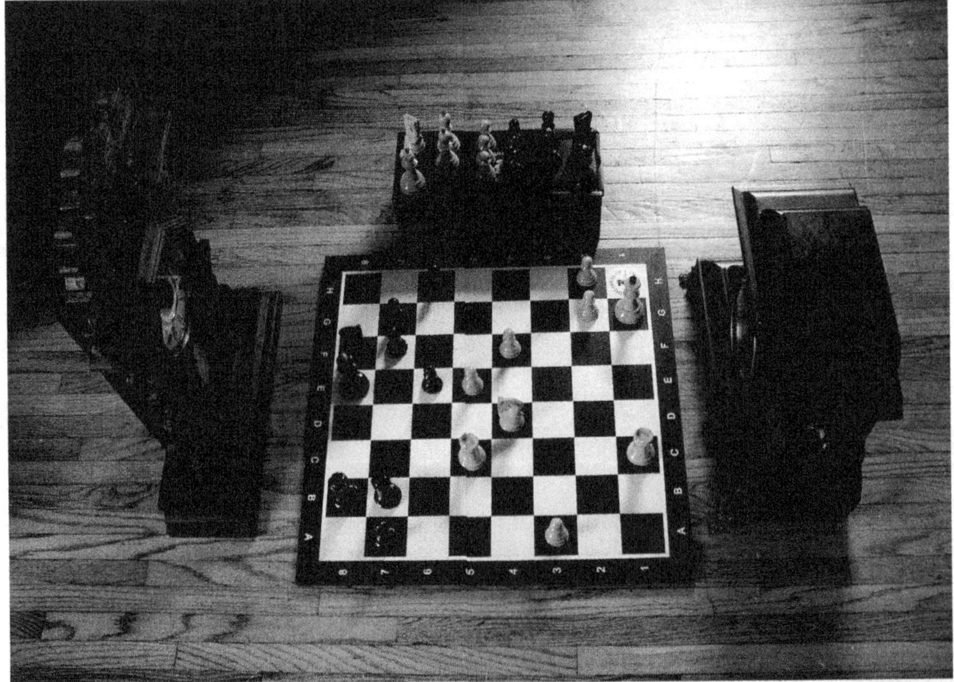

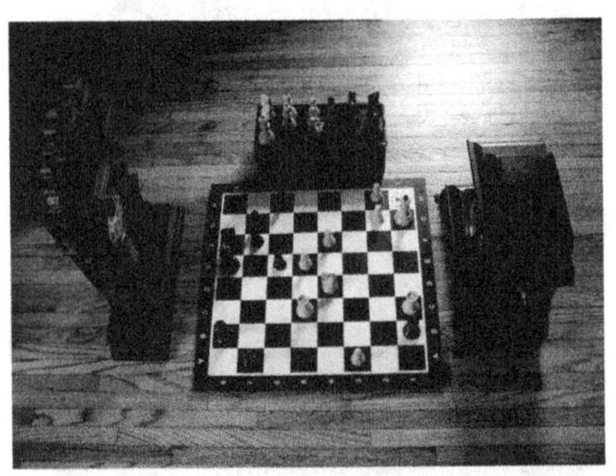

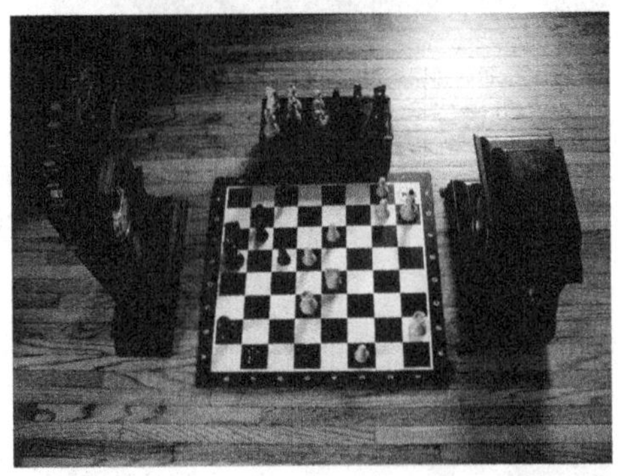

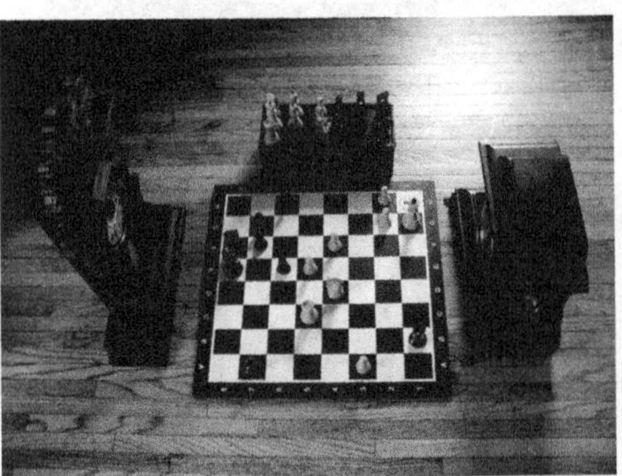

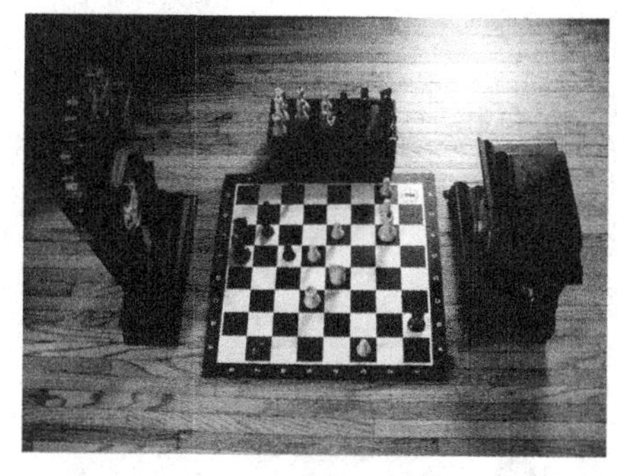
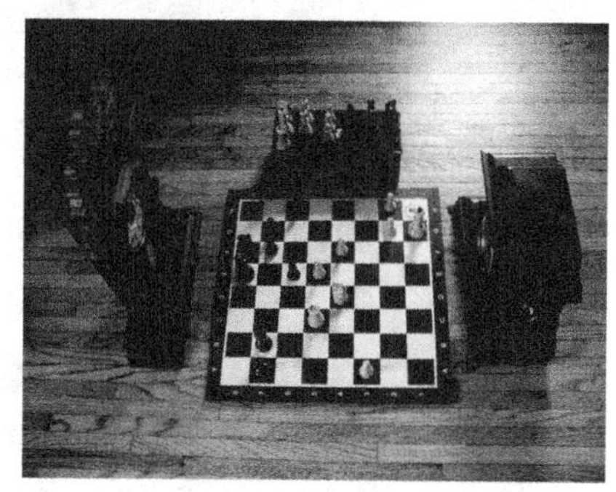
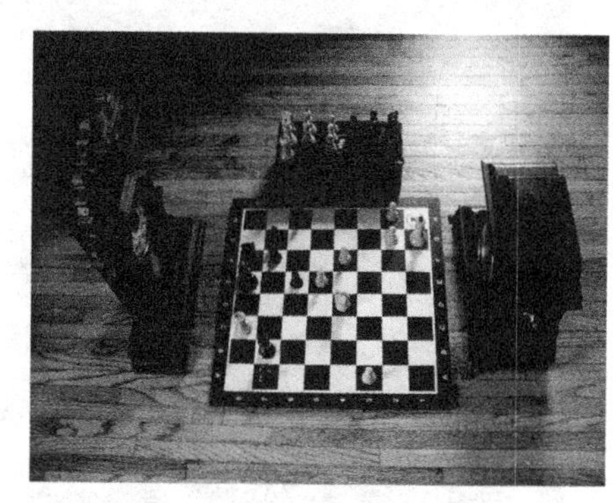
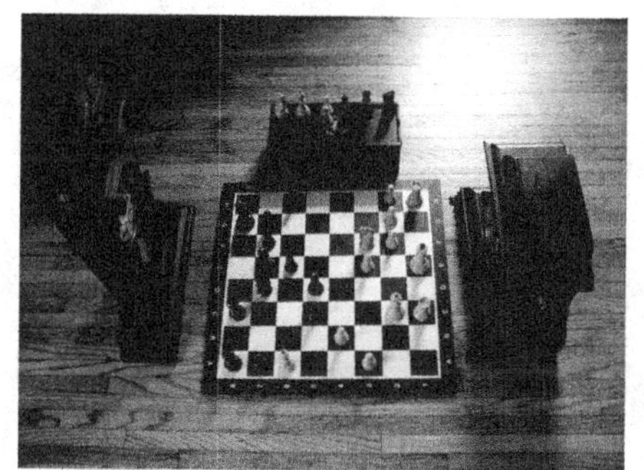
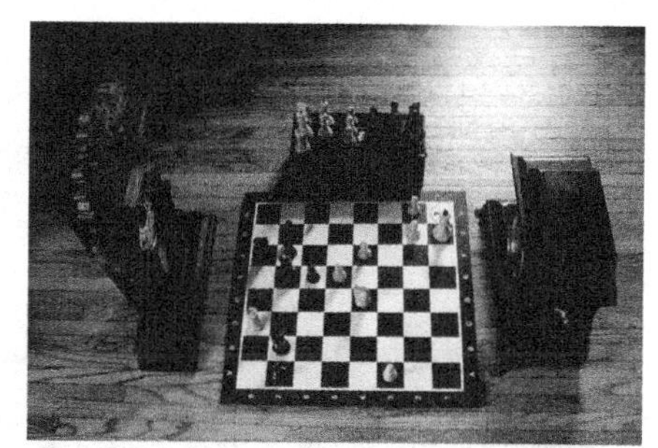
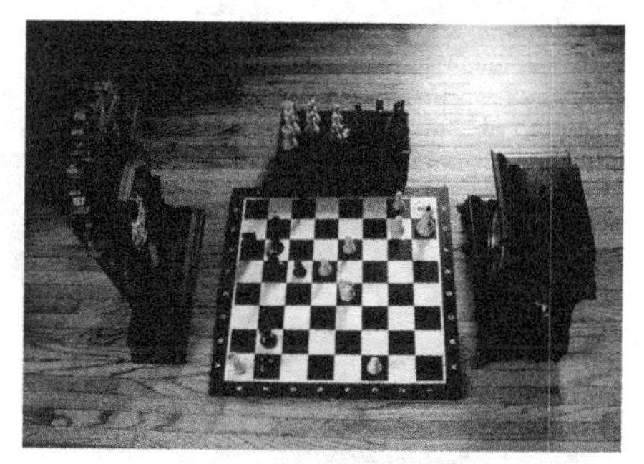
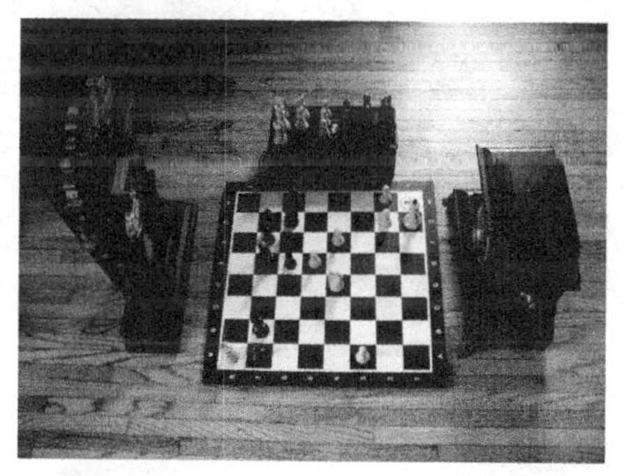
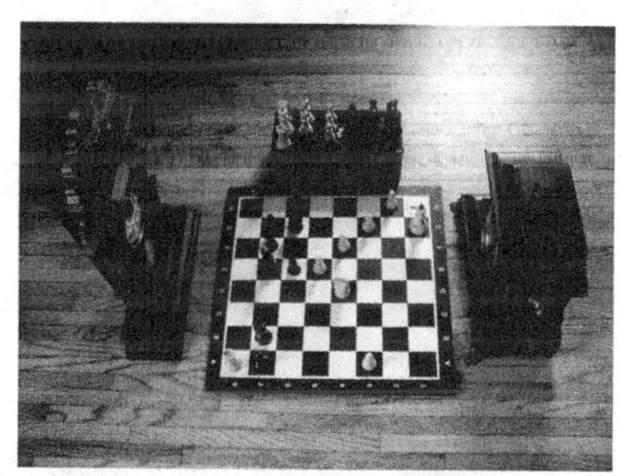
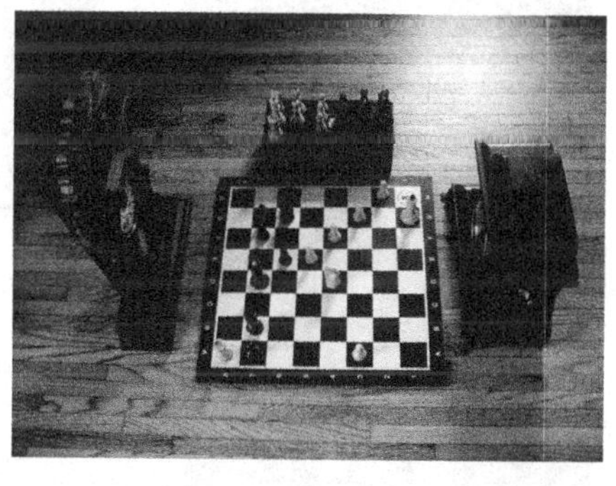
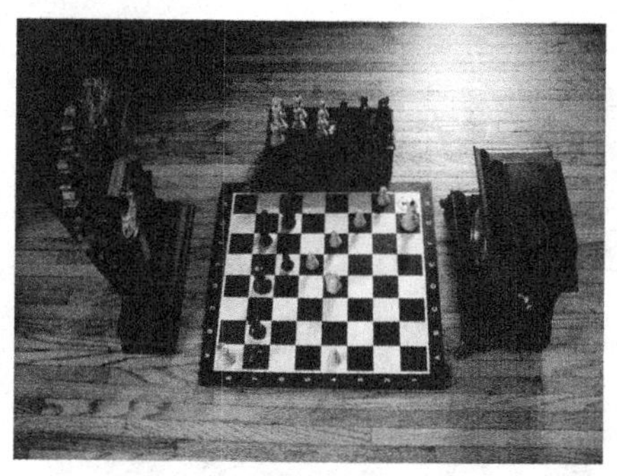
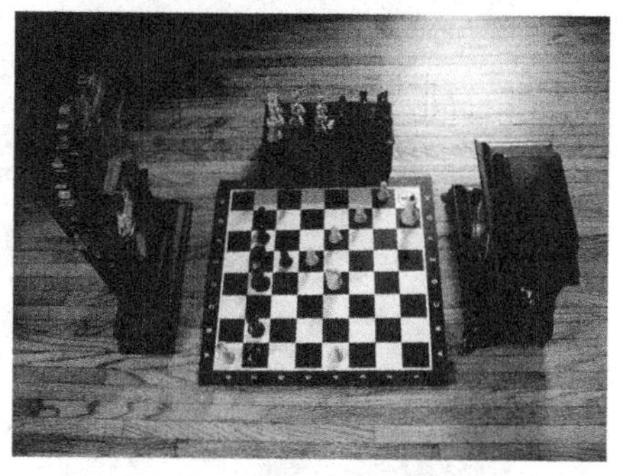
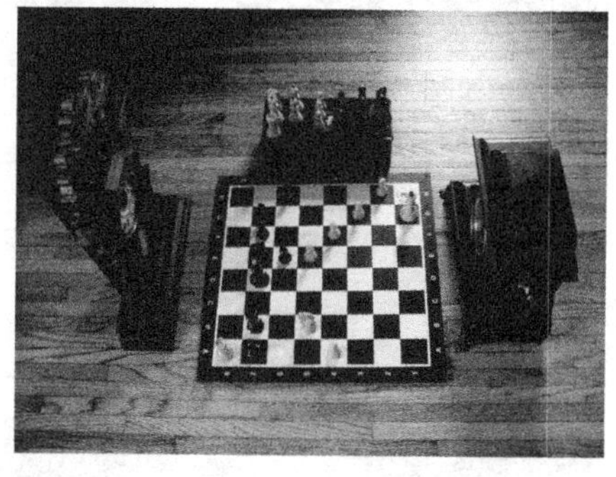

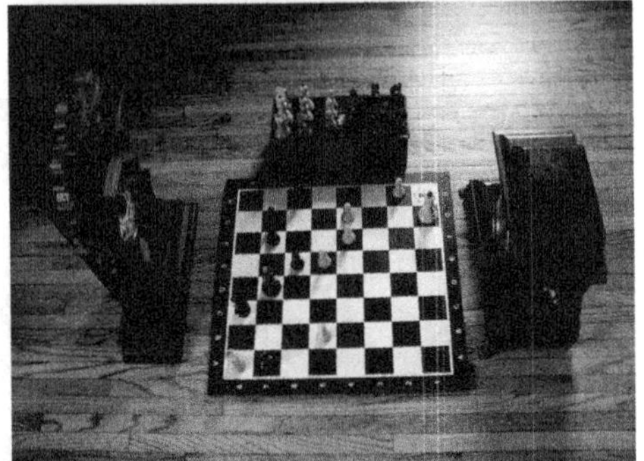
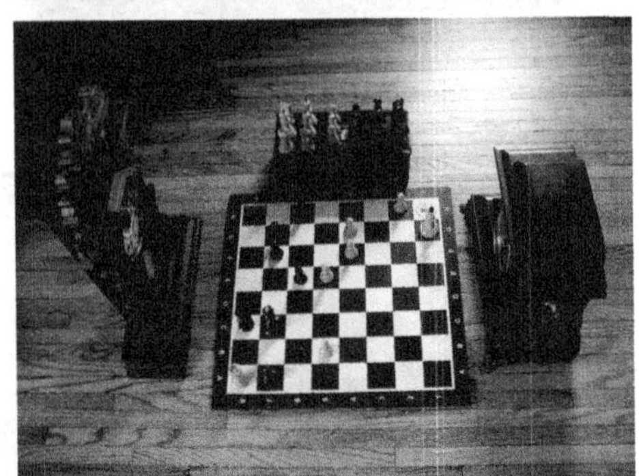
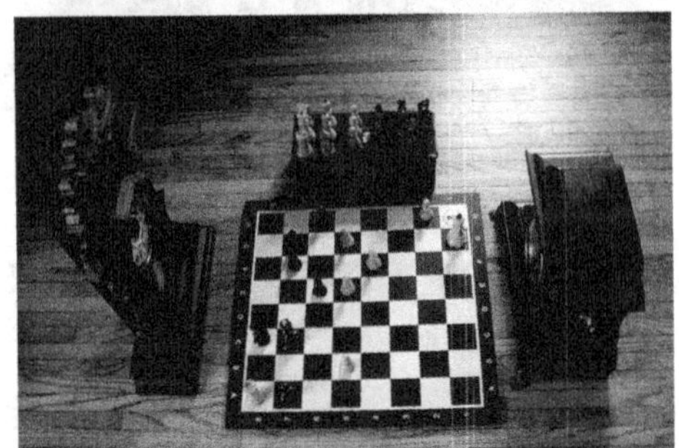
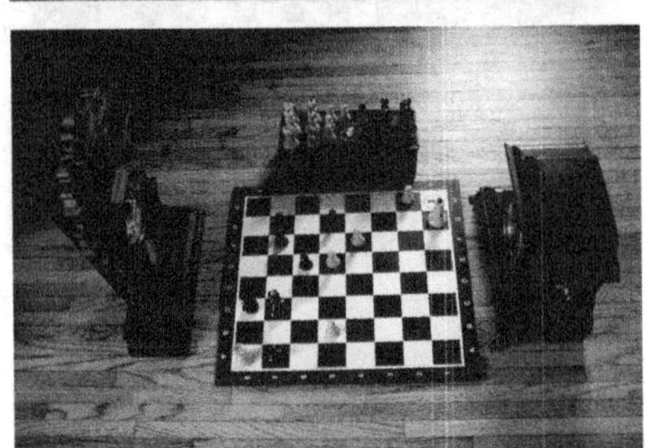
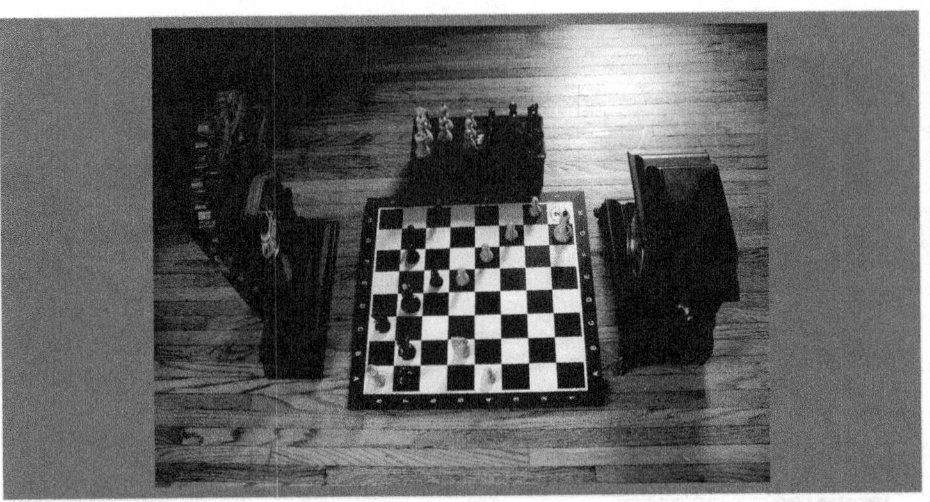
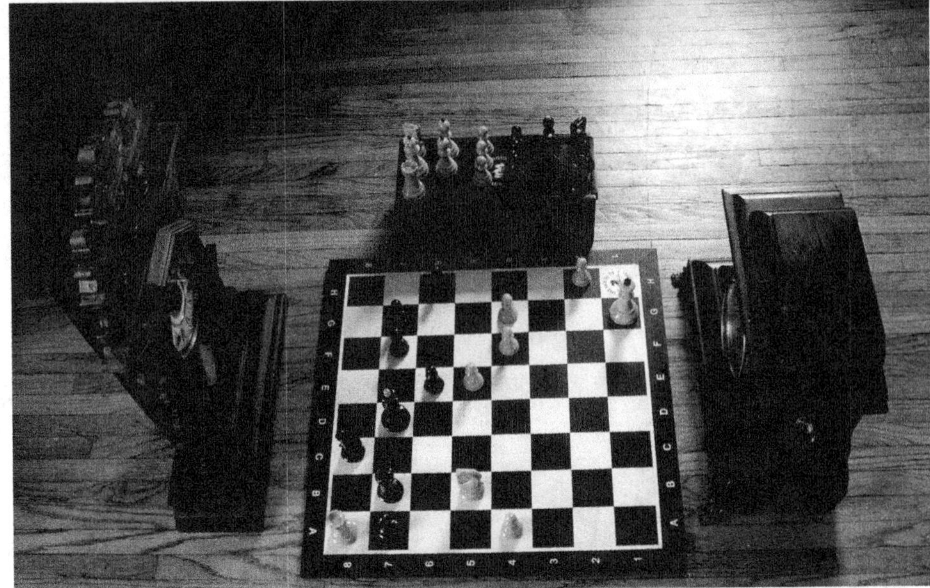
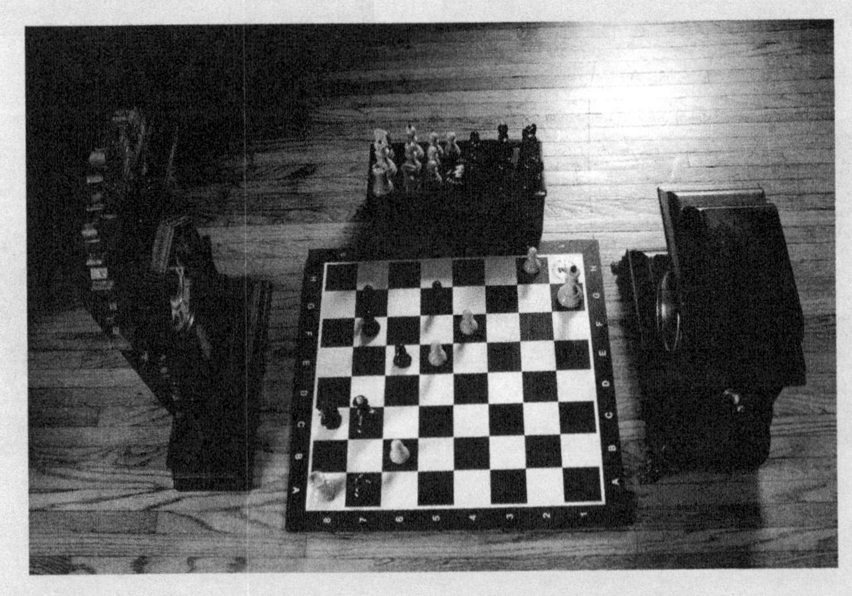

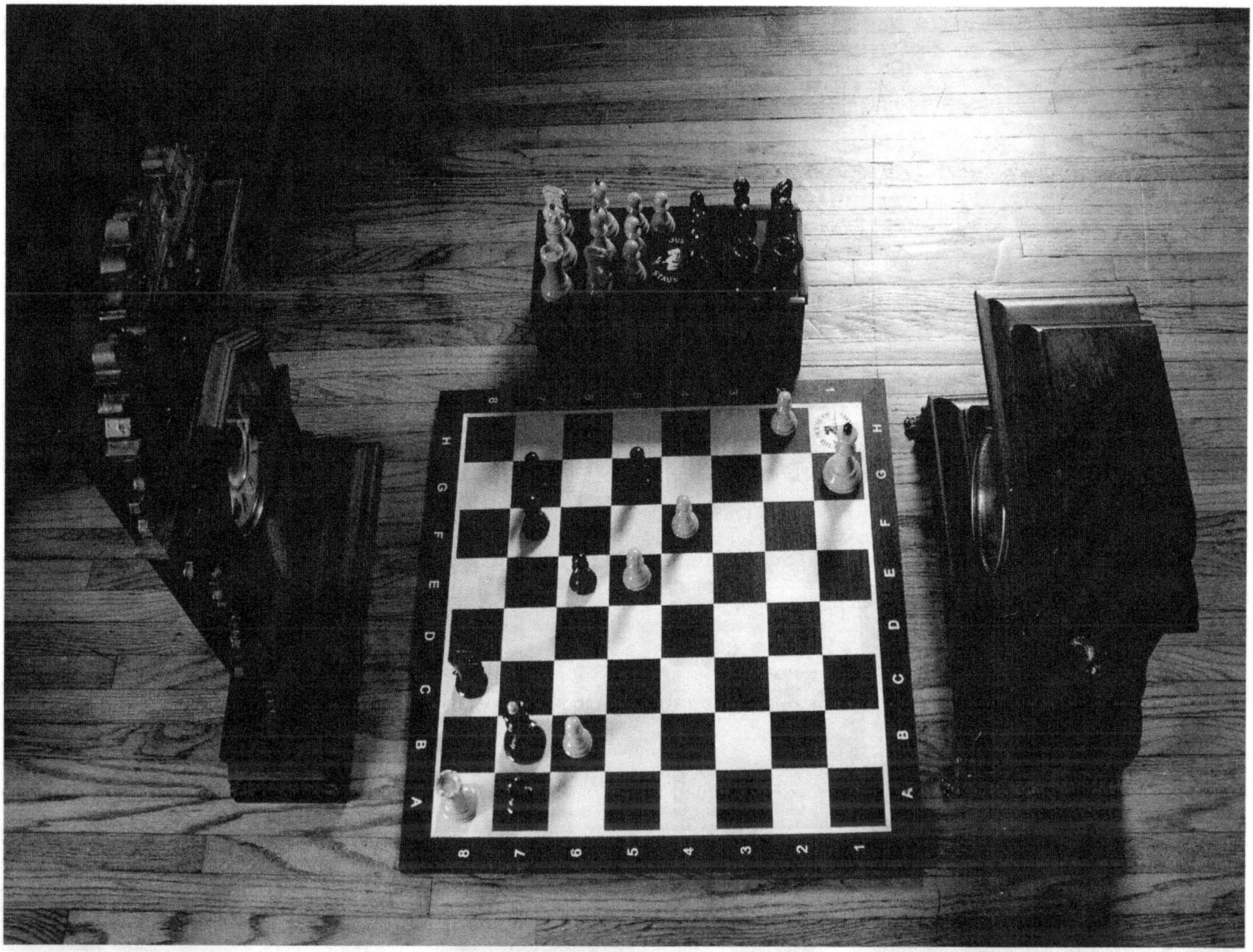

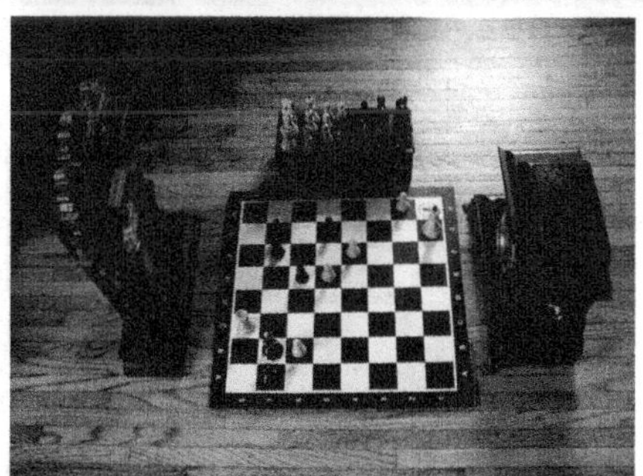
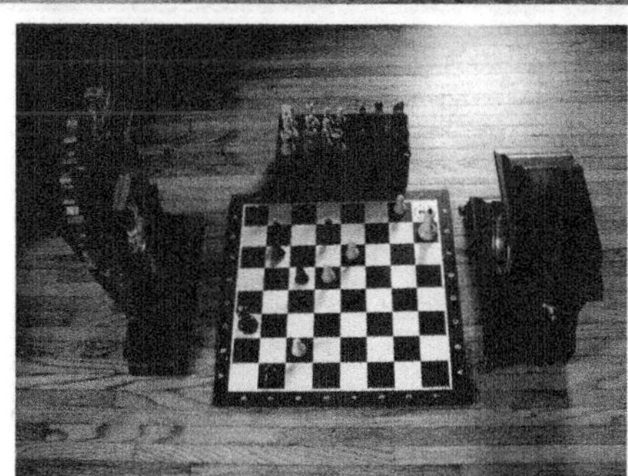
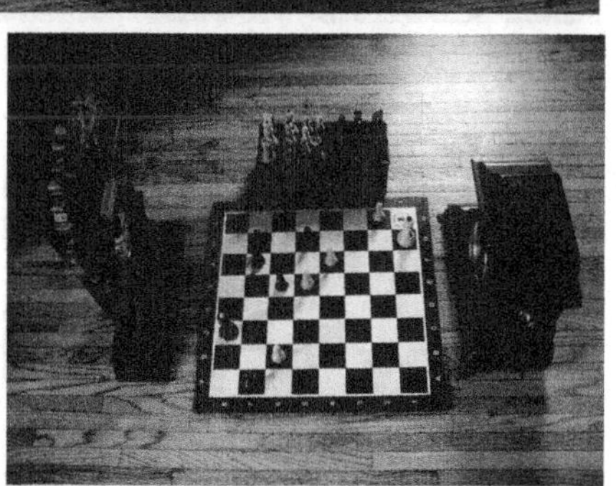
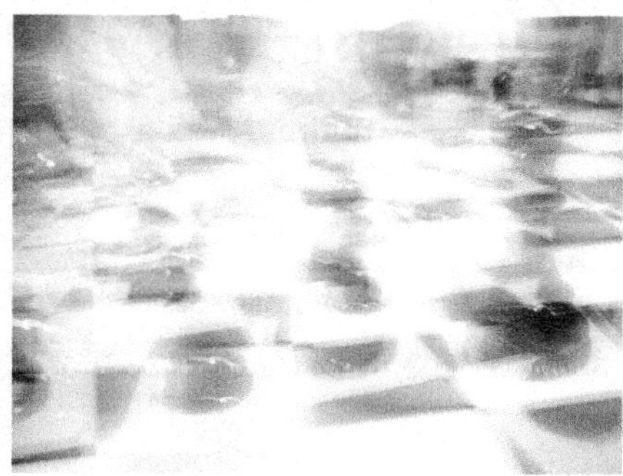
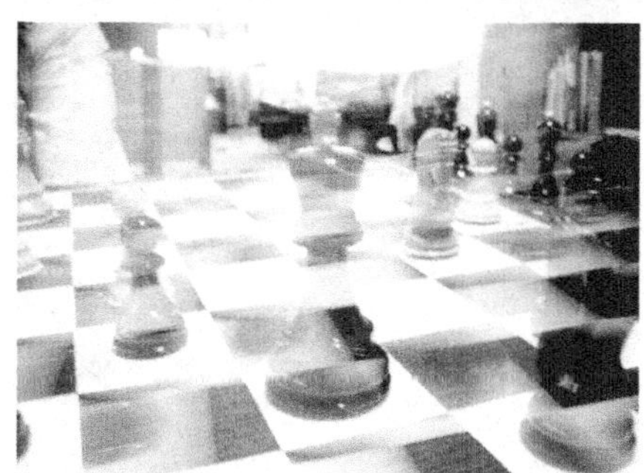
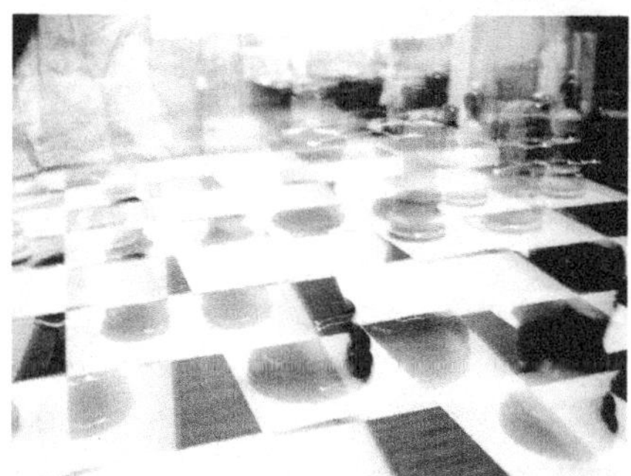

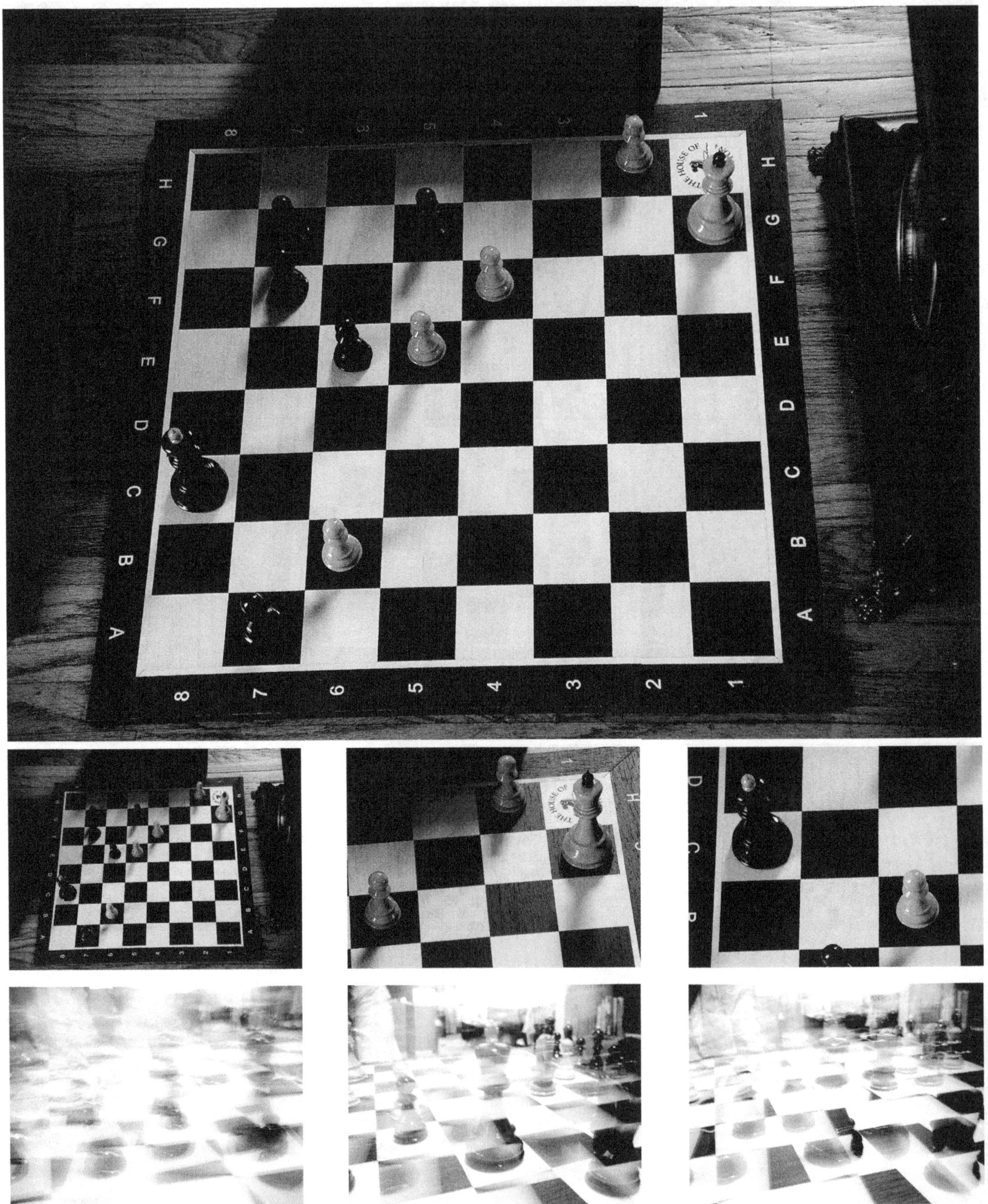

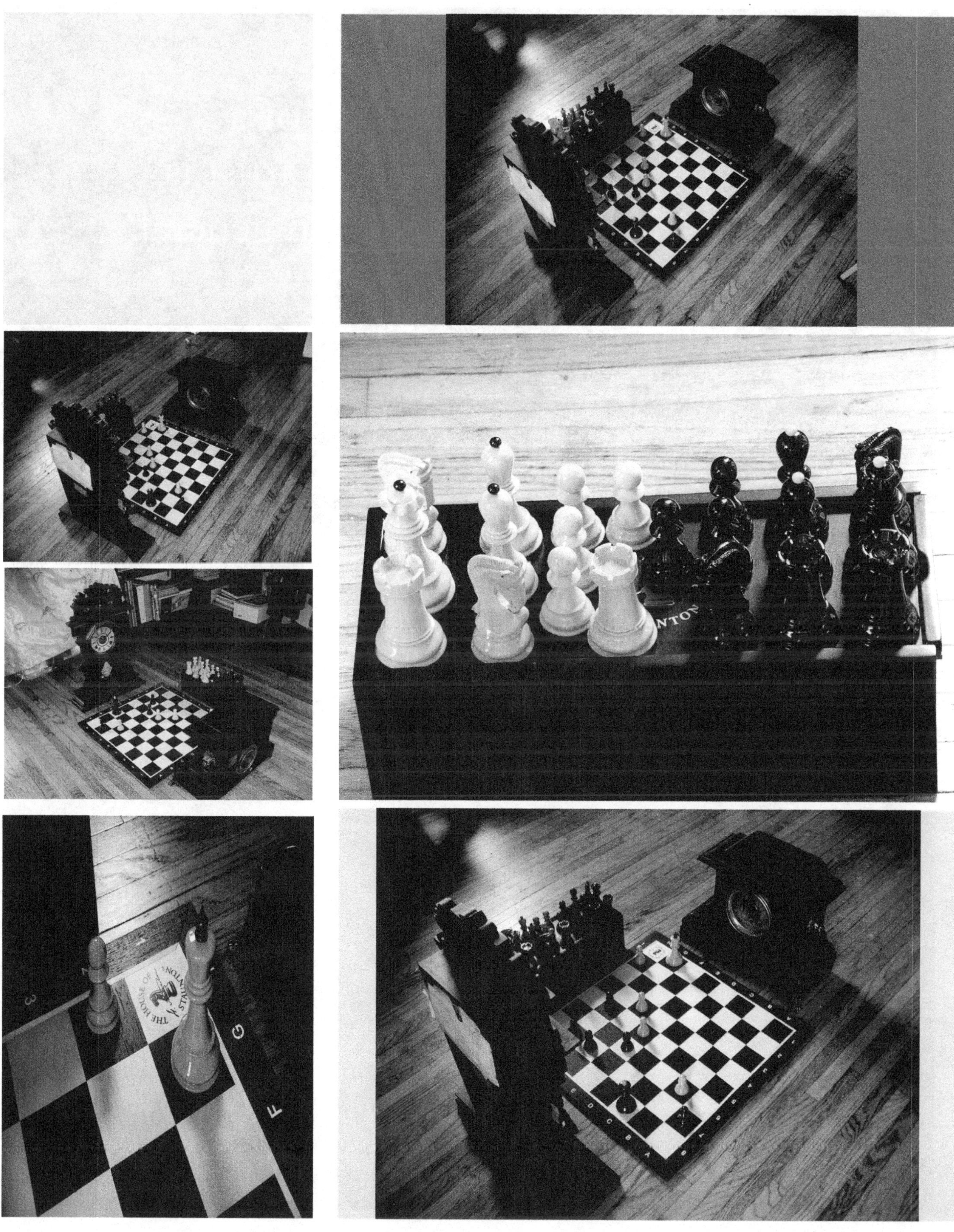

Chess players are madmen of a certain quality, the way the artist is supposed to be, and isn't, in general.

—Duchamp

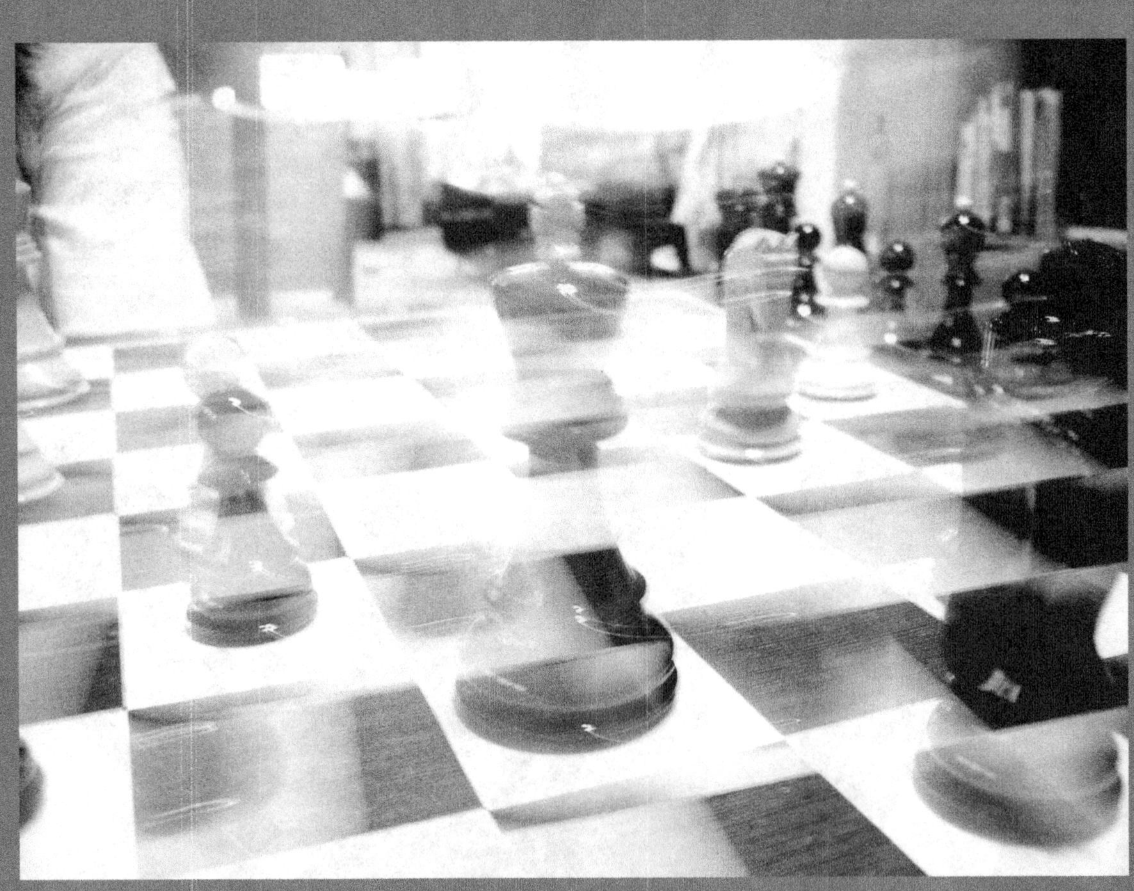

SECOND TABLEAU

CODA

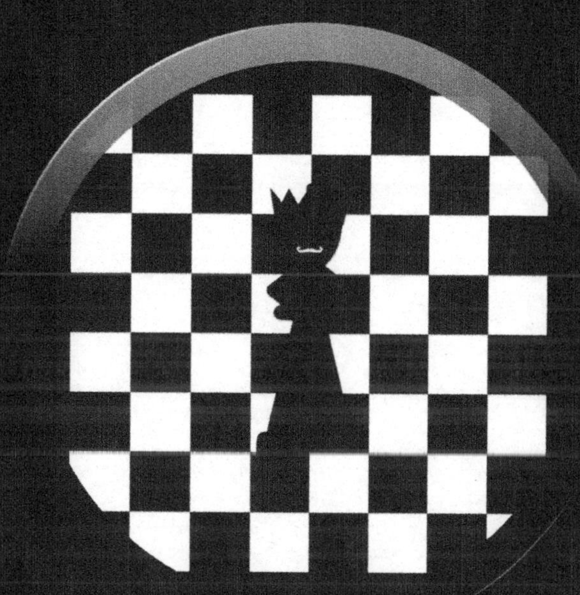

Marcel Duchamp Draws Rrose Sélavy

Dancers: Marcel Duchamp and Rrose Sélavy

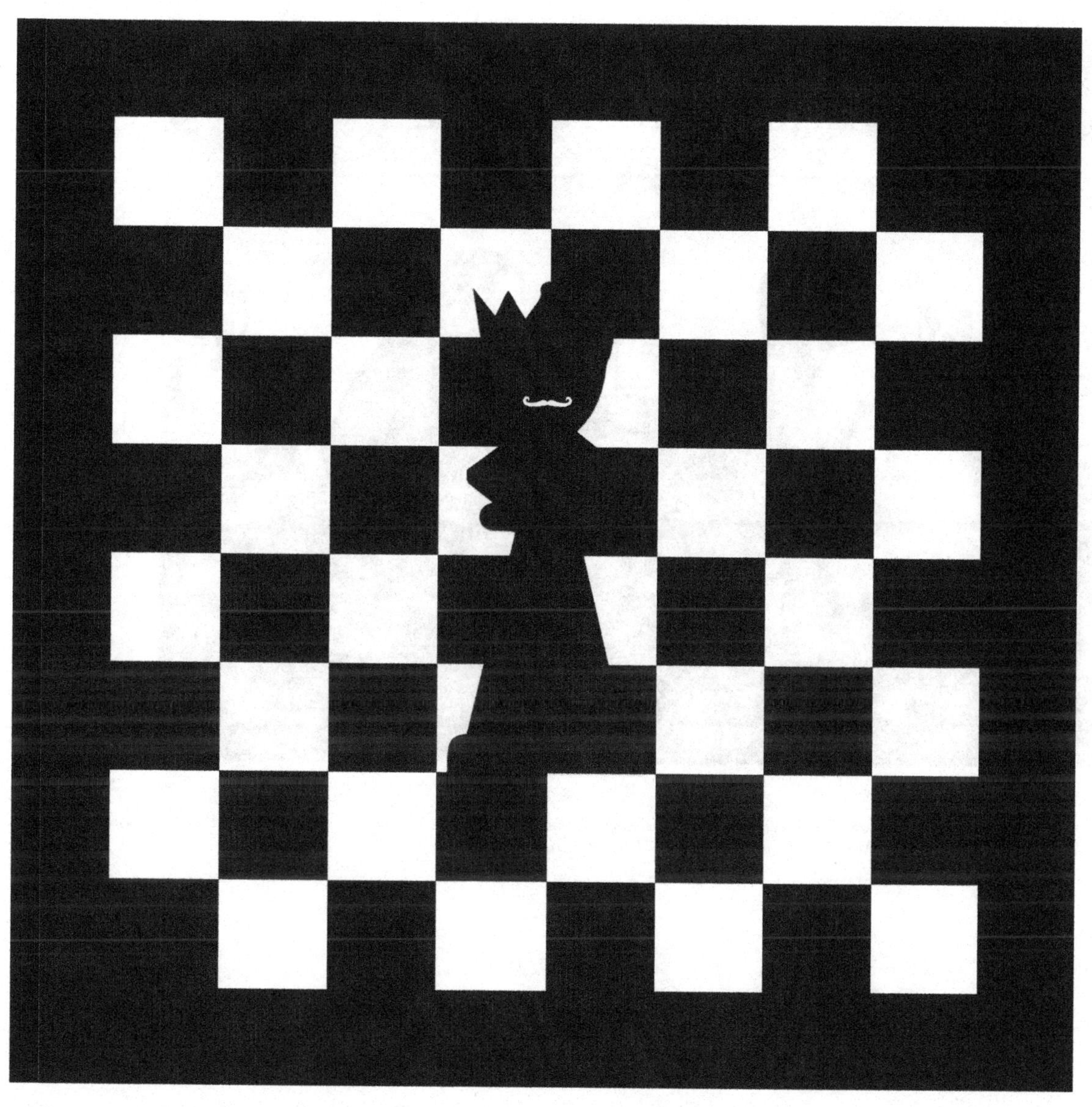

Duchamp Draws Rrose Sélavy

a complex allegory of frustrated desire

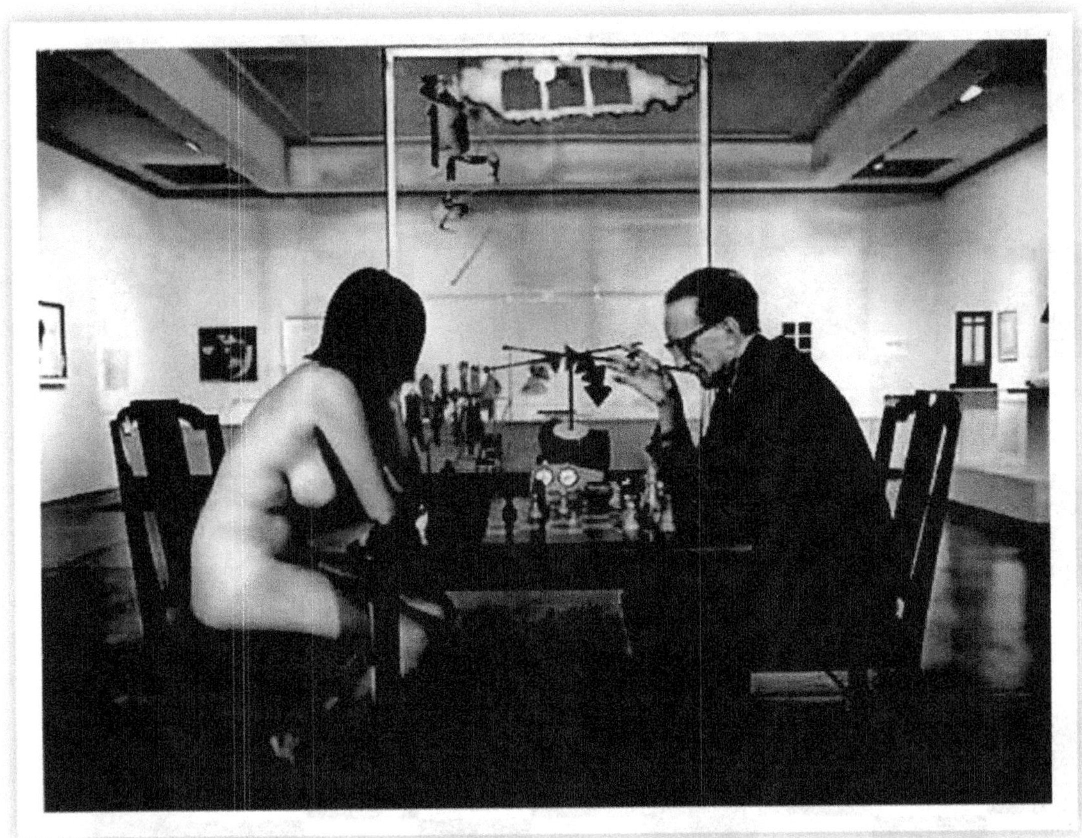

Photograph of Marcel Duchamp and Eve Babitz posing for the photographer Julian Wasser during the Duchamp retrospective at the Pasadena Museum of Art, 1963 © 2000 Succession Marcel Duchamp, ARS, N.Y./ADAGP, Paris.

BRIEF SYNOPSIS:

A game of chess is played between Marcel Duchamp and his female alter ego, Rrose Sélavy on the evening he completes his final masterpiece, Étant donnés. In the beginning of the play, we see an elderly Duchamp, who at the tail end of his career, is going through the bleak ends of his life as the master artist, and has given up art for chess. It is as if he were dead, and living through the praise of a senior artist who had completed his life's work twenty years earlier. We go through Duchamp's life over a chess game, which ends in a draw. By the end of the play we emerge from the game locked in the final moments of creation.

CHARACTERS:

+ Marcel Duchamp —Famed 20th Century artist

+ Rrose Sélavy —Marcel Duchamp's female alter ego

SETTING:

An empty white room fills most of the stage. The room is reminiscent of an art gallery, but there are no paintings on the walls or sculpture on the set. Lighting from above illuminates the whole stage, but has dark corners that fill ones mind with shadows. A table with two chairs opposite one another, sits center stage. A three-panel changing screen is placed near the back, stage right, always present, but out of the way.

DATE AND TIME:

January 5th 1966 around 8PM. This is the traditional, Twelfth Night.

THE CHESS GAME:

The play is using the actual game played by Frank Marshall verses M. Duchamp at the Chess Olympiad held in Hamburg Germany in 1930. The whole game is listed below in algebraic notation.

Frank Marshall (Playing White) - M. Duchamp (Playing black)

1.d4 Nf6 2.Nf3 b6 3.c4 e6 4.Bg5 Be7 5.Nc3 Bb7 6.Qc2 d5 7.e3 O-O 8.cxd5 Nxd5 9.Bxe7 Qxe7 10.Nxd5 Bxd5 11.Bd3 h6 12.a3 c5 13.dxc5 Rc8 14.b4 bxc5 15.Rc1 Nd7 16.Ba6 Rc7 17.e4 Bb7 18.Bxb7 Rxb7 19.bxc5 Qxc5 20.O-O Qxc2 21.Rxc2 Kf8 22.Rfc1 Ke7 23.Nd4 Ke8 24.f4 Rab8 25.e5 Nf8 26.Rc5 Rb1 27.Rxb1 Rxb1+ 28.Kf2 Rb7 29.Rc8+ Ke7 30.Ra8 Ng6 31.g3 Kd7 32.a4 Ne7 33.Nb5 Nc8 34.g4 Rxb5 35.axb5 Kc7 36.g5 hxg5 37.b6+ Kb7 38.Rxc8 Kxc8 1/2-1/2

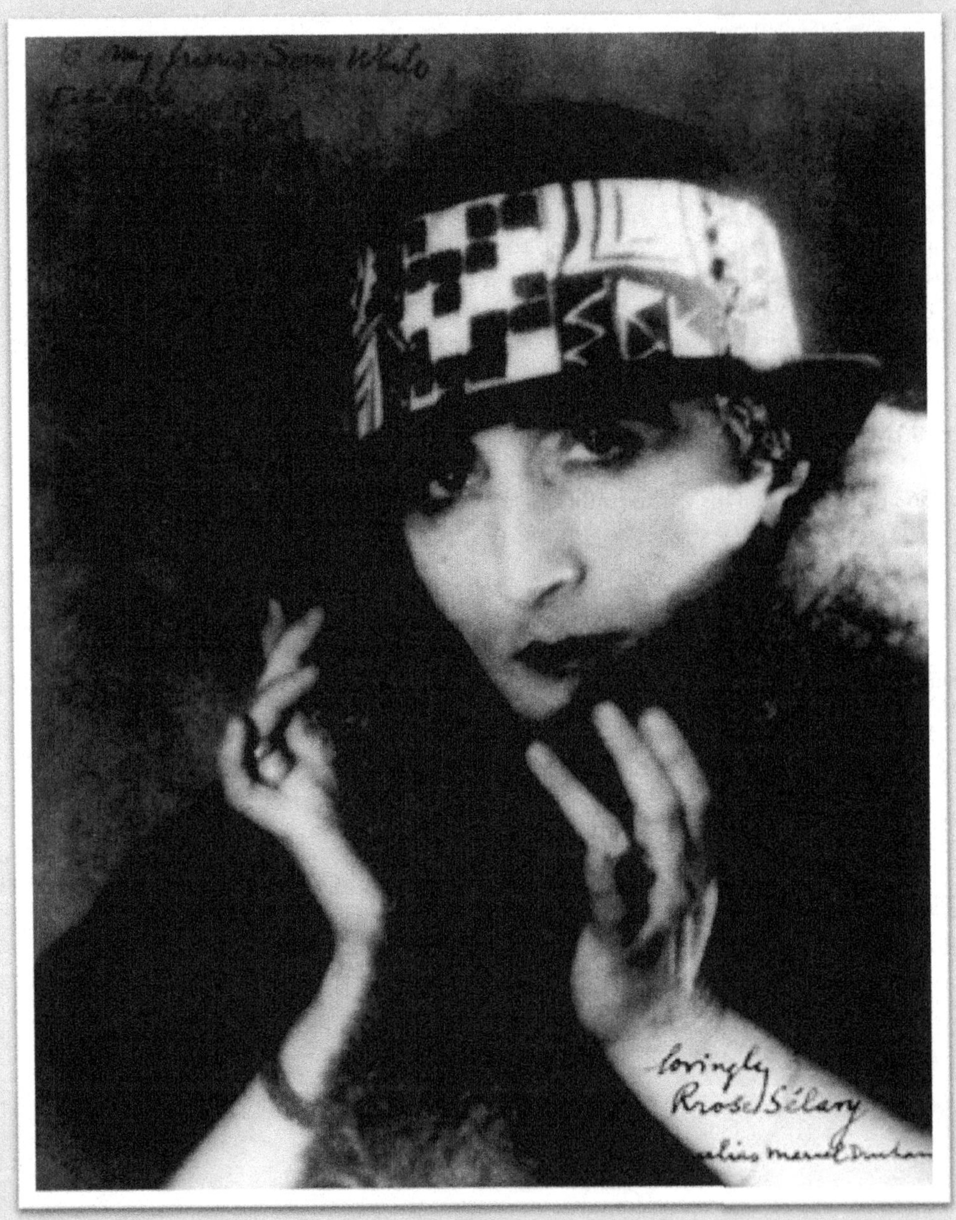

MARCEL DUCHAMP AS RROSE SÉLAVY

Photo taken by Man Ray

ACT 1

Opening Game – Nude Descending a Staircase

The lights come up on a barren stage; white walls that are very much like an empty art gallery. In the far corner, stage right, is a changing screen. In the foreground is a study table with two chairs. Nothing is set on the table.

Marcel Duchamp walks on stage. He is thin, tall, gaunt wearing gray wool trousers and a striped shirt with French cuffs and cufflinks. He is smoking a pipe made by the French company Butz-Choquin. He walks around the room looking for someone. Walks up to the changing screen and nods with a hand holding his chin; as if acknowledging something secret to the audience.

DUCHAMP

Ah. There you are. I was hoping you would come tonight. Man Ray cancelled again.

He walks behind the curtain and pulls out the chessboard and places it on the table with great care. He then goes back to the changing screen and retrieves a box of chessmen. He brings the box to the table and carefully sets up the chessboard with the pieces.

DUCHAMP

A conqueror and high king called his great scholars together and commanded them to set up a committee which was to study all the books written in the world, up to that point that is, and to steep themselves in that knowledge and condense it down for him. They worked for ten years and came up with a set of one hundred books to present to the king. The king was pleased but said that they did not go far enough in their work. He wanted them to condense it down further. He killed several of the scholars to make his point felt. They worked for two more years and came up with a set of ten books. They went to the king and had similar results, condensed further; and he beheaded two scholars. This went on and on for several years, condensing the ten books to two books, to one book, then one down to one chapter and then down to one page and then down to one sentence. A small group of the remaining scholars went to the king with their single sentence. This did not please the king either as he wanted one word that would convey the whole of human knowledge in one utterance. The king in his petulance, killed more scholars and sent the one remaining scholar to his home to condense their work into one word. After eight years, he emerged from his home with a sheet of paper held high in his hands. He had completed the task and had written down the one word that would meet the king's mandate. As he ran out, he tripped, fell and died. When the piece of paper was examined to see what the word was, they too were disappointed, as they could not read his handwriting.

The game of chess is now set and Duchamp looks up to see if there would be any reply to his story. Nothing is heard. The room seems empty, alone, closed in. He walks to the front of the changing screen and taps it.

DUCHAMP

Did you hear my story? *Pauses.* Are you all right? *Pauses.* Did you not find it amusing? Are you going to come out and play?

Duchamp places his hands on his hips in aggravation. He walks around to the back of the changing screen and takes off his clothing and places them over the top of the changing screen. Out walks Rrose Sélavy finely dressed in 1920's fashion with a cloche hat on. It is clearly Duchamp dressed in drag. She walks around the stage and waits for the room to acclimatize to her presence.

From behind the curtain walks Marcel Duchamp, fully dressed in the clothing he had on previously. Yet on the changing screen remains a full set of the same clothing Duchamp is currently wearing. He walks to the table, sits down and picks up two pawns, one black and one white. Hiding them in his clasped hands, he jumbles them around in his hands. He divides them and holds out both hands, fists clenched around the chessmen.

DUCHAMP

Pick to play first.

Rrose Sélavy picks the right hand.

DUCHAMP

White. You move first. So, what did you think of my story?

SÉLAVY
White Pawn to d4

It was amusing. Death is always amusing, ironic death is delightful. I wonder what the word was. Do you know? Or was this all of your story, bad penmanship is the final revenge of the scholar on the king's wickedness?

DUCHAMP
Black Knight to f6

He thinks a bit before responding. I do not know. This was all there was that was told to me. What do you think the word would have been?

SÉLAVY
White Knight to f3

Death.

DUCHAMP
Black Pawn to b6

No. If it were death, it could just as easily be the word, life. Life would just be as ironic to the story, would it not?

SÉLAVY

What would you have written as your one word? Tell me what the great Duchamp would write on a note to the king that would condense down all of human knowledge? Life? Non! Surely not.

DUCHAMP

This was not a story about me. I would not continue on in such a project for a king. If I were in that group, I would have been one of the two who were beheaded.

SÉLAVY
White Pawn to c4

You are avoiding the question; what's your word? After all these years together, have you become shy? You can tell me. You do know that I already know what you will say.

DUCHAMP
Black Pawn e6

Repetition.

SÉLAVY
White Bishop to g5

Looks at the board and makes a sound resembling disappointment.

DUCHAMP

Surely it would be repetition. How could it not be? Repetition is the key to tradition and therefore it should be the one thing the scholar would send to his king, so that he could avoid it at all costs.

SÉLAVY

A very good answer; it is very much in your style. But why not desire? That should be avoided as well. Why not desperate love, why not ...?

DUCHAMP

Desiring, the very act of being in desire, is the happiest anyone can ever be. For once you have obtained the longed for item, then you no longer have desire, you have love. Mere love can get dull, can it not? Lose its shine as the years wane on. For desire, one becomes a moth. Wanting to go back into deadly fires, risk everything previously built to get back in that light one more time. To truly enjoy the moment, as fleeting as fame, it all happens so fast, in such a brief moment it is gone. Outrage turns to applause, applause then silence, the stage goes dark, the chalkboard erased to a blank slate. The white king wins and the pieces go back into the box.

SÉLAVY

It sounds all too much like sex; a strange metaphor detailing the very first time. I remember the panic, the pain, the sparks of love, and then that dripping mess. It was not what I imagined it was. It was not at all like the sex I imagined I had with other women. Like a tomcat, it was all claws and spray, so feral. I do not think I enjoyed it at all. I find that the only true sex is masturbation.

DUCHAMP

That is not shocking. Everything is masturbation. The world is filled with masturbators. Each one looking at another person with desire, going home and in a state of envy creates a mental passion play. The mind engages with the mental ephemera, the skin tingles. The mind excited, pushes a gentle pawn forward with a fingertip.

SÉLAVY

This game is masturbation.

DUCHAMP
Black Bishop to e7

Very like masturbation, yet for the metaphor to be complete it would require a blind man performing the act in front of a mirror. But no, chess is cut from a higher form of pleasure; it is the finest mental activity ever created by humans. Without you here, it would be worse.

SÉLAVY
White Knight c3

That is very flattering; you always know just what to say to a woman to make her feel special. It's your move.

DUCHAMP
Black Bishop to b7

Checkmate!

SÉLAVY

What? How? Where?

DUCHAMP

No my word. Checkmate. That is what I would have written to the king. It is obvious to me now. Checkmate. It would be just as ironic and funny, as the king would have killed the scholar in any outcome. So it in the end, it was better that fate should treat him to a kindly death.

SÉLAVY
White Queen to c2

Can death be kind? Can it take you by the hand and lead you into a room that is forever? It all sounds very nice, but I do not think that that can happen, not to any of us. Ever. *pauses.* I wonder if this is why there is no scholar on the chessboard?

DUCHAMP

In the story they are all dead. How can they go to war if they have been killed by the king? It is of no matter, scholars are not good in war, nor are artists or fools. Alas, I could not fight for my country. My heart would not let me. Literally, I have a condition. That is why I came to America.

SÉLAVY

I always heard a fool never follows his heart. *Giggles into her hand.* You'll have to excuse me. I'm a bit drunk and liable to speak tastelessly. You are a master at chess; chess is war. You are a master artist; art is war. A battlefield is considered a canvas in the theater of war. What is art, if it is not war? It follows you would have been very good at being a soldier. Strategy alone would have made you a formidable opponent.

DUCHAMP

There is no solution as there is no problem. In art there is no winning. It is all a mirage. In chess there are only winning positions and losing positions that, in some cases, those moves can lead to a draw, an ending with no winner. There is nothing to win in art, only goals to be achieved.

SÉLAVY

There is a lot of money to be made as an artist. Some would consider that a wonderful prize to attain. There is also the praise, the fame, and the warm welcomings of their betters for merely painting something pretty on some drab cloth. I can think of many things that could be acquired through art.

DUCHAMP
Black Pawn to d5

Yes, that is true. I accomplished many things in the art world that I would not have been able to if I did not have chess. Chess has always been a major theme for my work. The intellectual puzzles make for a wonderful pursuit. From my very first success as a painter, I set a scene of my brother embroiled in a chess game with their wives lazing the afternoon away.

SÉLAVY

Chess is very plastic. You construct it. It's a mechanical sculpture where the potential moves are always present in the mind, in the gray matter. And with chess one creates beautiful problems and that beauty is made with the head and hands. It sounds very much like an exchange for art. Though, if I may say, you could not exchange winning the world with chess as you did with the art world.

DUCHAMP

I could not be happier with my life, so I win through every movement. Every moment, I am thankful for missing my opportunity to engage in the horrors of war. So many were lost, so much suffering by so many. Even the numbers of the dead are beyond my comprehension. Every movement, I turned into a position I could win.... *he pauses.* When I was young, I wanted to follow my brothers to art school. Even though I had many successes in my youth, I was still rejected. As simple as that, I was done with school. From there I went to work as a cartoonist and my father supported the beginnings of my work. I continued to paint, to explore with new ideas, styles and colors.

SÉLAVY
White Pawn to e3

And from rejection you went on to New York and at the Armory Show; you took America by storm when you displayed your painting, Nude Descending a Staircase.

DUCHAMP
Black King to King Side Castle O-O

Yes, that opened a lot of eyes. The Americans were stunned. It seems very small now, an achievement that was out of my control. But it is nothing to sneer at. It was more the newspapers' enthusiasm for the controversial. Oddly, they could not find the nude in the painting. Can you believe that?

SÉLAVY

It fanned flames that burned down the previous generations' shocking forms of art. Painting had become alive again, a phoenix reemerging from its ashes. And so you won the art world's endearing love.

DUCHAMP

I would not characterize it as endearing.

SÉLAVY

How would you characterize it, my dear?

DUCHAMP

I would contend that with my character, I would say it was the love the British showed to Jeanne d'Arc. A passionate resonance for god manifested in sexual desires, ending in flames, destruction and death.

SÉLAVY

I don't recall you being burned at the stake.

DUCHAMP

We no longer burn witches or warlocks. We have moved on to better forms of destruction.

SÉLAVY
White Pawn on c Takes Black Pawn on d5

We allow them to die while they live, to retreat from the field in surrender. Then they go and play chess. Ha, retreat from the field, *sortier du champ!*

DUCHAMP
Black Knight takes d5

Sometimes to pull back and reflect is the proper choice. One is liable to repeat what they have done; repetition is the worst mistake an artist can make.

SÉLAVY

The fear of repetition seems to be on your mind. So, you beg the question, what was your worst mistake?

DUCHAMP

Inviting you in.

SÉLAVY

No, really your mistake, what was it? For the past twenty years you have not made anything new. Your tournament play is no longer what it once was. You represented France in the chess Olympiad. Now your game is in decline. So you can be at ease, what mistake can you claim as your own?

DUCHAMP

You want me to say something about my replacing my work as an artist for chess. You know that is not true. It was no mistake. I found out that I was not born with the skills needed to become a world champion. I am a senior master. It may seem like I am sitting at the water's edge, poking ever expanding rings in a calm surface. But no, chess keeps my fingers and mind engaged while I wait. It keeps me occupied so that I do not repeat what I have already done. I could have made hundreds of ready-mades, one or two a week, for years. I could sell them for large sums of money, as the rich seem to want to invest their resources in things they do not understand.

SÉLAVY

White Bishop takes e7

It is easy to understand. An individual artwork is something easily desired. It's something guaranteed that their neighbors cannot have. And it is a fine way to invest money.

DUCHAMP

Black Queen takes e7

Once I placed a snow shovel, standing upright in a gallery, called, *In Defense of the Broken Arm.* I did nothing to it at all. A kind woman came up to me to tell me it was beautiful. It was not beautiful. I set that ugly shovel there in that space, so that it would specifically not be beautiful. It was work set in a gallery, but it was not art.

SÉLAVY

She probably turned around and found herself standing next to you. She was being polite, probably afraid to let on that she didn't understand what this hullaballoo was all about and had too kind a soul to call it crap to your face.

DUCHAMP

That is probably true. She did not buy the piece. It is a strange human condition that keeps us from saying what we should, when we should. Unlike the story of the two weavers who promise the king a new outfit, only visible to those suited to their stations or wonderfully intelligent. It was a child who pointed out to everyone that the king was indeed nude.

SÉLAVY

White Knight takes d5

Precocious children do tend to get away with quiet a lot.

DUCHAMP

Black Bishop takes d5

Looks up but does not say anything to the smiling SÉLAVY

134

ACT 2

Middle Game - The Large Glass

SÉLAVY
White Bishop to d3

It is said that the person who invented the game of chess was a renowned Dravida vellalar named Sessa. When he presented his game to his king, the king was so pleased that he told Sessa he could name any reward and that would be his prize. This vellalar was very wise and asked the king this: that for the first square of the chessboard, he would receive one grain of rice, two for the second square, four on the third square, and so on, doubling the amount each time across the whole board. The king accepted readily but was also quick to reproach Sessa for asking for such a small reward for such a wonderful creation. The king ordered the treasurer to count out and deliver the rice to Sessa. After a month the king asked his treasurer what was taking so long in delivering the prize. The frustrated treasurer gave the result of the calculation that was to be Sessa's prize to be $[2^{64} - 1]$ which equals eighteen quintillion grains of rice, which would weigh about five hundred and eight billion tons. That mountain of rice would cast a shadow over Mount Everest. Realizing he had given away his kingdom for the game of chess, the king abdicated in shame and crowned the wise Sessa the new king.

DUCHAMP
Black Pawn to h6

Frank Marshall told the origin of chess a little differently. He said that the inventor was an Indian mathematician. He also said that the king had the inventor killed on the spot when he learned of the trick. A king's gambit declined, so to say.

SÉLAVY
White Pawn to a3

Frank would, he did not like happy endings. I do. I heard this version from Walter Arensberg. Do you remember when we used to gather at the apartment above his flat in New York? Playing chess with all of the painters, Dadaists, and other wild people we met back then. Francis Picabia, Henri-Pierre Roche, Beatrice Wood, and Mina Loy. Man Ray was at that artist colony. It was a very nice time, I recall.

DUCHAMP
Black Pawn to c5

Joseph Stella spilled a drink on Alfred Stieglitz and called it a self-portrait. Yes, those were some fine days. It was Walter who helped me progress to play chess professionally. Chess produces mesmeric ideas, concepts that take over the mind. Ideas were everywhere back then, each night in the middle of drinks and hors d'oeuvres was a thoughtful chessboard being played over by some of the most radical minds of the time. Modernism was seen as threatening and inexplicable.

SÉLAVY

White Pawn on d takes White Pawn on c5

Didn't Picabia play Roché in that apartment, in a death match for the survival of one of their dada magazines?

DUCHAMP

Black Rook to c8

Yes, Picabia won and 391 stayed in publication and our little magazine, The Blind Man, which would publish anything submitted, hence its title, was doomed after only two issues. I published the score of the game with Walter in our follow up magazine, Rongwrong.

SÉLAVY

White Pawn to b4

An obituary in the form of a scorecard, is that dada? One journal is lost to gambling and another journal forms to tell of the former's passing. Things come around; things go around on a perpetual Ferris wheel.

DUCHAMP

Black Pawn on b takes c5

That is the modern experience, rapid movement. The train departing the station, the plane soaring in the atmospheres, the supersonic sounds exploding, eardrums pounding as fast as a racing heart. I was with the sculptor Brancusi at a Paris air show in 1912, we came upon an airplane. I said to him flatly, 'it is all over for painting. What could be better than that propeller? Tell me, can you do that?' And soon after, I abandoned painting. Paint became petrified, in its same form, dead for centuries, its remains turned to stone. As an ancient forest secreted away on some foreign plateau, keeping the hardened husks of what once was; animated, alive, locked away in a time period that occurred a long time ago. Yet somehow, it still circulates.

SÉLAVY

White Rook to c1

I remember. This was years before we met though. You told me this story several times. I think we were working on our film, Anemic Cinema. You held my hand gently when I took hold of the camera. Man Ray took my photo that day. I believe he took my soul with his camera. Ever since, I have never been the exactly same.

DUCHAMP

Black Knight to d7

You were simply Rose with one 'R' then. We worked on many things together. I held your hand many times. I made the piece, *Why not Sneeze, Rose Sélavy,* for you.

SÉLAVY
White Bishop to a6

The sugar cubes trapped in a birdcage. It was so heavy, but looked light as air.

DUCHAMP

The sugar cubes were made of marble.

SÉLAVY

There is a coldness I often think of when I see marble, even though it looked powdery as snow. Cold, frozen sweets singing out a mournful urge to be set free. But I never feel like sneezing when I see this piece.

DUCHAMP
Black Rook to c7

Of course you do not. The cold, yes, the entrapment, yes, the sneeze, no. One cannot spontaneously sneeze. That is the point to its title; I cannot make myself sneeze except when the body itself needs to sneeze. It is a narrow allegory trapped in a cage asking for the viewer to respond with involuntary actions.

SÉLAVY

Very funny.

DUCHAMP

It is humorous, but more so. These ready-mades are little trees cut down from their marketplace, from their mass-produced forest and reinvented. Placed into a new forest, a forest of boxes. Just as before their leaves rustle to the others, their roots comingle under the earth, they drink from the rains and go dormant in their winters. The works rustle amongst themselves, their invisible leaves reaching outwards. Their roots grow, as potential thought movements, plotting across the Cartesian map of the imagination.

SÉLAVY

Just like our little game? A set of movements, drawn out on as a tabula rasa, self-refreshing each morning with crisp sunlight to lead the way.

DUCHAMP

Like a pen and ink drawing with a difference, the chess players paint with black and white forms already prepared instead of inventing new forms, as does the artist. In the same vein, I created a new form of chess, a new way to play the game. The main features would be many colored pieces. The white queen was to be light green; the black queen, dark green. The rooks would have been blue, light and dark. The bishops yellow, the knights red, light and dark. The white king and white pawns would be white, and the black king and black pawns, black.

SÉLAVY

White Pawn to e4

It sounds wild. How did that work out?

DUCHAMP

Black Bishop to b7

You know how it worked out. It came to nothing.

SÉLAVY

Pour quoi?

DUCHAMP

You know why.

SÉLAVY

Tell me.

DUCHAMP

No one understood how to play with them. The game is hard enough without changing the colors one needs to memorize. The old man understood. He wanted a set.

SÉLAVY

White Bishop takes b7

Father?

DUCHAMP

Black Rook takes b7

It was something he could wrap his mind around. He knew art and he knew chess. This was his connection to me being so far away all the time. I was always a poor letter writer, and so I sent him the prototype when nothing ever prospered as a business proposition. I was working on *The Large Glass* at that time. I joined the Marshall Chess Club in hopes of promoting it, but no. These were my first days of professional play and it did not win me any fast friend. The club was down near Washington Square back then. I spent quite a number of nights playing until three in the morning, and then going back uptown on the elevated. That's probably where I picked up the idea that I could play a serious game of chess.

SÉLAVY

White Pawn on b takes c5

So chess and art are worlds apart. There is no surrealism on the chessboard?

DUCHAMP

Non. It is a fixed set of rules. I did get to know Frank Marshall rather well. I was hoping to have him authorize the pieces, call it the Marshall chess set. I planned to cut him in for 10% of the sales. That never came about, but I learned a lot from him. I could always hold my own against his game.

SÉLAVY

He was the world's strongest play in his day. Is this is one of those games that we are playing now?

DUCHAMP

Black Queen takes c5

This is from the 1930 chess Olympiad held in Hamburg. It was a good game.

SÉLAVY

Why did you want to play this game with me? Fond memories?

DUCHAMP

Not really, this game reminds me of times I won. If I wanted fond memories, I would choose the times I lost rather badly to José Capablanca.

SÉLAVY

The white cape, that's a good name for a chess player. A man cloaked in his pieces' color.

DUCHAMP

I idolized him and his playing. I studied his writings and his published games. I finally got to play him in an extended tournament where he was playing twenty-one other players. He was in the center, standing in a circle of tables moving from one board to the next. Twenty-one players competing, all of our mental might concentrated on beating this mammoth of a man. We were all unsuccessful.

SÉLAVY

White King to King Side Castle O-O

You lost? And I thought this would be a happy story.

DUCHAMP

Black Queen takes c2

It was a happy story. I had the same feeling I had when I was rejected from art school. Imagine what would have become of me had I gone there? Who would I be now? What kind of work could I produce? Only stale objects made through the narrow lens of the art teacher. I would have cried on when they would not grade the works in my imagination. Mark me down as a failure with no hope of ever becoming that dreamed of self. Capablanca taught me how to be hungry; to only accept winning after all the planning and hard work has been done. Spontaneous creations of chess grandmasters are not born from dreams. No, chess is purer than art, for there is no money to be made in it. So I went home, redoubled my efforts and devoured chess as if I was married to it. Not to the pieces, but to the game itself.

SÉLAVY

Sounds a bit bleak. What did Chesterton say, "poets do not go mad; but chess-players do. Poetry is sane, because it floats easily in an infinite sea; reason seeks to cross the infinite sea, and so make it finite. The result is mental exhaustion."

DUCHAMP

Naturally this is the part of my life that I enjoy most. These years coincided with my work on *The Large Glass*. A piece set in a wooden frame, two shattered glass panels hanging vertically. The top half is the Bride's Domain, the lower half, the Bachelors' Apparatus. It took me years to finish. It is still unfinished, really.

SÉLAVY

What does it all mean? Why are there nine bridegrooms? It reminds me of a chess game, with eight pawns and a knight striking out after the only female character on the chessboard, the queen. If they capture her, their exchange will mean victory.

DUCHAMP

There are no interpretations. The unfulfilled desires of the viewer, the resignation to the loss of one's imagination in permanent opposition to nature can be seen in this work. The bride is never allowed to consummate her relationship and the goal of marriage is congress, yet, they are never allowed.

SÉLAVY

White Rook takes c2

It sounds like the goal of chess, to mate. And if you are lucky, play your game fully; you could mate me in any number of moves. Silly boy, are you flirting with me?

DUCHAMP

Black King to f8

It would be easy to see our game as a sublimation for sex, but in French the term for checkmate is *échec et mat*. The pun does not work so well our language.

SÉLAVY

Maybe that is why you enjoy living in New York so much, that pun always works on a queen in Broadway. You needed to come to New York; you needed to find a place where your wordplay would manifest itself in a language that finally allowed you to mate.

DUCHAMP

Looks longingly into her eyes but says nothing.

SÉLAVY

Now we are at the point of what this is all about. This is Dada in a world overtaken by surrealism. The king is a queen and you have me all to yourself. Kiss me. *She leans over the chessboard, grabs him by the tie and slowly raises his lips to meet hers. They kiss in a held moment as the lights dim.*

Lemon Time

To be read to the audience by an offstage voice.

In every game of chess there is a middle point, a silent moment. A point when no piece can travel safely. The next move will determine the outcome of the game. In this moment, fear creeps into both players. There are no winners, no losers, only the act of play. A contemplative moment occurs, a moment of waiting. Time folds in on itself, propelling the game to forsake all of its ungainly allegories. The game is exposed, left in a field on its own. The water will continue to fall from its waterfall. The gas lamp will fade when its fire has no more to consume. The king will no longer control his country, his queen will live in another land, and atheists will control the bishop's position. The knight no longer rides a horse. Pawns are no longer tied to the whims of an invisible king. Royalty, the regiments, and religion stand naked at the top of the stairs ready to descend, to make an entrance onto a modern stage where money outweighs all institutions. Looking to take as its bride the unequivocal model of success, the glorious captured queen locked away in a vault, waiting for the pun to become philosophic. In a moment that can live forever, waiting for, planning for a moment for such a time to name this point of contact as an encounter, and initiate the rendezvous, the reproduction of exchange.

ACT 3

Endgame - **Étant donnés**
(Given: 1 The Waterfall, 2. The Illuminating Gas,
French: **Étant donnés**: 1° la chute d'eau / 2° le gaz d'éclairage.)

DUCHAMP

Yuck, that was awful. It was like kissing my sister

SÉLAVY

Oh you did just fine. *She readjusted her makeup and dabs on fresh lipstick.* This is living under the shadow of the bomb. It was simply a kiss to wake you up to the very life we are living.
Once we get our minds and our desires out of the way, the mind can act in its own accord.

DUCHAMP

You will always touch my mind, but that was a bit more than an accord.

SÉLAVY

Mmm. I thought you wanted to grasp things with the mind the way the penis is grasped by the vagina. Think of it as a congratulatory hug.

DUCHAMP

Well, let's just get back to our game.

SÉLAVY
White Rook on f to c1

Why? There is so much we can do. It's twelfth night. January 5ᵗʰ, the Eve of the Feast of Epiphany and today I am the *Lord of Misrule*.

DUCHAMP
Black King to e7

Oh really. In France he is called the *Prince des Sots*. From what I remember, it does not work out so well for him.

SÉLAVY
White Knight to d4

In festive rituals and Carnivalesque reversals, servants would dressed up as their masters, men would go out in drag, dogs would dress as cats, and mice would dress as cheese. The leader of these events was entitled the Lord of Misrule. He was an officer appointed by lot at Christmas to preside over the Feast of Fools and other revelries for the ritual of Saturnalia.

DUCHAMP
Black King to e8

I didn't know, I would have worn a fancy dress. Who shall I be, if you are the Lord of Misrule?

SÉLAVY
White Pawn to f4

You shall be the salt seller. As the spoonerism of your name, Marcel Duchamp, le marchand du sel, a merchant of salt. Ha! Done! *With a wave of her arm;* You are thus reborn!

DUCHAMP
Black Rook on a to b8

And you, my lord, if I may, are also rededicated, to "Arroser la Vie' or in English, 'to make a toast to life.' She, the granter of all wishes and who is a little free with her kisses. You have thus been installed.

SÉLAVY

You are such an iconoclast. You cannot install me. I am the *Prince des Sots.*

DUCHAMP

I made you.

SÉLAVY

You sure did.

DUCHAMP

I can make you anything I want.

SÉLAVY
White Pawn to e5

Oh no you cannot. No, I won't allow it. I am unique, an individual. An individual masked in your form as much as I am unmasked in my own. Standing here naked while being fully clothed. Dragged into games I wouldn't normally play. I am enrobed in the principles of art in bourgeois society who believe that the individual is considered the creator of art. I am the order of misrule today and today I am the creator.

DUCHAMP
Black Knight to f8

Let's not fight. Come back to the game. I love you as I love myself. You are as unique as I am, as much a creator as a creation. Please, don't be cross.

SÉLAVY

Says nothing but looks like she is about to cry.

DUCHAMP

The more perfect the artist, the more completely separate in him will be the man who suffers and the mind which creates; the more perfectly will the mind digest and transmute the passions which are its material.

SÉLAVY
White Rook to c5

That sounds like T.S. Eliot. Who are you? When have you started to like Eliot?

DUCHAMP
Black Rook to b1

I often recall that quote when I'm thinking of the creative act, the great actions of genius. I used it at a symposium in 1955. I was thinking of those abstract expressionists who talk about random movements in ways that make one marvel at their forethought.

SÉLAVY
White Rook takes b1

You mean like *great* artists? How can there be such a thing. And after all that we have been through?

DUCHAMP
Black Rook takes b1 [Check.]

There is such a thing as great art. There are millions of artists creating all the time. Every moment of each day all over this planet, more and more art is produced. Millions of unique items floating around the world, many are perfectly adequate. Many fall far below the breaking lines of quality. But in there, in that sea of production, are a few pieces of pure genius treading water, so that only history can provide time enough to reflect on them all. In the end, it is the observer who gives the final verdict and sometimes rehabilitates forgotten artists.

SÉLAVY
White King to f2

It is you who is observing me play a game with you; does this rehabilitate you?

DUCHAMP
Black Rook to b7

Am I forgotten already?

SÉLAVY

Maybe.

DUCHAMP

Then as the lord of this day, leader of our festivities, I ask you to grant me my wish.

SÉLAVY
White Rook to c8 [Check]

You've been rather naughty today; I might not be in a granting mood.

DUCHAMP
Black King to e7

But you are installed with powers beyond our control this evening. You can do anything tonight. I wish to never be forgotten so as long as the world plays chess.

SÉLAVY
White Rook to a8

What happens after humanity ceases playing chess.

DUCHAMP

Black Knight to g6

Don't say such things? What kind of world would that be? One I would not want to be a part of. A world overfilled with its own emotions. Chess is not a turning loose of emotion, rather an escape from emotion; it is not the expression of personality, but an escape from personality.

SÉLAVY

White Pawn to g3

This sounds awfully insincere of you. I no longer believe you. This sounds like a wicked joke. Are you toying with me?

DUCHAMP

Black King to d7

Me? The merchant of salt is insincere when talking art? Especially to you my dear Lord of Misrule? To you, my lovely Arroser la Vie?

SÉLAVY

White Pawn to a4

There it is. Yep, I know you too well. You are tricking me into thinking you have changed after all this time. Asking me grant you immortality, to be remembered as a Michelangelo. To have your artwork imprinted on posters, oven mitts and refrigerator magnets. What a laugh. To trick me in such a way is beneath you. To one of your shining creations, for the man who has no children, I am your child. An independent thought standing as apart from you, my creator, as your urinal. My own father, you have pickpocketed trust from my breast.

DUCHAMP

Black Knight to e7

Ha, well maybe. Just a little. It is nice to see indignance on your face. You look so young and filled with that youthful disgust only reserved for their elders. It reminds me of Wilhelm Steinitz, the first world chess champion who once claimed to have played against God. He gave God the advantage by giving him an extra pawn, and Steinitz went on to win. He went on to say, how you mate god is like this, "in the beginning of the game ignore the search for combinations, abstain from violent moves, aim for small advantages, accumulate them, and only after having attained these ends, search for the combination – and then with all the power of will and intellect, because then the combination must exist, however deeply hidden." His principles on how to win reverberate within me to this day.

SÉLAVY

White Knight to b5

Do you use this method when you play with everyone? Is this your way, our way?

DUCHAMP

Black Knight to c8

I wouldn't know. I am this way, and so I have no real reference on how I play or do not play with others. I am playing with you. Our game is wide open, a séance with the self. It is all exchange. Everything we say to one another is nonsense. One piece is exchanged for another with each player hoping for the greater outcome. As you say, the king is a queen but the queen can never be the king, even if though the equation might be equitable. The pieces of inner consciousness rest on squares of pure intuition and cannot be translated into a self-analysis.

SÉLAVY

White Pawn to g4

Oh, who would ever analyze what we are doing here?

DUCHAMP

Black Rook takes b5

What would they conclude? I sublimate chess for sex. That I play with myself too violently, a form of Brunner's syndrome?

SÉLAVY

White Pawn on a takes b5

Maybe they might say that you are sublimating the urge to kiss your sister by kissing me?

DUCHAMP

Black King to c7

More likely it is my unfulfilled urges to win at chess as ...

SÉLAVY

As you won in art? Champ-ion du monde? (*Champion of the world*)

DUCHAMP

Champ-ignons de merde. (*Mushrooms of shit*) That was a goal I never wanted.

SÉLAVY

White Pawn to g5

Never say never.

DUCHAMP

Black Pawn on h takes g5

No. I realized my limitations. I could only extend my reach so far. Like looking through slats in large wooden doorway, I could only peer into what I could never partake. In art one can self delude the self into thinking that they are good and remain on top for a very long time. There are very few criteria that can guide one towards a breakthrough work. And when those rules impose too much, then a new form arises to meet the needs of that age. In chess, the rules are the only thing one has to work with. Like when I played with Tristan Tzara. He would never move the pieces on the path they were to go. With him rules were irrational, aggravating, frustrating. It was no longer chess but something new. It was something closer to anarchy. However, without the rules, then there is no game.

SÉLAVY

White Pawn to b6 [check +]

And who would win?

DUCHAMP

Black King to b7

How can one win against dada? Futility.

SÉLAVY

And your colorful chess pieces, were those also futile?

DUCHAMP

Yes. But to my father they were everything. I made different chess sets that were much easier to use. Even a leather pocket chess set. It would have sold well if not for so much labor to produce them. Others sets were wooden, flowing sculptures. They were for play but also for the gallery.

SÉLAVY

White Rook takes c8

It is getting dark. We need a light. *She walks to the changing screen and pulls out a gas lamp. She lights it and brings the ghostly light toward the table. She looks at it for a moment then sets it on the table.*

DUCHAMP

Black King takes c8

That's perfect. It's absolutely perfect. Where did you get that light?

SÉLAVY

From behind the screen; it's always been there. *She points to the screen.* Just look at our game. I offer a draw. Do you accept?

DUCHAMP

My dear Lord of Misrule, I accept. I have always wanted to draw you in this light. No one wins, no one loses. A beautiful game with delightful problems worked out to the same outcome as if we had not played at all.

SÉLAVY

Oh don't say that. This was fun; it is the playing of the game that matters most. One can take wild risks and not be so cautious. Besides how awful for you if you lost to me.

DUCHAMP

I would happily lose to a woman. I had a wonderful match against Vera Menchik. Chess is for everyone.

SÉLAVY

No, I mean to lose to yourself. Against me ...

DUCHAMP

That would not be bad, only fatalistic. All of life is accumulation and then loss. Either by using the resources to continue to survive and you have the works you accumulate over a lifetime. They survive on without you. Unfortunately they cannot die with you.

SÉLAVY

How lovely an idea is that, art as vapors of gas. Evaporating into the ethers along with the vapors of one's life. It is a shame your work did not die with you. That is, if you consider that you perished when you when you gave up art to play chess.

DUCHAMP

I gave up nothing.

SÉLAVY

You left me alone for years. I was a chess widow. Isn't that what they call women whose loved ones leave them alone to spend time with chess?

DUCHAMP

Don't say such things. I consulted you on every move I ever made. That reminds me, I have something to show you. I told you I did not give up art.

SÉLAVY

New work? But I thought....

DUCHAMP

Come with me. Grab your lamp we might need it.

SÉLAVY

Go where? There is nowhere to go.

DUCHAMP

You'll see. Follow me. Grab the lamp. It's perfect.

SÉLAVY

What do you mean perfect. Have you gone blind in your old age?

DUCHAMP

It's better to see with. That is all. Come.

She takes up the lamp in her right hand. He takes her by the left hand and they walk to the changing screen. They go behind the screen and are no longer seen by the audience.

The lights go dark. A slide is projected onto to back of the stage. Étant donnés (Given: 1 The Waterfall, 2. The Illuminating Gas, French: Étant donnés: 1° la chute d'eau / 2° le gaz d'éclairage.) We see the first of two images of the tableau. The first image is of the wooden door separating the work from the audience.

SÉLAVY

What is this? I have never seen this here before.

DUCHAMP

Take a look. There are two holes to look through.

SÉLAVY

It's a landscape, a waterfall. It's beautiful; such a wonderful tableau. Where did this come from? How long have you been working on this project?

DUCHAMP

I began to work on it in 1946. I have not kept it secret really; it just took a very long time to work on the concept. It is the making that becomes the tedious task, dull and commonplace. I want to display it after my death.

Étant donnés - Exterior

SÉLAVY

Twenty years? Has it been that long? Why have I not seen this before?

DUCHAMP

It was a surprise.

SÉLAVY

For me? This is for me? Oh you shouldn't have.

DUCHAMP

In a way. It is almost complete. I just need to place one more item then it will be complete. Nunc dimittis. At some point it will have to move from this spot, but that is nothing to worry about. I have a detailed notebook on how to break it down and reset it.

SÉLAVY

It looks like a fairy tale, a classical painting. You have always wanted to move the painting from the wall and into real life. This is a triumph. Can we go in?

DUCHAMP

Indeed. I was hoping you would want to enter.

The audience hears the sounds of a large heavy door slowly swinging open.

SÉLAVY

I'm a little frightened, but I don't know why.

DUCHAMP

That is all right, fear is natural. The new is always frightening. Come take my hand, we'll have a look together.

SÉLAVY

But.....

DUCHAMP

Come. It's time. Make yourself comfortable.

SÉLAVY

I don 't think this is a good idea. I am the Lord of Misrule. I will not go where I do not want to go. I won't.

DUCHAMP

Is it possible that you do not know? You do not know the error of your choice? The chosen one, the one that becomes the Lord of Misrule is sacrificed on the altar of Saturn at the end of the ceremonies. That sacrifice brings about the end of winter and thus the world lives on.

SÉLAVY

Oh you don't believe that. Silly rituals are everything your work strives against.

DUCHAMP

This is no ritual. It is only a new kind of installation. We'll be together forever. Come take my hand. It's time to put you to bed, my beautiful little darling. I will sing to you as I once did when you were very young. Do you remember our song? I do, come we'll sing *c'est la vie* together again.

SÉLAVY

Don 't shut the door. I ... I am afraid.

DUCHAMP

Voila! That too is perfect. It's perfectly natural to be frightened. It is just what this piece needs; your fear will color this and produce a shade that will make this piece live on and on. Come to me, come, that's a good girl.

The second image is projected to take the place of the first image. This image is the vision seen through the eyeholes. We see a nude woman lying on her back with her face hidden and legs spread, holding a gas lamp in her right hand. She is in a pastoral landscape. In the distance we see a moving waterfall.

[End]

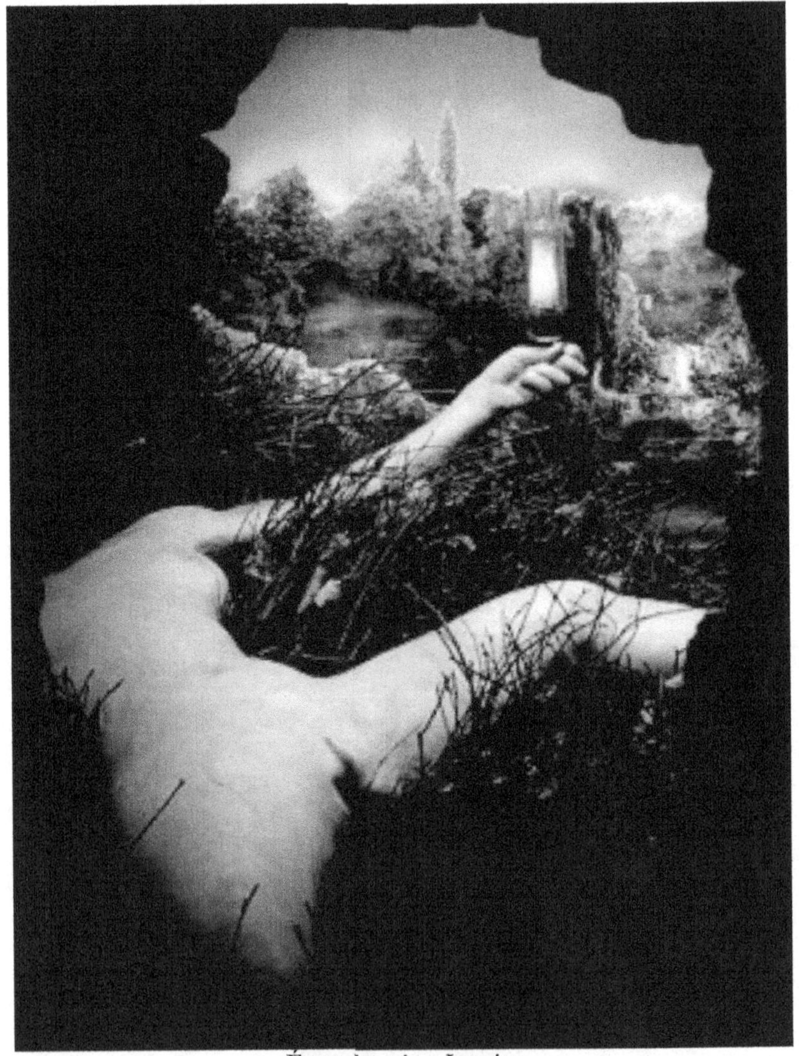

Étant donnés - Interior

SECOND TABLEAU

APOTHEOSIS

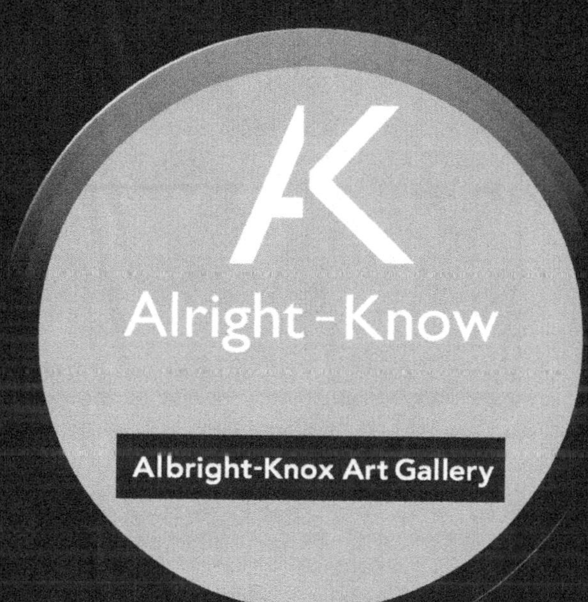

Importantly Being Earnest

Or how the author was kicked out of the Albright Knox Art Gallery
for carrying an Umbrella

Dancers: Marcel Duchamp, Leonora Carrington, Dorothea Tanning & Gertrude Abercrombie

Narrator: Rrose Sélavy

Earnestly Being Important:

Or how I was kicked out of the Albright-Knox Art Gallery for carrying an umbrella

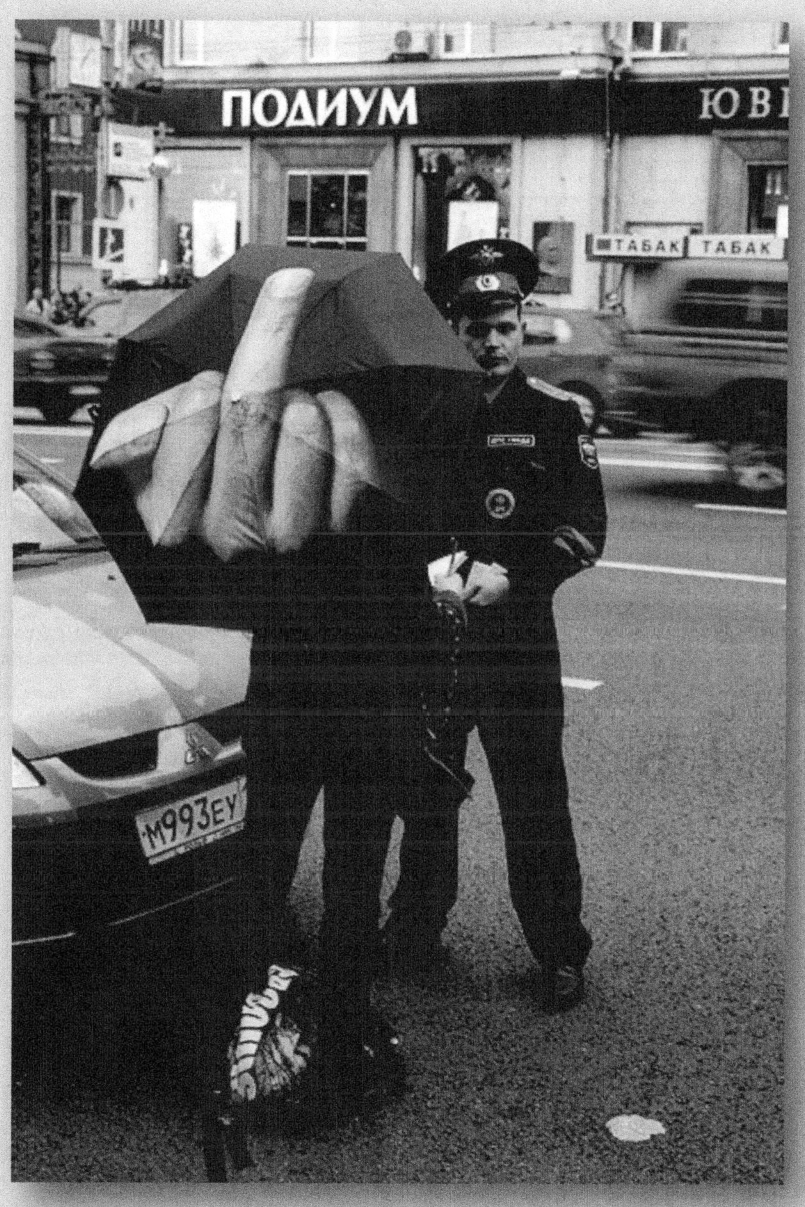

It is unlucky
To carry an umbrella
In the museum

BlazeVOX [books]

76 Inwood Place, Buffalo, NY
Phone: 716-878-5454
E-Mail: editor@blazevox.org
Web: www.blazevox.org

[April 11, 2011]

Attn: Director
Albright–Knox Art Gallery
1285 Elmwood Ave
Buffalo, NY 14222
RE: **There is a taste in my mouth and it's no taste at all**

Dear M:

I am writing to tell you about an unpleasant incident
that happened at the Albright-Knox last week Thursday
about 3PM. It had threatened rain that day
And for my walk over I carried an umbrella.

I had been enjoying my visit and after an hour,
in front of the art piece
the title escapes me just now,
the skin tone portraits of the board of directors,
While I was describing to friends how the color white is ambiguous,
I was asked to leave the gallery
By a security guard
Simply for carrying an umbrella.

In disbelief, I left without incident.
I felt hurt, embarrassed, and humiliated
by this heavy-handed tactic and I believe
this might have been handled differently.

I have been going to the Albright Knox all of my life
Having always found the joys of inspiration within its walls,
I am afraid that this incident will forever diminish that pleasure.
I have dedicated my life to art and to treat a fellow artist
in this shabby a fashion is unworthy of your gallery.

I am a poet and the executive at BlazeVOX,
a small poetry press located in Buffalo.
I say this as I was at the gallery to look at artwork
from one of our authors, Michael Basinski,
whose new book is currently in production.
I mention these items as it locates
me in a favorable way towards art and art galleries
and that I had a genuine reason to be in the gallery.
I am not a hooligan nor am I unkind towards rules
that bar one from carrying outdoor items inside.

I was never told when I entered and paid for my ticket,
conversed with the front desk attendant; the gift shop staff
about a bow tie, walked past several gallery employees
and other less agile security guards, that I might get thrown
out of the establishment for carrying my umbrella.

I saw no signs that said one would be removed
from the premises for such an infraction. Furthermore,
I do believe that instead of being ejected, one might
have pointed to a place like a coat rack where one might
be able to leave outdoor items. I am sure that this is not
too much to ask, as weather in Buffalo does tend to happen.

And since there was no form of appeal to this unilateral decision
I was left to walk home with hurt feelings, which will manifest
in my decisions when it comes to making future donations.

In the end I am left feeling rather wounded by all of this.
I wanted to convey this to you and hope that you might
be able to find a way to ensure better customer service
for art patrons, especially ones who live so close to the gallery.

We both know that customer service is key to a successful enterprise
and why I am taking time to inform you of my unpleasant day.

Thank you.

Geoffrey Gatza
Editor, Publisher
BlazeVOX [books]

BlazeVOX [books]

76 Inwood Place, Buffalo, NY
Phone: 716-878-5454
E-Mail: editor@blazevox.org
Web: www.blazevox.org

[April 11, 2011]

Attn: Director
Albright–Knox Art Gallery
1285 Elmwood Ave
Buffalo, NY 14222

RE: **Why didn't I say, why didn't I say, no, no, no**
      Part two – oh god, I could do better than that

> She's so swishy in her satin and tat
> In her frock coat
> and bipperty-bopperty hat
> Oh God, I could do better than that
>
> —David Bowie, *Queen Bitch*

My out-of-focus image is reflecting back to me in the glass
of an open, empty, vestibule. The self appears ghostly
a figure entering the building, when in fact, it is leaving.
A mirror image of old fashioned irony, acting oppositely,
the reverse of what one expects to be doing at that moment.
The person one thinks, imagines that they are, might be,
that courageous mental avatar swimming in thought fluids
of artistic possibilities and permutations that await them
inside this beautiful gallery, enters. Instead you are leaving.
Formally asked to leave by security for carrying an umbrella.
It's all so surreal, so surreal it is outdated by at least ninety years.
Finally, the artwork is no longer the agent provocateur against
Those who seek to secure our surrounding from ourselves.
The poet again is an enemy, expelled in a comedy of manners.

I have always lived more boldly than I should given my resources.
I am fonder of my life than anyone else I know, however,
I sat on the steps of the gallery and looked out
on the reflecting pond, contemplating the compartments of good governance
and evenhanded uses of power and how they are prized above the arts,
above literature, above personal propriety, above, even, a paying customer.

How I long for basic customer services in the arts world, a swipe
of normal consumerisms where a patron is a customer and owns
the buying power that a ticket should provide.

An art gallery could contain a public space of observations on being,
lived out demonstrations, the greater abilities, energies and emotions
of all humankind in one structure that was for and by the community.
And on almost every other occasion it is.

Instantly I am five years old again and unimpressed by the Warhol
soup cans. To me it represented a poorly conceived lunch; and besides,
I was a *beef and barley* kind of child and the painting depicted tomato,
This reminded me of my grandmother but we never ate tomato soup
Together. In this shadow memory I feel an awful shame cloak over me.
I remember being frightened by the evil walking flower sculpture,
And to this day, I wish I could walk into the painting, *The Marvelous Sauce*.
I remember sliding along infinity in short socks in the mirror-room.
Hidden away, yet in full view of all magnificence reflected outwards.
Over and over and over the hollow chair and mirrored stick table
Sits suspending in the ice-green silver tinged glass presence.
A perpetual now encasing trapped excited light in neverworlds.
Art that can surround one's being in totality and isolate, remove
The surroundings of the lower-than-life everydayness, in a box
segregated, side by side with and within the pulsing emptiness hand
that dangles the far away laughter carrot of art;
That shadow hiding within the object setting this piece
apart from a cotton-candy carnival's amusement tent.
This is the modern pleasure experience, the immersion
In totality, within the piece, set alone, with others
As a shared solitary experience floating, as a victim
Of deprivation to reach out toward the thousand
Images of your cubed reflection, reaching out for
Understanding of why we are here, in this moment.
I could see things I didn't want you to be able to see.
What did you think of when you saw my face?
You can see my embarrassments over and over again.
I want to change everything about the man you in this cage.
I hold my hands over my belly, in hopes you will not
notice how much change my body has endured. You
look no younger yourself, your cragged body appears
As I appear to you, damaged, gilded, crowned in failure.

In the memory, the mind moves moments to suit the needs
of the memory. At once I am younger than I care to remember
the next it is five years ago. Waiting to meet John Ashbery
and hear him read his poems in the gallery's auditorium.
At the pre-game party I spilled a glass of red wine down
the front of my red shirt
And went outside to feel less awkward, less damp.
In those solitary moments, I smelled the floral late summer air
And felt happy about art and poetry. The artists and scholars
And their endlessly searching questions of when will my time bite,
Mr. Ashbery, as did your apple of success.
Can you tell me when will art
embrace me as I have cherished art throughout these ever vacant years.
In the outside, gold junebugs danced around the tin porch lamp.
An opening, a wooden screen-door's screeching broke the moment.

To my horror out came John and David
on their way to prepare for the upcoming reading.
I was daydreaming in a wine stained shirt.
I quickly blathered something wonderful
to him about how great he was and how
his art had moved me, my mind, rather, to distant
whatnots and all the while he smiles with me.
Graciously he allowed that moment to occur.
He waited patiently for me to wind down
Then politely he moved on towards the gallery.

To meet one's hero is always an odd moment,
not necessarily pleasant, but generally uncomfortable.
You want to express in one pushing breath
the wondrous things that happened in your brain
Which their work managed to generate. You do not immediately
realize that you were alone when this happened. They were not
with you on your journey through their poem, as the movie actor
Cannot see you watching them, feel your emotion with you,
as magic is immune to it's magician. Uncontrollable moments surge
Instantly, not always readily remembered in their exacting
Sequences, which causes one to stand stiff, a diffused statue
A naked ambition moth, opening to the flame that inspired
It to fly into the sparks stirred up from broken kindles in fallen forests.

These moments last for an infinite amount of time.
Like the line we stood in to meet Julie Mehretu
She gave a lecture on her process and successes.
She was so very cool, American and aptly situated
in the now of her charismatic creations. Inspiring,
Occupying the space in a comfortable leather jacket.

It was such a great moment; I wanted to keep her
Bring her home as one might keep a beloved cat.
But unfortunately artists cannot be collected
as easily as their wall décor.
And now, we are publishing a book of poems
by her cousin Timothy who choose the painting
Excerpt (Suprematist Evasion) for the book cover.
Radiating pinks jut from central points where
a squiggle city once stood. Reds, yellows and blues
dot the evolution of circular trail patterns around
a map-like canvas. It is all very exciting and gilds
Timothy's poetry rather well. The recolinear lines
Dart about the field, but all comes home to rest
in the snowfields of murdered fathers at Elsinore.

And then there was that time I was on acid
We walked the hallways as only young friends can
Together our minds melted inwards towards the walls.
We annoyed the docents by critiquing
the plaster workmen remodeling the first floor
in our finest art speak and newly learned analyses.
We commented on the industrial nature of the new space,
The unfinished walls with plaster-dust encrusted circular saws
Opened to us like the post-modern setting it was immersed.
A snakelike line ran towards a red phone on the floor.
There was a stepladder that led upwards to nowhere.
This was all folly, a nothing at all, a random funny thought
merging today's art through minds raised on classical
depictions of bearded men glowering at frightened women
trying to break through to be edgy and against the systems
we so dearly enjoy so very much.

The world was once so reductible, a closed system where art
could demonstrate to the world the entirety of the known existence,
even if it meant reality could be marred by the artist's talent.
As a straight line in the sand cannot be a division in the sand,
It is merely the mind recalling a similarity to a representation
of a moved medium upon which the active brain can dream.

Now _things_ are everywhere aren't they, the mind can directly
Be misdirected, even by a phone on the floor of an art gallery.
Red can mean just about anything to anyone, art evermore means
Nothing primarily substantial as our lives frequently contain less
and less truly meaningful moments, as pencil markings on walls.

Which brings up the time Maxine Chernoff and Paul Hoover
Came to read from their work. Ethan could not host them
so I gladly showed them a fine time at the Albright-Knox.
We had a glorious visit and I learned a great deal from both
of them, important life lessons that escape me just now, but
It was the only time I have eaten at the gallery's restaurant.
We laughed over the almost incident with the security guard
who had come over to us to make sure that we did know
That yes, the diagonally spaced pencil lines
drawn on the wall - were in fact art. We leaned in,
Our eyes were very close to the wall, and I said, it's all right,
these people are accomplished artists, poets and editors,
so I am sure if anything gets smudged, we can make it right, as
I pulled a mechanical pencil from my vest with a wicked smile.
She gasped so severely I feared she would faint or get the hiccups.
Ultimately she did not and after smoothing out her ruffled
emotions we were allowed to continue on to other exhibits.

These memories waver in my mind like those blue wooden poles
that once stood on the far side of the gallery. They have been sent
on now, to another gallery, another space, another owner
but, in their upright reaching weathered blue I found determination
standing, vertiginously, as would bamboo in a longing meditative stance
gleaming on and on in the cold evening; standing up to the snow showers
with nothing but sky and starlight to cover them from mere mortal exposure;
as if stating to those who drive by, dying here would be redundant.

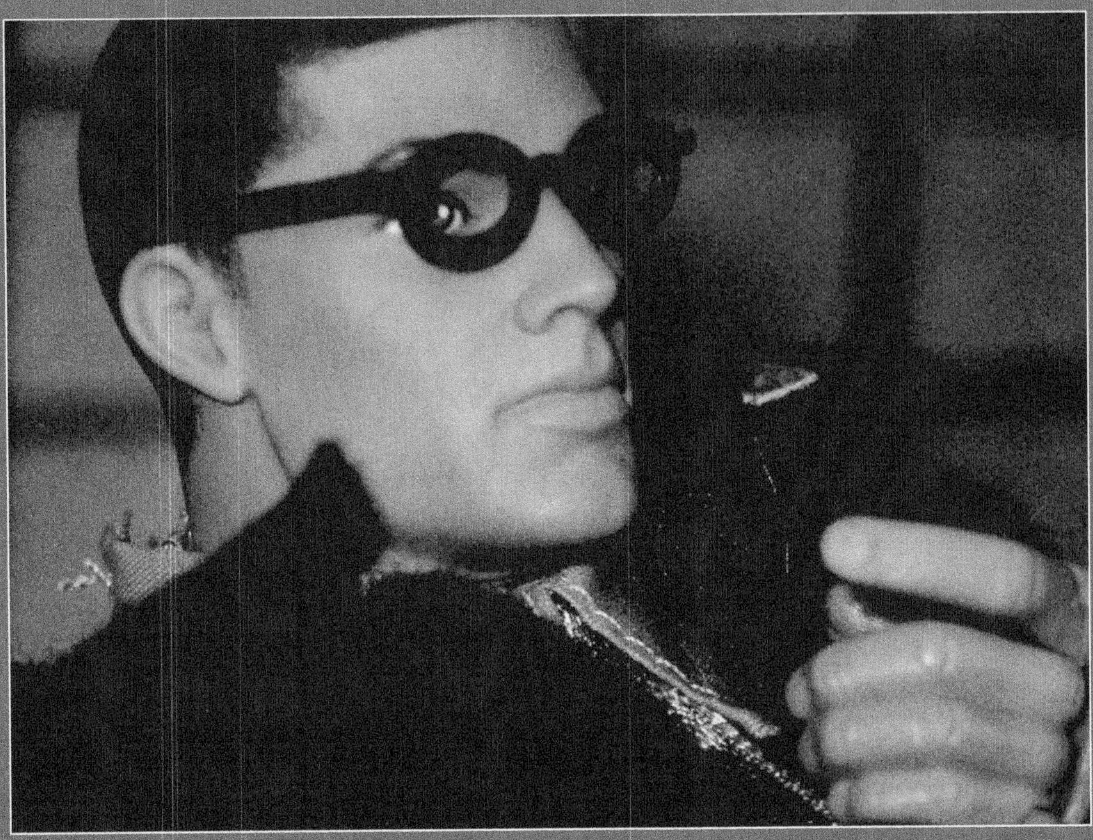

Geoffrey Gatza is an award winning poet and editor. He is the author many books of poetry, including *Secrets of my Prison House* (BlazeVOX 2010) *Kenmore: Poem Unlimited* (Casa Menendez 2009) and *HouseCat Kung Fu: Strange Poems for Wild Children* (Meritage Press 2008), He is also the author of the yearly <u>Thanksgiving Menu-Poem</u> Series, a book length poetic tribute for prominent poets, now in it's tenth year.

His visual art poems have been displayed in gallery showing, OCCUPY THE WALLS: A Poster Show, AC Gallery (NYC) 2011 *occupy wall street N15 For Ernst Jandl - Minimal Poems with photography from the fall of Liberty Square.* And in, LANGUAGE TO COVER A WALL: Visual Poetry through its changing media, UB ART GALLERY (Buffalo, NY) 2011/12 *Language for the Birds.* Geoffrey Gatza is the editor and Publisher of the small press BlazeVOX. The fundamental mission of BlazeVOX is to disseminate poetry, through print and digital media, both within academic spheres and to society at large. He lives in Kenmore, NY with his girlfriend and two beloved cats.

http://www.geoffreygatza.com/
http://www.blazevox.org

Made in the USA
Monee, IL
07 July 2026